Child to Parent Violence and Abuse

A Practitioner's Guide to Working with Families

Helen Bonnick

Child to Parent Violence and Abuse: A Practitioner's Guide to Working with Families

© Pavilion Publishing and Media Ltd

The author has asserted their rights in accordance with the Copyright, Designs and Patents Act (1988) to be identified as the author of this work.

Published by:
Pavilion Publishing and Media Ltd
Blue Sky Offices
Cecil Pashley Way
Shoreham by Sea
West Sussex
BN43 5FF
Tel: 01273 434 943
Fax: 01273 227 308
Email: info@pavpub.com

Published 2019

All rights reserved. No part of this publication may be reproduced, stored in a retrieval system, or transmitted in any form or by any means, electronic, mechanical, photocopying, recording or otherwise, without prior permission in writing of the publisher and the copyright owners.

A catalogue record for this book is available from the British Library.

ISBN: 978-1-912755-25-7

Pavilion Publishing and Media is a leading publisher of books, training materials and digital content in mental health, social care and allied fields. Pavilion and its imprints offer must-have knowledge and innovative learning solutions underpinned by sound research and professional values.

Author: Helen Bonnick
Production editor: Ruth Chalmers, Pavilion Publishing and Media Ltd
Cover design: Phil Morash, Pavilion Publishing and Media Ltd
Page layout and typesetting: Phil Morash, Pavilion Publishing and Media Ltd
Printing: CPI Anthony Rowe

Contents

Acknowledgements 1
About the author 2
Foreword 3
Preface 5
Introduction 15

Part 1: Five impossible things to believe 29
    Chapter 1: How much? 31
    Chapter 2: It could happen to anyone 47
    Chapter 3: The impact on families 71
    Chapter 4: Punished for being a victim 81
    Chapter 5: Nobody's problem 89

Part 2: Four traps to avoid 101
    Chapter 6: The difficult parent 103
    Chapter 7: I blame the parents 117
    Chapter 8: We need the young person to engage 127
    Chapter 9: Just like domestic violence 137

Part 3: Three aspects of work with families 151
    Chapter 10: Understanding the issue of power 153
    Chapter 11: Full family assessment 167
    Chapter 12: Whole family intervention 185

Part 4: Two conflicting paradigms 227
    Chapter 13: Two conflicting paradigms 229

Part 5: One thing everyone can do 243
    Chapter 14: One thing everyone can do 245

Conclusion 253
    Chapter 15: A final word, and where to next? 255
    Appendix 1: Acronyms used 261
    Appendix 2: Programmes of work 263

Acknowledgements

I am eternally grateful to all those who have contributed to the journey of this book. The structure is based on a conference presentation I shared with Al Coates at Community Care Live; his contribution is much appreciated. Many people have allowed me to intrude on conversations, or to ask them unbearably painful questions; they have freely shared their knowledge and have in turn probed and pushed me into completing this work. I am most grateful of all to those who understood how important it was, and who believed that I could do it.

Stephanie, Demetria, Rachel, Sally and Jenny all agreed to be interviewed and recorded, and were gracious in responding to questions that must have seemed clumsy or unnecessary at times. People I have come to know on Twitter have taught me much too. Many other parents have shared their stories over the years, some in closer contact than others, and have contributed in their own ways to the case studies included here. It has been humbling to listen to experiences that many would find hard to tolerate once, let alone on a daily basis. Sandi and other practitioners have also spent long hours with me. All have wanted to contribute towards learning and future practice development.

It has been heart warming to be accepted into a larger body of researchers, practitioners and thinkers, all willing to share their knowledge as we journey together. I have enjoyed long discussions, shared train journeys, listened in at conferences and persuaded people to blog for me. Eddie graciously shared so much early on. Rachel and Amanda have always asked how my writing was coming along – for the last five years! Wendy and Al have picked my brains as I have picked theirs, in phone calls, emails, and meetings. It has been a pleasure to work closely alongside Jo and to learn from her at the same time.

Martin persuaded me to keep going, and helped me work out why I wasn't writing when I had become completely stuck. He and others: Jill, Wendy, Victor, Tracey, and Fiona have read chapters and offered suggestions, corrections, guidance and encouragement. Their contribution is far greater than they probably realise. Sue gave me a home away from home and free of distractions, to kick start this last year.

I am grateful to my editor, Ruth, for her work in finally bringing this to fruition. Thanks of course to Jon for technical assistance, and to Tom for professional advice. Lastly, Steve, who has patiently put up with my single-mindedness over the last year in particular, when he had hoped we might have retired to sunnier climes, or at least had days out together. I'm free tonight!

About the author

Helen Bonnick is a consultant, speaker and trainer on child to parent violence and abuse. She qualified as a social worker in 1983, and has since worked as a practitioner, supervisor and educator. She offers training and consultation services to local authorities, other groups and individuals. She no longer works directly with families, but always tries to respond to requests for advice. She contributed to the development of Home Office guidance on adolescent to parent violence and abuse, and writes a regular blog in this area.

Following an MA in child studies that focused on child to parent violence, Helen spent time building networks and consolidating training in this field. Her work culminated in the launch of www.holesinthewall.co.uk – an internationally accessed hub that brings together information on training opportunities, research findings, reading material, discussions and news features in one place for parents and professionals. The site now attracts 2,000 visitors per month.

Foreword

Dr Ruth Jones, OBE

I have worked in the field of domestic and family-based violence and abuse for over 30 years, in practice and in academia, most recently as Founding Director of the National Centre for the Study and Prevention of Violence and Abuse (NCSPVA), (now the Centre for Violence Prevention), at the University of Worcester. Over this time, I was aware of some 'child to parent violence and abuse' (CPVA), through the stories of some of the women I worked with, who talked about it in whispers, and as an add-on to narratives of domestic abuse. I do not recall it being talked of as a discrete form of abuse, nor do I remember it being talked about by practitioners, unless they spoke of the 'cycle of abuse', i.e. children acting out abuse they had learned from living in families affected by domestic abuse. Over the last decade however, CPVA has been more prominent as an issue in its own right, through research, and through parents increasingly drawing attention to it and asking for help. This has led to a need amongst practitioners, to know how best they can work with families experiencing it. I was thrilled then, to learn that this book was being written, and even more thrilled to know that it was being written by Helen Bonnick.

I first became aware of Helen when I discovered the 'Holes in the Wall', the online resource that she created, for parents, practitioners and academics. The resource gives easy access to relevant leaflets and information on projects, programmes and services, as well as a range of national and international research on CPVA. It has been a vital tool for my undergraduate and postgraduate students who study and research the phenomenon, and for my own research on CPVA. Information from Holes in the Wall has also helped me understand CPVA on a personal level. A few years ago, I experienced CPVA from a troubled teenaged son whose behaviour was abusive towards me and his siblings. Thankfully, this is no longer the case, but information from Holes in the Wall helped me greatly at that time. This was in contrast to my experiences of seeking help. I found a concerning lack of knowledge, understanding and response to the CPVA from many practitioners. I am grateful then that this practitioner's guide to working with families affected by CPVA has been written, and feel honoured that I was asked to write this foreword.

Foreword

I have been lucky enough to hear Helen Bonnick speak at several conferences, and I got to know her better when she agreed to be keynote speaker at a conference on CPVA I organised at the University of Worcester in March 2018. Helen spoke about evidence-based approaches and contexts for intervention in relation to CPVA, showcasing her vast knowledge of the issue, and her commitment to early intervention and relationship-based working to enable people to realise their own skills and build resilience. Much of what she talked about at that conference is expanded upon in this book.

After placing CPVA in context via an introduction that highlights the complexity of 'naming' the issue, the book explores 'Five impossible things to believe', and 'Four traps to avoid' to challenge some common, but deeply ingrained opinions, attitudes and myths that can make responding to CPVA difficult, including the notion of parent blaming. This is something I was very aware of when doing my own research on this issue. One particularly practitioner I spoke to about my research said, 'Oh…you are looking at those parents who can't control their children'. This is in fact, not what I was looking at, but is an example of a common misconception that results in parental shame; as identified by researchers talking with affected parents. A growing body of research consistently shows that CPVA can happen to any family, with any parenting style, and that it can have a devasting impact on parents, and on wider family members. Research also shows that an increased understanding of the nature and impact of CPVA amongst practitioners has led to their desire to know how to support families who experience it. The bulk of this book focuses on working with families affected by CPVA, allowing Bonnick to share the knowledge that she has built up over many years as a Social Worker and Practice Educator specialising in working with families, and a researcher, specialising in CPVA. The book concludes with some ideas about how knowledge and responses to CPVA could and should be further developed.

In conclusion, this is an original, timely and important book, that brings CPVA out of the shadows. It is primarily aimed at practitioners, but will also be beneficial to parents, academics and all who are interested in the phenomenon which is CPVA.

Preface

It has been suggested that this book should carry a warning with it: may not be easy to read. It has certainly not been easy to write. At a time when many social workers, as well as other professionals, feel under siege; resisting governmental controls, challenges within academia, and regular criticism within the press, why would you want to read something else that suggests an absence or error in practice? How to be honest in sharing the voices of those I speak with, while at the same time, honouring the profession of which I am a member, and the impressive work that takes place each day to enable children to remain safe? How to recognise the commitment of those who believe they can never get things right, because they will always be criticised one way or another? And indeed, that sentence could have been written the other way round, because this is a story of two parties, both feeling much maligned and misunderstood.

At the start, it all seemed quite straight forward. Practitioners had approached me for advice on many occasions, and even suggested that I write a book with guidance on how to respond to families experiencing violence and abuse from their children. I was deeply embedded in a network of academics, campaigners and parents, seeking to promote awareness and develop a proven response, having made a decision to commit time and energy myself to pursuing a greater knowledge and to bringing this issue to wider attention. The sharing of experiences (of both practitioners and parents) seemed a sensible way of framing my writing, illustrating learning with real experience. But in any arena where people are hurt and emotions are raw, there is a risk that things will be said that are later regretted. I would find myself pulling back, reframing a discussion, making excuses; and then I would take another phone call from someone who had just had a negative experience with a professional, and I would feel like rolling up my sleeves and going back into the fray. I was angry myself: angry that families were reporting that they could not access help; angry that my profession was letting people down; angry that I couldn't do anything to help. Angry is not necessarily a good place to start writing a guide to good practice!

I first knowingly came across a child who was violent to his mother in the 1980s, while practicing as a social worker in a generic team. We discussed it as a team, but were unable to offer a useful response other than to refer the family to the then equivalent of child and adolescent mental health services. The experience stayed with me, and when I had the opportunity to pursue some further study, I took the topic of access to help for families experiencing abuse from their children as the focus of my dissertation. I became like a dog with a bone. Completing my studies the question arose of how to take this further; and I was eventually persuaded to develop a website (www.holesinthewall.co.uk/) which now acts as an international resource hub for anyone interested in the subject of violence and abuse from child to parent. I have been privileged to speak at conferences and training events on many occasions, but each time I am as conscious as I was at the start that there is always more to learn, always another voice to listen to.

Listening to voices has thus been an important part of the development of this book. Parents do not speak easily of the abuse they experience. It is considered shameful and something to keep hidden. They may not think of it in terms of abuse at all. Yet when they do speak it can be as if a dam has been breached and years of pain come flooding through. The last five years, in Britain at least, have seen a gradual awakening in this respect. Greater media coverage – some good, some terrible – means that parents hear about other people in the same boat. This is a subject that is more talked about, and even pops up in story lines in television soaps. While it still carries shame, it is less hidden, and potentially practitioners will see more and more people coming forward and asking for help.

When I have worked with student social workers, I have been encouraged, and excited even, by their reflective skills, by their determination to bring about change, to question established practice, to continue learning. Social workers who I talk to about their experiences of working with child to parent violence and abuse are similarly open to new ideas, and new ways of working. This in turn encourages me to believe that, though there may be parts of this book that are challenging to our beliefs and current practice, we do as a profession have the skills of reflection that will permit an honest examination and response. I suppose what I am saying is this: folks, we seem to have got this wrong on occasions in the past when we didn't really have a grasp of what was happening. Now that we do know more, it gives us a chance to reflect on our thinking, to examine our practice, and to polish up the way we work. There's going to be some shocking and challenging stuff ahead, but I'd like to give you some pointers for good and effective work. I want to learn from when things have gone well, highlighting the positives, but not hiding from mistakes.

This will not be a weighty academic tome, but I will tell you where you can find more academic writing if you would like to explore ideas further. I hope that it will be both accessible and practical for anyone working with families, in whatever capacity, and wherever you are. It may also be useful in other ways for anyone wanting to know and understand more about children's violence towards their parents. It is full of stories from the front line. It is also full of headlines and quotes, to give a flavour of wider opinion, to remind us what the rest of the world thinks; sometimes shocking, but all used to illustrate the state of things, just where we are at the moment, and how far we still have to go. For instance:

'Parental Abuse the Most SHAMEFUL Domestic Crime of all!
The assault of parents – the very people who gave life, love and sustenance to their children – ranks among the lowest of the low … cases of parental assault cannot be tolerated. They should be brought to light, so that the authorities – and the long arm of law – can deal with the perpetrators. The question here is how much the law can actually do. If the endgame is the restoration of familial harmony, the adversarial, trial-based approach may not constitute a silver bullet.'
(Editorial, Straits Times, 2009)

We may feel very uncomfortable with the tone of this piece, and much of what I have to say will challenge the content too. But in essence it carries the eternal question, what on earth are we supposed to do?

A little background

Child to parent violence and abuse is far from being a new phenomenon, and mention of it – and how shocking it is considered to be – can be found in diverse places. Writers and conference presenters like to find the oldest recorded reference to make this point. Gallagher (2004) quotes Socrates: *'The children now love luxury: they show disrespect for elders and love chatter in place of exercise. Children are tyrants.'* (Socrates, 470–399 BC).

So why are we coming to this so late in the day? It is certainly not the first aspect of family violence to have taken people a while to accept. Intimate partner violence (IPV) in the seventies, child abuse in the eighties, elder abuse in the new millennium … all were met initially with a mixture of scepticism, antagonism, horror and, importantly, incredulity. But while each of those involve the abuse of one party traditionally considered less powerful, by a family member with presumed greater power and authority, child to parent violence and abuse turns our expectations upside down, featuring as it does, the abuse of those family members traditionally considered to hold the power, by those traditionally presented as weaker, more needy, and more subservient. For sure, as a child matures, the balance of power shifts towards greater parity in adulthood, but the prevailing expectation, is it not, is that the parent calls the shots and the child jumps to it. What that actually looks like day-to-day may be affected by where you live in the world, by your cultural background and family traditions, perhaps by your age, income, education, politics, personal circumstances or even luck; all influencing your style of parenting, the support available, and the bumps in the road along the way.

Preface

Many families report difficult times: toddler tantrums, teenage angst and rebellion, an awkward child, a disability, a loss of confidence leading to requests for help and advice. Some parents will resolve these within their own immediate support system, with help from family and friends. Some reach for parenting magazines or programmes on television. Universal family support services, where they are available, were imagined as offering easy to access help and advice, nurturing families to get through the hard times and identifying those who might need more help. GPs, health visitors and school staff offer listening ears and refer on as necessary. Parenting programmes have become ubiquitous and some local authorities may offer these in many different flavours. So with all this help available, if the child is still resistant to discipline, to warnings and consequences; still shouts, hits, breaks, and runs away; it must be something the parents are doing wrong; they're not trying hard enough, right?

Fourteen years ago, as I was reading message boards as part of my research, I was shocked at what parents were saying, but also a little sceptical. Story after story about asking for help and instead being investigated for abuse or neglect, and even having children removed, by members of a profession – my profession – founded on strong values and ethics, and the principles of the Human Rights Act. I was ambivalent about how to read and respond to such claims. These were anonymous stories. How could I verify them? For the last five years parents have been contacting me directly with the same stories. Some are parents with whom I have some sort of relationship, and in whose truthfulness and objectivity I have every confidence; parents who are often working within the health and social care professions themselves. But at the same time I have practitioners – and more of them – asking what they can do. They know this exists and feel helpless and powerless to respond.

Other writers have also documented the lack of guidance and policy for practitioners seeking to support families through their crisis:

'At a conference attended by over 200 social housing professionals focusing on action to prevent anti-social behaviour, more than two-thirds of the participants indicated that they had dealt with cases involving mother abuse in the previous twelve months. Discussions with social work practitioners revealed a similar familiarity with the problem often combined with a sense of frustration about the lack of guidance as to how to address the issue.'
(Hunter *et al*, 2010)

'Despite anecdotal evidence of practitioners being continually confronted with such cases, parent abuse has yet to reach the status of "social problem".'
(Holt and Retford, 2013)

I began to ask practitioners directly myself: if they were familiar with the issue, how it was encountered, what other issues were involved, whether they felt able to intervene to offer support, what training they had received … The picture that emerged confirmed what I already suspected; that this issue was much more widespread than we were aware, but it was hidden behind and within better understood family and personal problems, such as domestic violence, mental health problems and substance use, and so attracted little individual attention.

Listen to these two voices:

'By age 14, only 42% of entries to care are due to abuse or neglect, while 45% are accounted for by a mixture of acute family stress, family dysfunction and socially unacceptable behaviour. Alongside this, many young people face challenges with their mental and emotional health (64%), special educational needs (38%) and substance misuse (32%). The building of effective working relationships with young people and their families, and shoring up strained relationship within families is, therefore, a significant challenge to those working with adolescents.'
(Department for Education, 2017)

And now a social worker engaged regularly with children 'on the edge of care':

'At one point I was the social worker who'd get those cases where teenagers were being relinquished into local authority care … part of it was the violence, usually the older ones – it seemed like parents were a lot more comfortable saying, "My kid's doing this to me, doing that – I'm scared of him". … I think probably with our cases with adolescents, it's a feature with nearly every case. The majority. If it's mental health, identity issues, kids running drugs, there's almost always an element of CPV and I think there's a growing understanding amongst professionals, but not on a strategic high level.'
(Interview with Sandi, 2018)

Those working to support families understood that child to parent violence and abuse exists, they had some sort of language to describe it, but they felt ill-equipped, under-skilled or under-resourced to offer a proper response. And like the parents I spoke with, they had one question more than any other: 'But what should you do when it all kicks off?'.

In parallel, the last ten years have seen tremendous growth in awareness, knowledge, understanding and programmes of support around the world. The body of research literature has grown out of all proportion to its size a decade ago. Individual campaigners have shown great persistence and resilience, as well as ingenuity, spreading the word, impacting legislation or developing resources.

More and more agencies, local authorities and professional groups are looking to increase their knowledge and develop support through conferences and training events. Evidence-based practice is starting to emerge. Child to parent violence and abuse is still largely neglected in initial training programmes such as the social work degree, and yet I hear more and more stories now of practitioners who have got it right, whose empathy and openness have enabled them to support a family in a way that changes the story – for that family of course – but importantly for the whole field of work.

The idea for this book has been growing for a long time. It has been important that it has only now come to fruition, as my own understanding and ideas have developed over the years, working them out through study, through conferences and discussions, and through blogging on my website, Holes in the Wall, and as I have had a chance to reflect on my own sense of anger. It has been important to me to listen to the experiences and views of families affected by this form of violence and abuse and to bring their voice to the table. Mostly this has been from parents. I would have liked there to have been more input from children and young people, but that comes with its own problems.

We are learning that child to parent violence and abuse is an issue that crosses boundaries of race, of class, of status or income, of the type of family or the type of home. Being based in Britain, and grounded in British and UK legislation, there is naturally a particular cultural slant to what I have written, but I have tried to bring in examples from other countries and cultures whenever possible. Research from around the world shows many similarities, but also interesting levels of nuance and unfamiliarity. Some support programmes have travelled successfully across continents, with more or less tweaking to make them more culturally suited to their new homes. Pan-European research has explored different models of response. International conferences and networks have sought to expand understanding across the globe. This remains a small field in which to work, but one of the pleasures has been the openness to share ideas and knowledge from all involved.

Following an introductory chapter, setting the scene and discussing definitions and language, I have divided the book into five sections in which I develop an understanding of the main issues before moving on to a more structured approach to work in supporting families. Each section is further divided by chapter; and each chapter is written in such a way that it should be easily digestible and immediately useful.

I start with 'Five impossible things to believe': five core issues in understanding an issue that many people still find hard to accept, and which hopefully set the scene for future discussions. These five issues have been chosen as fundamental building blocks. They open up the topic to give a broader background knowledge.

- 'How much?' in which I explore an understanding of prevalence.
- 'It could happen to anyone,' a look at what we know about the profile of families affected.
- 'The impact on families', both emotional and practical and a little about wider impact.

Then two specific issues, which challenge our thinking further:

- 'Punished for being a victim', looking at the re-victimisation of parents by services.
- 'Nobody's problem', which explores the difficulties in accessing help.

The second section, 'Four traps to avoid', addresses myths and stereotypes, looking at beliefs and assumptions that can impact on the delivery of a service. They address frequently asked questions, but they are perhaps more emotionally challenging than the earlier section.

- 'The difficult parent', with a look at the dynamics in the practitioner/service-user relationship.
- 'I blame the parents', exploring what we know about blame and responsibility.
- 'We need the young person to engage.' Do we? What can we do when they won't?
- 'Just like domestic violence.' Many comparisons are drawn both in relation to our understanding of this issue and the responses we can adopt. I explore whether this analogy is a helpful one.

In the third section, 'Three aspects of work with families', we start to look more specifically at assessment and models of intervention, after some important consideration of the power issues at play here.

- 'Understanding the issue of power.'
- 'Full family assessment.'
- 'Whole family intervention.'

We then have a section on the difficulties emerging from our tendency to think in binary ways, 'Two conflicting paradigms'; and then, lastly, 'One thing that everyone can do'. The book closes with a final chapter for those interested in taking their learning further.

Background information and research findings are supported by testimony from professionals and from families who have given permission for their voices to be included, specifically to raise awareness of their situation and needs. Above all, this is a book which brings the families' lives to the fore, and documents what they say helps, what hinders, and what they want to celebrate or protest. Suggestions are made for further reading, for useful resources or links; and most importantly, each chapter includes pointers to things that individuals can think about further, or do themselves to develop awareness, to build a response, or to support families in their own circle or work.

There is no magic wand to wave to solve the problem of child to parent violence and abuse. If there was, we would clearly not be in this position now, and yet that is what we all want – for those affected to be able to wake up one day and for the horror to be over; to be able to live and love as a 'normal' family. No more walking on eggshells or hiding the bruises, no more excuses about missed outings or appointments, no more guilt, shame, sadness, and feeling unsure if you can carry on another day. Some things will work for one child but not another, for one day but not another. Some families will turn the corner. Some families may always live with some level of abuse, but it might be at a level they feel they can manage.

There are already many excellent programmes of work in existence. They may be few and far between and hard to access, but they exist and we are learning from them all the time; and as more work continues the body of evidence for their effectiveness grows too. There is much we do not understand. There is a long way to go. But there is hope, and that is the hope I want to pass on here.

'Our life now is unrecognisable compared to 4 months ago thanks to ASF-funded therapies. I was afraid. Now I am not. Priceless … I can actually hardly believe how different things are. Weeks and weeks since we had a violent episode.'
(Tweet, @suddenly mummy, 2017)

'He will always have issues and he will always have difficulties, but I do see him as a success story … We've come a long way in every respect. He's changed so much … We've come so far.'
(Rachel, interview, 2017)

'It just took finding the one SW who was horrified at the lack of support we'd had + who just got it done. She's amazing.'
(Tweet from parent, undated)

References

Gallagher E (2004) Youth who victimize their parents. *Australian and New Zealand Journal of Family Therapy* **25** (2) 94–105.

Holt A and Retford S (2013) Practitioner accounts of responding to parent abuse – a case study in ad hoc delivery, perverse outcomes and a policy silence. *Child and Family Social Work* **18** (3) 365–374.

Hunter C, Nixon J & Parr S (2010) Mother abuse: a matter of youth justice, child welfare or domestic violence. *Journal of Law and Society* **37** (2).

Introduction

Some words about language and meaning

'Our experience was not one of some occasional kicking or hitting out. By violence we mean proper scary, injury causing, potential death kind of violence on a regular basis. Hospital visits, scars, permanent damage to property and psyche.'
(Amanda Boorman, 2015, for The Adoption Social)

When described in this way, it is hard to imagine how such a phenomenon has managed to remain hidden for so long. And yet this is the situation we are in, with no agreement as to name or definition; and confusion all round as to what words and phrases to use to encapsulate the experience, let alone understand and respond to it.

Why is it so difficult to name?

This is a book about working with families experiencing child to parent violence and abuse, child on parent abuse, parent abuse … you may already be confused at the profusion of different names for this issue. Over the years I have found and listed over 30 different phrases and titles, including acronyms, for the experience of families where their young children and adolescents are violent and abusive towards them. It is as if this 'new phenomenon' is discovered for the first time on each occasion, and so, each time, a new name is coined by those involved in the work.

In 1979 Harbin and Madden used the phrase 'battered parent syndrome' to describe what they saw happening in families. At other times, in other places, we have learned about the 'tyrannical child', and about 'mother abuse'. 'Parent abuse' (PA) is a more inclusive term. In Australia it is known as 'adolescent violence in the home' (AVITH).

Where you live may have some bearing on your preferred terminology, as different countries and cultures vary in their positioning and conceptualisation of children's challenging behaviour and thus in the language used to name it, varying from filial violence, through child to parent violence, youth aggression in the home, parental abuse or assault. Some of the terminology – the use of *adolescence* particularly – reflects the presumed most likely age group to be involved. Language may also reflect your profession or theoretical approach: do you think of it as 'juvenile family violence' or as 'mother battering'? In Australia the use of the term AVITH includes recognition of property damage, and abuse of siblings and pets – as distinct from violence in the wider community.

There is a wider discussion about whether the term 'abuse', 'aggression', or 'violence' is more appropriate, or whether to use more than one. Not all abuse is violent. Not all violence is abusive. Wilcox (2012) writes: *'The term abuse is useful in that it reflects the nature of the behaviour and correctly locates the phenomena within the wider field of familial abuse (e.g. domestic abuse, elder abuse, child abuse). The use of "violence" alone reinforces the idea that parent abuse is solely about physical violence and ignores the multiplicity of behaviours occurring within a range of familial relationships'.*

Most books and papers begin not just with a name and definition, but also with an explanation of the chosen phraseology. I used to go with parent abuse. It seemed to encapsulate what I wanted to talk about, and was at that time in wider use (Wilcox, 2012). In her PhD thesis looking at domestic property violence as a distinct form of parent abuse, Murphy-Edwards (2012) also chose this phrase, and gives her rationale: 'A well-accepted template for describing interpersonal violence'. Yet time and time again I found myself having to field questions about abuse BY parents. It seemed the possibility of abuse of parents by children was too hard to believe, and so it was assumed the violence must be in the opposite direction.

Now I prefer the phrase 'child to parent violence' (CPV), or 'child to parent violence and abuse' (CPVA) – and the latter is the terminology I have chosen to go with for this book. It seems to me to make very clear the parties involved, the direction of the abuse, and the inclusion of abuse other than physical violence. For me it is also significant in including younger children, while embracing childhood up to the end of the teen years (and beyond in some cases). Coogan (2014) has more to say about this:

'While recognizing the validity of the term "parent abuse" to describe child-initiated violence and controlling behavior toward parents […] the term "child-to-parent violence" is preferred for three reasons:

1. *It encompasses a wide range of abusive behaviors, including acts of violence and controlling tactics.*
2. *It indicates that it is the parent who is the target of the abusive behavior by the child under the age of 18 years of age.*
3. *The term clarifies that it is the child who uses violence to disempower the parent.'*

However, even using this terminology is not without its own problems:

- As well as birth parents, I also want to acknowledge grandparents, kinship carers, step-parents, foster parents, adoptive parents, residential care workers and anyone else engaged in the parenting role.
- I want it to include damage to property or to siblings, or pets.
- And there are those who do not consider their child's violent behaviour to be abusive in the traditional understanding of the word.

Attempting any name is to squeeze a huge elephant into a tiny mouse box. Each family's experience will be different and each experience may vary over time. The words we use are at best descriptive. We do not as yet have an officially agreed name.

Does this lack of an agreed name matter? I would argue that yes, it does. It can make it difficult to have conversations and be sure we are talking about the same thing (particularly when using just initials). It does not help families better understand their situation or experience and ask for help; and it potentially hinders campaigning and policy development. A lack of agreement makes it difficult to collect data, and, 'if it can't be counted, it doesn't count'. Agencies need an agreed name to give something a code, and without a code there is no intervention. It certainly makes research problematic if you need to be running 30 different search terms!

Words are important

The minefield of phraseology is not confined to a name. Our use of language both talks about an idea and helps to form that very idea. If we are careless in the words we use we may also contribute to labelling, or shaming. I will try to avoid terms such as victim and perpetrator or abuser. We will come to see that this is too simplistic a distinction. I have also come across phrases such as smother-mother or helicopter-parenting, which mean different things to different people; but I find them problematic in that they have come to convey a very negative message. The idea of over-entitlement is more complicated, and is one which will be considered later in greater depth.

Just as words frame a problem, they also impact on how we anticipate a solution. Think of children as naughty, and we imagine they deserve punishment. Think of them as having poor mental health, and they deserve our compassion. Those two responses make uneasy bedfellows; but how we think about this issue can make all the difference in whether we have the energy to continue!

It's not just professionals who have problems with names

We should be aware that parents may not think of their experience as abusive at all, and when they seek help may use different phrases instead, such as the child being 'out of control'. They describe being unable to access help because they do not have the 'right' words for what they experience. Great sensitivity is needed as a pre-requisite for all work in this field, to hear what a parent is saying, and to avoid minimising their experience.

'Time and again, I was turned away without the help I so desperately needed because we all know what a "tantrum" looks like – a kid kicking his or her legs, crying and screaming, for maybe 10 or 15 minutes. By calling Devon's episodes "tantrums" I was unwittingly minimising what was actually going on and no one was taking me seriously … When I began to use the correct terminology to describe Devon's behavior, health care and mental health professionals, even police officers, were more receptive. "Rage" was a magic word that made people pause, listen to my story, and try to help. Instead of brushing me off, they called in psychiatrists and social workers. They made referrals for local services. They stopped treating me like I was just a high-strung mother.'
(Williams, 2018)

This is something we need to be aware of as we listen to and respond to families.

So what about a definition?

Just as we have problems with a name, there is no shortage of definitions of child to parent violence, yet no one definition which is universally accepted.

Credited as the first to name the phenomenon, Harbin and Madden (1979) used their term 'battered parents' to describe 'actual physical assault or verbal or non-verbal threats of physical harm'. Subsequent researchers have included financial, psychological and even sexual assaults and threats in their definitions, as well as acts of coercion. The intention to cause harm has been considered significant in separating this out from so-called 'normal' teenage behaviour, hence the definition employed by Cottrell and Monk (2004) of *'any actions by adolescents that are intended to cause financial, psychological or physical harm'*; and the focus from Howard and Rottem (2008) on physical or psychological attempts *'to dominate, coerce and control others in the family'*.

Those that are most encompassing focus on *a pattern* of violence and abuse, as separate from a one off incident; and they consider the impact on the parent or family and on the relationships between parties involved. The upturning of the normal power balance is crucial. Over time definitions have become more refined, but also broader. The definition I use a lot, and which I shall be employing in this book, is that from Holt (2015):

'*A pattern of behaviour, instigated by a child or young person, which involves using verbal, financial, physical and/or emotional means to practise power and exert control over a parent … The power that is practised is, to some extent, intentional, and the control that is exerted over a parent is achieved through fear, such that a parent unhealthily adapts his/her own behaviour to accommodate the child.*'

It is impossible to over-emphasise the importance of naming the impact on parents. Wilcox *et al* (2015) too call it: '*the most hidden, misunderstood and stigmatised form of family violence. It involves teenage and younger girls and boys who use physical, psychological, emotional and financial abuse over time to the extent that parents/carers* **live in fear of their child** [my emphasis]'. Reported in The Age, Victoria Acting Chief Commissioner, Shane Patton, said that the consequences of family violence are the same as terrorism, and it should be viewed with the same gravity: '*The ramifications are the same in the long run. We have death, we have serious trauma, we have serious injury and we have people impacted for the rest of their lives*' (Mills, 2017).

What are we talking about?

First, what we're not talking about. We're not addressing so-called normal teenage behaviour, nor toddler tantrums, nor a one-off explosion that is eventually resolved. This is not a book about elder abuse, nor abuse by adult children, and not particularly about families where everyone is violent to everyone else – though some of the suggestions would undoubtedly be helpful in those situations. I will talk about the violence that may be experienced in families with severely disabled children and young people, in so far as there is some overlap, but there are other more appropriate sources of help if that is the main issue.

An escalation, perhaps, within verbal abuse, or from verbal abuse to physical violence; it may happen suddenly, 'out of the blue", but, more likely, creeping up unannounced over time, to the extent that it may be difficult to identify the point at which it 'crossed the line':

'*A slow and steady erosion of you as their mum … then suddenly they are in control.*'
(Parent on CPVA programme, with thanks to Jo Sharpen)

All kids do that

How do we know when the line has been crossed, when behaviour has moved from being 'normal' to 'abusive'? Understanding age appropriate behaviour, distinguishing between tantrums and 'meltdowns', thinking about harm caused, looking at the escalating stages of conflict and the usurping of power – all these can help us to distinguish between the stresses that many families experience, as children test boundaries, learn to be independent individuals, struggle with the influence of other relationships, and come to maturity – and the point at which these things might be thought of as abusive. Price (1996) distinguishes six levels of adolescent aggression:

- The petulant child.
- A flair for the dramatic.
- The beginning of damage.
- Threatening gestures and serious damage to possessions.
- People get hurt.
- Serious danger and harm.

A different response is suggested for different levels of aggression. Many adolescents will employ level one and two tactics on a day-to-day basis, tugging at heartstrings to exert control and achieve their aims. Where this behaviour is recognised, and challenged, by parents with effective internal and external resources, simple management techniques can bring results. Without such capital, the child concerned can find they wield growing power in the home.

What does it look like?

The range of behaviours described by parents is wide ranging. I have collected examples together:

> Something that may sound petty to an outsider, but when being experienced on a daily – or hourly basis – takes its toll.
>
> A four year old can do a lot of harm when they are out of control.
>
> A sixteen year old, bigger and heavier than Mum.
>
> The verbal abuse, that goes on and on and on.

Pushing, shoving, tripping, punching, strangling.

Defiance, disrespect, disobedience.

Lying, stealing.

The looks, the silent treatment, the slamming of doors.

Demands for a lift, the hiding of car keys, the taking of a car, the grabbing of a steering wheel.

Rages, that last hours, or days.

The verbal abuse, that goes on and on and on.

Denial of the truth, denial of the remote control, confinement of a parent to one room.

School refusal, refusal to eat, refusal to wash, refusal to leave the house, refusal to speak to relatives.

Lighting fires.

A baseball bat, a phone, a knife. A knife.

Words of abuse, standing too close, threats of assault, inappropriate touching.

The incremental effect of tens, then hundreds, and thousands of pounds lost, through damage repairs, debt payments or theft.

Crockery, a television thrown across the room, a cherished photo broken, a christening bracelet missing.

The verbal abuse, that goes on and on and on.

Threats to self-harm, threats to harm another, threats to kill, threats to run away.

The verbal abuse, that goes on and on and on.

How does it feel?

Words can be carefully chosen, but they can still be sterile. To *define* or *describe* child to parent violence and abuse is one thing; to actually convey a sense of what it *feels* like, what parents *experience* on a day-to-day basis, demands a different voice. Most texts on this subject include some level of testimony from parents. But parents don't sit there waiting for researchers or help to arrive on a white charger. They post on message boards, they call helplines, increasingly they blog and tweet and Facebook each other, they speak at conferences, they tell their story with their words and reclaim some degree of power by so doing. Yes, when you read it sometimes it is hard to believe. Sometimes you think you can put your finger on something and say, 'that, that's the problem'. But it is rarely that straightforward, and the very nature of the beast is that we cannot, and sometimes choose not to, believe that this is really happening. I have included at the end of this chapter some places you can find further testimony from parents.

In the meantime, listen to Jenny. Her son, Adam, was bullied at school, because he was quiet and didn't fit in. He had physical health problems which caused him psychological distress, and for which he held his parents partially responsible. His growing violence at home culminated in him pushing his mother down the stairs, breaking her nose.

'It feels like suffering a bereavement.
He wasn't the child I had imagined.
It is only me that he hits. The worst thing was when he said that he does not respect me …
He is close to his sister. She thinks I take too much from him. She gets cross with me.
He treats me as a housekeeper, someone to provide pants and do the cleaning.
I know that sometimes I say too much – I ask him to do something he has already done. I am stressed. When I am less anxious it is calmer.
He is fine at school or out somewhere else, but it is all difficult at home. He will throw things when he is angry or frustrated, throw them down the stairs, or turn his room upside down. He will push me but he hasn't hit me for a while since we have been working at things. He will still make a fist and go as if to hit me. He makes me afraid. I am scared of him. I don't know when it will all start. He can be fine. We have happy times as well. We can do things together as a family. But then you are waiting for it to happen.'
(Interview with Jenny, 2015)

The issue of intent

This discussion is one which seems to have been building over the last year, as members of the adoption community in particular have shared their experiences.

'And … with a pretty clean slap in the face we're back into deliberate provocative #CPV and yep, I still have no idea what to actually do.'
(Tweet from Pedalling Solo, @PedallingSolo, 27rd March 2017)

How do we understand the actual intent of children and young people to do harm, or to control the narrative within the home? 'Intent' is something that features widely in definitions of CPVA, and within many articles and publications. Indeed, it has been seen as fundamental in understanding the processes whereby a child may usurp the position of authority within the home, and create an environment where parents are scared of them and alter the way they live.

Intervention programmes work on the basis of a child or young person's capacity to acknowledge a sense of purpose in their actions and to decide to change. We may well be able to think of scenarios where a child or young person demonstrates clear intent in their thinking and actions around violence and abuse.

> Emil has poor control of his temper, and this has involved him in offending behaviour, which has in turn brought him to the attention of the youth offending service. He meets with his social worker and talks about the way he uses behaviour to control his mother and sister in the home to achieve his goals. He knows that they are afraid of him, and chooses to continue to use controlling tactics because there is a pay off.

But for many, this is a thorny subject, warranting greater analysis; and some would contest whether 'intent' should even be included within our definition of CPVA, or alternatively, whether there is, in fact, more than one phenomenon happening. Some parents may feel uncomfortable about labelling their child's behaviour as malign, and prefer phrases such as 'trauma-fuelled violence' or 'signs of distress' to the term CPVA. Observers may point to the child's past experiences as having determined their responses, (explaining, rather than necessarily excusing the behaviour). But to what extent is it then beyond a child's control to change? Is there a difference between intent to act in a certain way, and intent to harm? How much agency can be ascribed to young children, particularly those who have learning difficulties, or who have experience of trauma in their lives?

In 2018, Thorley and Coates released an analysis of responses to an online survey about families' experiences of CPVA. The question of intent was, for them, a difficult one, and they sought to untangle the issue by creating an umbrella term of Childhood Challenging, Violent and Aggressive Behaviour (CCVAB), distinguishing within this between CPVA, where there is evidence of clear intent to use power to control and to cause harm; and *'Conduct Disorder confined to the family context',* for *'children who are unable to regulate and moderate their verbal, emotional and physical responses to the environment'* a distinction perhaps between instrumental, and expressive violence. The latter group would include children with experience of early trauma, diagnosed conditions such as autism spectrum disorders (ASD), and other trauma, attachment or learning difficulties.

In making such a clear separation, we must be careful to avoid a direct causal link and inevitability between conditions such as ASD and violence and abuse – something which Gallagher (2018) and others have been keen to challenge. Bonnie van Metre of the Kennedy Krieger Center for Autism and Related Disorders states *'Children do not engage in self-injury, aggression, property destruction or seriously disruptive behaviors solely because they have a disability. Challenging behavior has a message … it communicates a need … behavior serves a specific function'*. A further risk is that we construct the two 'types' as binary opposites. Many children without experience of early trauma, using violence with clear intent, would fit the description and diagnosis for conduct disorder; and children with early trauma and issues such as reactive attachment disorder may work hard to control many aspects of relationships and their surroundings in order to feel safe.

> *'After the 8th hospitalization, Mary came home with a murder plan. She'd written it down with pictures and words while inpatient. Despite our best efforts to monitor and keep our cupboards locked, she found a weapon. And she planned to find it, planned to use it, all around her father's work schedule. When Luke wouldn't be here to protect us. She wasn't out-of-control. She was casually discussing getting rid of the people who cause her the most emotions. Because love hurts Mary. She fears it. She hates it.'*
> (Herding Chickens blog, 2017)

Kate Iwi argues (2018) that part of the difficulty with the idea of intent is in the way we are conceptualising it. She also suggests that trying to separate the two is unnecessarily divisive. And so the jury is still out on this distinction. The reality may be that some children are able to, and do, move from one to the other. I used to think of this in terms of a line, with extremes at each end and most somewhere in between. I am inclined these days to think more in terms of Venn diagrams.

What is clear, listening to parents, is that the experience of the violence or abuse can be exactly the same, whether it comes from a place of high anxiety in the child, or deliberate and malicious intent. While we would want to exclude children and young adults with severe learning difficulties from consideration here, I believe that it is important to start from a position of recognising and seeking an understanding of the levels of violence and abuse, and the impact of this; before we can move on to thinking about the different types of intervention that might be needed: how they might differ, and similarities that might exist.

What can you do?

Reading testimony from parents can be overwhelming after a while, but I would suggest that the more we read and learn about the experience of child to parent violence and abuse, the better we will be able to respond at work, or indeed in our private lives. To read more does not make us inured, but begins a process of realisation that there is a lot of this happening, which in turn can make us more ready to hear and believe parents, and families, when they do come to us for help.

Check out what parents are telling you as opposed to what you are hearing. Are they the same? Do parents have the words that you recognise, or are they using different terminology? What questions would help make this clear?

Find out more

Many parents are now blogging about their experiences of child to parent violence and abuse.

- Hannah Meadows: CPV stories https://hannahmeadows.com/cpv-stories/.
- Raising Devon: https://raisingdevon.com.
- Herding Chickens: https://heardingchickens.wordpress.com
- The Mumdrah Diaries: http://mumdrah.co.uk/category/the-mumdrah-diaries/ particularly the post *Collateral Damage*, http://mumdrah.co.uk/collateral-damage/.

For further testimony from parents, there are numerous websites, blogs and message boards, for instance:

The Institute for Attachment and Child Development, 'Why my child with reactive attachment disorder acts differently with you than with me': https://www.instituteforattachment.org/why-my-child-with-reactive-attachment-disorder-acts-different-with-you-than-with-me/.

The Silent Suffering of Parent Abuse: When Children Abuse Parents
https://wehavekids.com/family-relationships/The-Silent-Suffering-of-Parent-Abuse-When-Children-Abuse-Parents
On this site there are 508 comments from individuals around the world talking about their own experience of abuse.

Most research publications include testimony. A good place to start is the research report, *'It all Starts at Home,'* from **Jo Howard and Naomi Rottem** (2008). Available at: http://apo.org.au/system/files/3995/apo-nid3995-59656.pdf.

For more visual renderings, there are a number of films and documentaries that cover the issue of CPVA. *In Cold Blood* is a docu-drama series from Singapore, exploring the impact of extreme and shocking behaviours, and highlighting issues such as family violence. The episode, **Parental Abuse**, was published in 2013. https://www.youtube.com/watch?v=RNGw-vuFqR0.

For more information about research into children and young people who display harmful sexual behaviour, see the DMSS Research paper from **Di McNeish and Sara Scott** (2018) https://www.csacentre.org.uk/index.cfm/_api/render/file/?method=inline&fileID=E2C17C42-5084-47CC-902E94451079C6B6.

Yvonne Newbold opened up the discussion in the UK about the experience of violence from children with severe learning difficulties. You can read more about this on her website: http://yvonnenewbold.com.

Jerome Price includes many vignettes in his book *Power and Compassion: Working with difficult adolescents and abused parents* which explore ways of working with families of aggressive teens. Some of these offer strategies for work, some are examples of, for instance, escalation or different types of abuse.

Tantrums vs. meltdowns?
There are many places you can find writing about the distinction between tantrums and meltdowns. See for instance *'Dealing with your Child's Meltdowns'*, a blog post on '**The Curly Hair Project** website, https://thegirlwiththecurlyhair.co.uk/2015/03/03/dealing-with-your-childs-meltdowns/.

James McTaggart, an educational psychologist, has produced a chart comparing different models of understanding behaviour, and the way this plays out in different fields of expectations, beliefs and management: https://twitter.com/JamesEdPsych/status/1027184323521331200.

Eddie Gallagher offers a list of situations when a child might apparently use violence towards a parent or carer, making distinctions between those that might be included in a discussion of CPVA and those outside this definition. (The list appears in different orders in different publications.)
http://www.eddiegallagher.com.au/violence%20to%20parents.html.

References

Coogan D (2014) Responding to child-to-parent violence: innovative practices in child and adolescent mental health. *Health and Social Work* **39** (2) e1–e9.

Cottrell B and Monk P (2004) Adolescent-to-parent abuse. A qualitative overview of common themes. *Journal of Family Issues* **25** (8) 1072–1095.

Gallagher E (2018) *Who's in Charge? Why children abuse parents and what you can do about it.* London: Austin Macauley Publishers.

Harbin HT and Madden DJ (1979) Battered parents – a new syndrome. *American Journal of Psychiatry* **136** (10) 1288–1291.

Herding Chickens (2017) *What are we Fighting for?* [online]. Available at: https://heardingchickens.wordpress.com/2017/06/11/what-are-we-fighting-for/ (accessed February 2019).

Howard J and Rottem N (2008) *It All Starts at Home: Male adolescent violence to mothers*. Inner Couth Community Health Service Inc and Child Abuse Research Australia, Monash University.

Holt A (Ed.) (2015) *Working with Adolescent Violence and Abuse Towards Parents*. Oxford: Routledge.

Iwi K (2018) *What Do We Mean by 'Intent' in the Context of Child to Parent Violence?* [online]. Available at:https://wp.me/p1sWM6-1j5 (accessed February 2019).

Mills T (2017) Quarter of all youths committing family violence are boys bashing their mums. *The Age* **8 December**. Available at: https://www.theage.com.au/national/victoria/family-violence-treated-same-as-terrorism-under-new-police-strategy-20171207-h00lvl.html (accessed February 2019).

Murphy-Edwards LJ (2012) *Not Just Another Hole in the Wall: An investigation into child and youth perpetrated domestic property violence* [online]. Doctor of Philosophy Thesis, University of Canterbury, New Zealand. Available at: https://core.ac.uk/download/pdf/35469378.pdf (accessed February 2019).

Price J (1996) *Power and Compassion, Working with Difficult Adolescents and Abused Parents*. New York: The Guilford Press.

Thorley W and Coates A (2018) *Let's Talk About: Child-parent Violence and Aggression (CPVA)* [online]. Available at: https://www.academia.edu/37078253/Lets_Talk_About_Child_to_Parent_Violence_2018_Summary (accessed February 2019).

Wilcox P (2012) Is parent abuse a form of domestic violence? *Social Policy and Society* **11** (2) 277–288.

Wilcox P, Pooley M, Ferrando M, Coogan D, Lauster E, Assenova A, Mortenson A & Christoffersson I (2015) *Responding to Child to Parent Violence: Executive summary* [online]. Available at: http://www.rcpv.eu/78-rcpv-executive-summary-may-2015-english/file (accessed February 2019).

Williams K (2018) *Why This Mom Uses the Word "Rage" and Not "Tantrum" for her Child with Developmental Trauma Disorder (a.k.a. Reactive Attachment Disorder)* [online]. Institute for Attachment and Child Development. Available at: https://instituteforattachment.org/rage-not-tantrum/ (accessed February 2019).

Part 1:
Five impossible things to believe

Chapter 1: How much?

One of the first things people want to know about CPVA is 'How big a problem is it?' The second is, 'Is it getting worse?'. It is disappointing to have to keep replying to both that we just don't know.

- Journalists are interested in figures to back up their stories.
- Campaigners want to bolster their cause and garner support.
- Academics seek integrity.
- Commissioners are required to justify their spending.
- Families are relieved to know that they are not alone.

How would we know?

In order to be taken seriously, there is a need for any cause to gather data. In this case the maxim 'If you can't measure it, you can't manage it' has been what has driven people of late. We want to know, but can we ever hope for a truly accurate figure?

Given the lack of agreement on what to call this form of violence, it is amazing perhaps that we have the amount of data that we do, but what we have is a real mish-mash of statistics, some now quite old, others more recent. There are conclusions drawn from asking questions of the general population, as well as from specific groups of people affected by the issue; some analysis looking at numbers and some more interested in the experience of violence; and as well as academic work there are annual and special reports from those agencies engaged in work in this field.

All of this has been collected in different ways, using different definitions of CPVA, from a range of sample sizes and age groups, or populations that are very specific. The conclusions that have been drawn are sometimes at odds with each other in different types of research. This makes it difficult to draw accurate conclusions in terms of numbers perhaps, but all together, it is interesting in itself as an indicator of how wide ranging an issue it may be, and as a historical record of the growing awareness of the issue. You will repeatedly hear the figure of 10% – ten percent of families with adolescents experiencing violence and abuse on a regular basis – but where does this figure come from, and how reliable is it?

While practitioners in other countries had been documenting their findings for some years, the interest in Britain in the issue, in comparison to other aspects of family violence, remained low, and it was not until 2009/2010 that a new wave of academic discussion concerning CPVA emerged here. Initially 'discovered by accident' in research into other issues (Holt, 2009; Galvani, 2010; Hunter *et al*, 2010; Selwyn *et al*, 2014), CPVA became a topic for research and discussion in its own right and spawned a serious of papers, conferences and networks. Links were made with the publication of figures from annual reports of a number of charities (Family Lives, YoungMinds), raising the profile further. While in the UK we saw the publication of findings from two major pieces of research: *Adolescent to Parent Violence and Abuse* (Condry and Miles, 2013) and *Responding to Child to Parent Violence* (Wilcox *et al*, 2015); we are still playing catch-up with other countries in terms of the impact this has had on policy and practice. But as awareness has increased at a local level, new data has begun to be gathered that enables a more rounded and nuanced understanding of the difficulties faced by so many families, and the sorts of intervention that might help them move forward.

Lies, damned lies and statistics

Before looking at some of the numbers, a general word about data. Statistics can be presented in misleading ways, whether through mischief, lack of time or ignorance. Tabloid newspaper headlines are a particular example of this! How we feel about numbers may be determined by our own experience, personal or professional, and our relationship with the subject. Some people find it easier to think of numbers in more concrete ways – a classroom of children for instance, a personal friendship group, or perhaps the local town population. There will continue to be question marks over the reliability of much of the data we use, and we need to be aware of this in the claims we make for it. Honesty, shame, timing, who or what we ask, who is doing the recording, what they understand, how it is recorded, these factors all impact on the answers we receive. To what extent is it reasonable to extrapolate generally from figures garnered from a particular population, in a particular place, at a particular time? The very notion of children being violent and abusive towards their parents lies so far outside of most people's model of family life that they find it difficult to conceive of it as an issue at all; and some people will argue that the figures we have are a wild over-statement. Others point to the fact that, since it is so difficult to talk about, they represent only the tip of the iceberg. In discussing prevalence, we neither want to create a moral panic, nor bury our heads in the sand.

So let's look at the data we have, where it comes from, and what it can tell us.

General population self-report surveys

Through the 1980s and '90s, there was an emphasis on counting acts of violence or abuse, generally using the Conflict Tactics Scale, or a serious of questions included in a larger survey. A number of largely American studies asked respondents in the general population about their experiences of different aspects of violence, variously as victims and/or perpetrators; and from these surveys we glean figures of anywhere between 2 and 25% of teens perpetrating violence in the home against parents. Straus *et al* (1980) found a total of 18% of children aged 3-17 years old had hit their parent in the previous year, a figure that becomes 10% when confined to adolescents. In another study from Gelles and Straus (1988), the figure of 10% reappears, again including young children. Much of the later discussion refers back to these surveys for statistical purposes, despite the fact that this includes all types of violence and ages, and as little as one act of violence a year. Looking only at more severe acts of violence, across a number of different surveys, the figure drops to 2-5%, and it has been suggested (Gallagher, 2008) that, in taking a less all-encompassing definition, and cross matching a range of different data, this figure represents a more accurate picture.

At risk population surveys

It would be expected that responses from these surveys would give a higher figure for the incidence of violence towards parents. Gallagher (2008) looked at studies including family conflict and violence in their remit, and found figures ranging from 10-75% in research into groups such as substance using youth, young runaways, or those in a residential training establishment. He found the data to be inconclusive for similar reasons to the broader surveys, but notes that a figure nearer 20-25% (for more severe violence) does emerge overall, and has more credibility when viewed against that of 3% for the general population. From this we can suggest that certain groups of young children are more likely to be using violence and abuse at home, compared to the general population.

Police, court and clinical data analysis

Researchers have examined data from police records, courts, hospitals and clinical practice, often including individual case studies too; and we also see this when it is released following requests by journalists for particular stories. Weight of numbers as this accumulates arguably gives a better sense of the overall picture, but this too must be treated with some caution. Families come to the attention of, or seek help from, one agency rather than another for a variety of reasons. By the time they seek help the situation may be well established. Some agencies will then operate their own filtering system in the recording and processing, both of people and data.

Some countries are ahead of others in the collection and dissemination of data regarding wider aspects of family violence. A research team at Monash University (Fitz-Gibbon *et al*, 2017) examined records from the Melbourne children's court which showed 6,228 applications for a family violence intervention order where the respondent was 17 years or younger, between July 2011 and June 2016. In 45 of these, the respondent was aged 10-11 years old. The recent Royal Commission into Family Violence report (2016), by the Victoria government in Australia, included significant information about adolescent to parent violence, such as 1 in 10 police family call outs related to adolescents using violence in the home, and has led to money being found for preventative work. Since the publication of this report, figures collected for family violence include CPVA, revealing that 7000 youths were reported for family violence in 2016-17 (Mills, 2017).

In contrast, from Canada, the Chief Public Health Officer's report – *A Focus on Family Violence in Canada* (2016) includes only a few lines on parent abuse, and no statistics. Within Britain, Condry and Miles (2013) had to manually sift through police records for their research. They found 1,892 cases of adolescent to parent violence reported to the Metropolitan Police in one year (2009-10) looking at adolescents aged 13-19 years old.

We have information about links with poor mental health, and other diagnoses both from research looking at the reported incidence of CPVA among those being treated in hospital (Laurent and Derry, 1999), and the mental health profile of those known to be using violence towards their parents. This distinction is an important one to make when we talk about the influence of different factors in explaining CPVA. Gallagher (2018) has reported on findings from his own clinical sample, which has grown to over 500 cases; and other programmes working with families have also released information and analysis about the work they are engaged in (Routt and Anderson, 2014).

As these studies accumulate over time and the total population studied increases in size, it is from this dataset particularly that people have started to draw conclusions about the prevalence of abuse by gender of parent and young person, by race, class, family characteristics or parenting style, health and wider offending behaviour. The data from this work tends to give a different slant to our understanding to that from the general population surveys. For instance, the distribution by gender appears more equal in surveys than when clinical data is examined – the answers to questions perhaps reflecting the different ways in which men and women feel about, and experience, the use of violence and abuse. There are, of course, arguments that clinical data is in itself not completely objective, depending on cultural perceptions of, tolerance of, and responses to violence.

Emerging from other research

Holt (2009) unearthed some troubling findings in a research study into the experiences of parents whose children were involved in the youth justice system, and who had received 'parenting orders'. She was surprised to find that parents, both mothers and fathers, spoke about violence and abuse from their children 'in passing' as if it were of no consequence, that it had been continuing for quite some time, and that there was little wider acknowledgement of this as an issue or of how to respond.

A study of families supporting a family member using drugs or alcohol, also turned up unexpected findings in relation to the levels of violence and abuse from children towards their parents and carers. Galvani (2010) reported on this in the final report, and then went on to conduct further follow up research as a result.

Similarly, Hunter *et al* were engaged in a review of Family Intervention Projects when they began to find more and more parents reporting violence and abuse from their children, often following an experience of intimate partner violence. They went on to publish a further paper in 2010 examining their findings in greater depth.

Beyond the Adoption Order (Selwyn *et al*, 2014) was a ground-breaking report into adoption breakdown in Britain, yet it was also significant in lifting the lid on the true level of violence and abuse experienced by adoptive parents from their children. They found that up to 30% of the families surveyed experienced violence and abuse on a regular basis, some 3% to the extent that it became unsafe to carry on, and children went on to live elsewhere.

'We were surprised to find that 19 parents (27% of the most challenging group), without prompting, reported worrying behaviour shown by their child around the use of knives. Parents described children who had used knives to threaten, intimidate, or control others … One mother for example, described how her son would pick up a knife, make eye contact with her, then slowly and deliberately put it back down. Another described how her daughter ran her finger up and down a knife during an altercation with her father.'
(Selwyn *et al*, 2014)

Reports such as these started to suggest that this was a more widespread and complex issue than had been understood. Some involved a small sample size and so it was difficult to make generalisations to the wider population, but it was clear that for particular groups of families, in particular circumstances, this was a regular and serious problem that demanded greater attention.

Specific research

Around the world we now see a growing body of research specifically targeting the issue of CPVA, much from Spain, the US, Australia, and Britain in particular. Studies have examined samples of school-aged children (Ibabe *et al*, 2013) and university-aged young people (Gamez-Guadix and Calvete, 2012); families where an individual suffers from mental illness (Sporer and Toller 2017); or is using drugs or alcohol (Calvete *et al*, 2015); or has come to the attention of the police (Ibabe *et al*, 2014); adoptive parents and special guardians, amongst others groups – and significantly the body of work as a whole also includes interviews with practitioners (Holt and Retford, 2013; Coogan, 2016). Less concerned with numbers as such, attempts have been made to draw conclusions, often about risk or predictive factors in either the child's or family life. Suggestions are made as to who is most affected and in what ways. The human and economic costs of abuse are documented. Comparisons have been made as to different responses and their effectiveness.

The first large-scale research data in Britain, from the Oxford adolescent to parent violence and abuse (APVA) study, was published by Condry and Miles in 2013. Condry and Miles physically counted reports to the Metropolitan Police of physical violence to parents (including step parents and grandparents) or property from 13-19 year olds over the course of one year, 2009-2010. The figure of 1892 incidents is important in demonstrating that this is not an insignificant problem, but the data should be handled with care:

- This is only what police recorded.
- It is only what parents reported.
- We know that calling the police may be a last resort.
- Culture, race, class etc. all have an influence in determining who reports to the police and how they, in turn, respond.
- The understanding of domestic violence and APVA influences the way police respond.

'Responding to Child to Parent Violence' (RCPV) was a pan-European three-year research project which reported in 2015, investigating policy and practice in five different European countries, with the aim of raising awareness of child to parent violence, and finding out how countries across Europe deal with it (Wilcox *et al*, 2015). This project developed a significant bank of resources including films and toolkits for practitioners who work with young people and parents experiencing this problem.

Smaller scale surveys have also been commissioned to explore the issue further, particularly, in the UK, from the adoption community. Thorley and Coates followed up an earlier online survey (2016, reported in 2017) into adopters' experience of CPVA, with a larger survey of parents generally in 2018. The organisation Special Guardians and Adopters Together (Schroer, 2018) similarly commissioned a survey into the stress, health and well-being of their peers, highlighting anger and rage meltdowns as the most common problem faced, and CPVA affecting 69% of respondents.

Annual and special reports

Around the world, charities working to support families often operate helplines and online advice and support. A look at the annual reviews and reports for some of these reveals a high level of stress for families with teenagers, with significant numbers seeking help because of behaviour and relationship problems. In their annual report for 2013-14, **YoungMinds** reported receiving 33,239 calls to the telephone helpline during the year. Of these, 11,483 were unique callers, and CPVA features on the top five reasons for calling. Daphne Joseph (manager of the parents helpline) reported in a radio interview on BBC West Midlands that about 52% of calls are to do with children and young people using violence, and that mental health concerns were a prominent issue.

The organisation **Family Lives** has been particularly important in raising awareness, and they too are regularly called on for media interviews. Their annual reports specifically mention child on parent violence, in case studies and in the high proportion of parents calling the helpline regarding teenagers' aggressive behaviour. In 2010 they released a report focusing on this in its entirety, updated in 2011 with recommendations to government. They show a steadily increasing number of visitors to their website and helpline, with a commensurate rise in the number of calls about children's physical aggression.

4Children (now part of Action for Children) examined the incidence and effects of family conflict in their 2012 report, *The Enemy Within*. Surveying 1,018 families with children, they suggested up to a fifth of families had serious or frequent arguments with teenage children – not in itself necessarily indicative of CPVA, but the report also comments that adolescent to parent violence was found to be a growing problem. From this survey it is extrapolated that 4 million families in the UK experience regular conflict and violence in the home.

In their national policy report, *In Plain Sight* (2014), **CAADA** (now called Safe Lives) drew attention to the link between children's experience of witnessing domestic violence, and then going on to use violence themselves.

Drawing on 877 children's cases captured by front-line specialist children's workers and supplementary data from 331 children, from four specialist services, they found that children suffered multiple physical and mental health consequences as a result of exposure to domestic abuse. A quarter of the children were found to exhibit abusive behaviours themselves, mostly once their exposure had ended.

From reports such as these we learn more about where families go for help, and the difficulties they are having in finding appropriate support. We also generate a broader understanding of who is affected, but more of that later.

So what figure sounds reasonable to you?

A strange question perhaps, but we should acknowledge our own assumptions and leanings. Perhaps we are becoming more used to figures of around 25% when talking about the prevalence of intimate partner violence, of childhood sexual abuse, or incidence of mental distress, and yet they would have seemed unthinkably high just a few years ago. If we pause to consider some of the other statistics thrown at us on a daily basis, many involving factors that are seen to increase the risk for CPVA, how does our thinking change?

- Three children in every class have a diagnosable mental disorder (YoungMinds, 2018).
- More than 68,000 children in England are diagnosed with conduct disorder (Public Health England, 2016).
- One in seven teenagers experience some form of neglect (The Children's Society, 2016).
- Around one in five children are exposed to domestic violence in the home (NSPCC, 2018).
- One child in every class is bereaved (Child Bereavement UK, 2019).
- In some parts of the country, as many as one in four children are living in kinship care arrangements (Nandy and Selwyn, 2011).
- 46,000 children are thought to be involved in gangs (Children's Commissioner's Report, 2017).

None of these issues, in itself, suggests that a family will go on to experience CPVA. However, each of them is indicative of levels of stress in the lives of young people and their families, and we should be concerned about them in their own right. They are presented to consider what vulnerabilities in family dynamics they might go on to create, and to place a 3% figure for CPVA into perspective.

So what about 3% now? That would be one child per class in a typical British secondary school using violence or abuse at home. If you work in that field, might you think it too low? A figure of 10% gives me around ten families that I know well. That may feel impossibly high, but probably reflects reality. Cottrell (2004) testified to the way in which individuals routinely started telling her about their personal experiences as soon as she mentioned her work. As I talk to people about my interest, more and more parents open up about their own family life.

Make it useful, make it real

Big data is useful in indicating a need, generating a demand from training or the redirecting of resources, positioning something in a hierarchy for dwindling funds; and of course for demonstrating change, whether worsening or improving. On a national scale, governments may be obliged to take notice of new understandings and respond in some measure (for instance with violence against women and girls (VAWG) guidance); but of more value is to augment it with local knowledge, specific up-to-date statistics and interpretations pertinent to local demography or agency remit. At the 2014 RCPV conference in Galway, different agencies testified to their own findings regarding prevalence:

- Cuan Saor, a women's refuge, saw 89 families in March 2014, 18% of whom reported having had experience of CPVA.
- A substance use agency asked families about CPVA, and 8% had identified it as an issue in 2013.

A quick reflection on caseloads may suggest figures as high as 30% for some agencies. A parent visiting A&E with her son spoke to the nursing sister at length as she took the family history. She was told that on every shift the staff might see 2-3 families affected by CPVA (personal communication).

Better still is solid data, as agencies start to gather and analyse their own statistics in this way.

During a conference on responding to children's violence to parents, there was a discussion about the problem of how little data is available across sectors. Gudrun Burnet, Senior Business Partner (Domestic Abuse), who is the lead on domestic abuse and violence against women and girls at Peabody, realised that it would be possible to change the data sets within the organisation's IT system to capture much more detail quite easily, went back to work the next week and did it! The housing provider is now able to produce figures on reports of abuse to family members by teens (male or female) as well as by adults.

'The re-structuring of the delivery of services for young people in Surrey was identified as providing a key opportunity to raise awareness of adolescent to parent abuse (APA) amongst practitioners and professionals and a study was undertaken by a practitioner with particular interest in youth justice, more broadly the areas of aggressive behaviour in adolescents, intimate partner violence in adolescents, domestic abuse, and young people who display harmful sexual behaviour.

The aim of the study was to explore the prevalence of APA encountered by practitioners during their work for a front-line service. An online survey was designed to capture quantitative data with which to establish the prevalence of APA, in addition to capturing information about offence, victim and perpetrator characteristics. Surrey Youth Support Service (SYSS) gave permission for the dissemination of the online survey to SYSS practitioners. A favourable ethical opinion was obtained from The University of Portsmouth, which confirmed that the proposed research was ethically compliant. Relevant permissions were sought from SYSS and practitioner's participation was voluntary and consent was fully informed.

A total of 66 practitioners employed by SYSS in May 2014 participated in the study. This represents approximately one third of SYSS practitioners. Eighty-two percent of the sample recalled working with an average of six young people referred to the SYSS who had displayed APA. This represents approximately just over one case (1.24) of APA per year, per participant. Data from SYSS report that the average number of cases open at any one time is 9.8 and that the average length of a case is 6.75 months (0.56 years). This would suggest that SYSS practitioners work with an average of 17.4 cases per year. Therefore, the sample rate of 1.24 cases of APA per year, per participant, represents seven percent of a participant's annual caseload. These findings demonstrate that APA is moderately prevalent within SYSS and an intervention directed at this form of family abuse would be desirable. This research is being further developed as part of a professional doctorate thesis.'

(Beth McCloud, Professional Doctorate Student, reprinted with kind permission)

Is it getting worse?

Reading the media, and other reports, might well lead one to believe that this is an issue that is getting worse year on year.

'Sharp rise in parents being abused by their violent children.'
(Hunte, 2017, ITV News)

'Police figures show a surge in the number of under-18s treated as 'suspects' in violent crimes against their parents, with offences including assault, robbery and sex attacks.'
(Barrett, 2015, The Telegraph)

In the week following a mother's death in the London Borough of Tower Hamlets in 2014, at the hands of her young son (Arkell, 2014), children's services received 70 calls (personal communication) from parents about violence and abuse from their children. No one would suggest that this was an increase in experience, but it shows how little we might know about the true figure.

Annual reports appear to show a year-on-year increase in parents calling for help. Barrett, writing in *The Telegraph* newspaper (2015) claimed that data from the Metropolitan police records show an increase of 61% in violent crime by young people under 18 against their parents, in the two years between 2012 (895) and 2014 (1417). But what does this actually tell us? How do we interpret figures such as this?

Many would argue that CPVA has always been with us, and recent reports of an increase merely reflect our growing awareness, a change in the way we think of and understand it, and in the way it is recorded. Others point to changes in society and the way we live our lives, which may indicate a likely increase.

A speeding up of life, increases in stress, exam pressures within education, consumerism, materialism, more children staying at home longer as housing costs rocket … all these have been proposed as links to poorer mental health, increased levels of expectation and entitlement, or conflict within the family. Families move across the globe because of war, or for personal or economic reasons. Families split up and re-form. More children are taken into care. Early intervention services are cut at times of austerity. Children spend more time indoors because of the fear of risks in society – or they spend more time outside because of cramped housing condition. Online activity exposes children to new risks. Parents reportedly feel disempowered through the discouragement of smacking, without alternative systems being suggested. Parenting styles change. A risk-averse or over-involved parenting approach denies opportunities for children to fail, and learn resilience. What is considered 'normal' changes.

In the middle of all of this, let us not be accused of trying to make a point. The picture is not overwhelmingly bad, and we do need to take care in how we read beyond the headlines, drilling down into the details of a report. So, the headline figures for teenage girls self-harming are indeed deeply shocking; but overall, the *Good Childhood Report* (The Children's Society, 2018) suggests that the general level of happiness among teens remains much the same, or is improving. The Relate report into the state of family life (Marjoribanks, 2016), recognising the fundamental importance of family relationships in terms of general well-being, found 91% of parents considered their relationship with their (birth) children to be good – though this number drops to 61% for step children. A piece in The Conversation (Williams, 2014), admittedly from 2014, urges us to reject the cherry picking of the tabloid press focusing on 'feral youth', and teenage violence and dysfunction, and to read the full *Longitudinal Study of Young People in England* (Department for Education, 2014) in full to get a more rounded picture of what is going well and not so well in young people's lives.

Whatever else is going on, we should be pleased that more people are talking about their experience of child to parent violence, that parents feel more able to ask for help, and that there are better recording systems in place. Is there more child to parent violence than in the past? Without reliable and comparable data we can never say for sure. We may not be able to back up the claims that *'the number of parents being abused by their children has nearly doubled over the last five years'* (Hunte, 2017), but it is probably fair to assume that there has been some increase in the last couple of decades.

There are many benefits in the gathering of data. We just need to be careful about the claims we make about it. Perhaps we will never be able to ascertain a real figure for the number of families affected by violence and abuse from their children, or about the rates of increase; but to start collecting information now, wherever we work, can only be a gain.

What can you do?

- How about a survey of staff about their workday experience?
- An audit of case files, or new referrals?
- Or a decision to ask families routinely about their experience? This needs to be planned carefully to ensure there is an appropriate response to the answers given.

- Altering data collection methods for the future.
- Supporting a doctoral student (or, indeed, undertaking doctoral or other research).
- Liaising with other local agencies to scope wider statistics.

Find out more

A good overview of the studies can be gained by reading some of the literature reviews.

Gallagher E (2008) *Children's Violence to Parents: A critical literature review* [online]. Monash University: http://www.eddiegallagher.com.au/Child%20 Parent%20Violence%20Masters%20Thesis%20Gallagher%202008.pdf. Gallagher's Master's thesis gives tables comparing different surveys and studies and shows how he came to his figures. He offers a comprehensive analysis and commentary of the reliability of early statistics.

Hong JS, Kral MJ, Espelage DL & Allen-Meares P (2012) The social ecology of adolescent-initiated parent abuse: a review of the literature. *Child Psychiatry and Human Development* **43** 431–454.

Kennair N and Mellor D (2007) Parent abuse: a review. *Child Psychiatry and Human Development* **38** 203–219.

Safe Lives (2015) *Getting it Right First Time*: http://www.safelives.org.uk/sites/default/files/resources/SafeLives%20top%20 tips%20sheet%20FINAL%20FOR%20WEB_0.pdf. This top tips sheet is for routinely asking about the experience of violence/abuse. Although this is designed primarily for use where there are adult perpetrators, it is still useful as a starting point.

Simmons M, McEwan TE, Purcell R & Ogloff JRP (2018) Sixty years of child-to-parent abuse research: what we know and where to go. *Aggression and Violent Behaviour* **38** 31–52. (This is the most recent and probably the most comprehensive.)

Walsh JA and Krienert JL (2009) A decade of child-initiated family violence: comparative analysis of child-parent violence and parricide examining offender, victim and event characteristics in a national sample of reported incidents, 1995-2005. *Journal of Interpersonal Violence* **24** (9) 1450–1477.

ADCS (2018) *Executive Summary: Safeguarding pressures phase:*
http://adcs.org.uk/assets/documentation/ADCS_SAFEGUARDING_PRESSURES_PHASE_6_EXECUTIVE_SUMMARY_FINAL.pdf .

References

4Children (2012) *The Enemy Within: 4 million reasons to tackle family conflict and family violence* [online]. Available at: http://www.ersab.org.uk/easysiteweb/getresource.axd?assetid=174516&type=0&servicetype=1 (accessed February 2019).

Arkell H (2014) Teenager arrested after his mother is found dead at their home in East London. *Daily Mail* **12 February**.

Barrett D (2015) Children as young as seven accused of violent 'crime' on parents. *The Telegraph* **6 May**. Available at: https://www.telegraph.co.uk/news/uknews/crime/11586949/Children-as-young-as-seven-accused-of-violent-crime-on-parents.html (accessed February 2019).

CAADA (2014) *In Plain Sight: Effective help for children exposed to domestic abuse* [online]. Available at: http://www.safelives.org.uk/sites/default/files/resources/Final%20policy%20report%20In%20plain%20sight%20-%20effective%20help%20for%20children%20exposed%20to%20domestic%20abuse.pdf (accessed February 2019).

Calvete E, Orue I & Gamez-Guadix M (2015) Reciprocal longitudinal associations between substance use and child-to-parent violence in adolescents. *Journal of Adolescence* **44** 124–133.

Child Bereavement UK (2019) *Why We are Needed – Statistics* [online]. Available at: https://childbereavementuk.org/about-us/why-we-are-needed-statistics/ (accessed February 2019).

Children's Commissioner (2017) *On Measuring the Number of Vulnerable Children in England* [online]. Available at: https://www.childrenscommissioner.gov.uk/wp-content/uploads/2017/07/CCO-On-vulnerability-Overveiw-2.pdf (accessed February 2019).

Condry R and Miles C (2013) Adolescent to parent violence: framing and mapping a hidden problem. *Criminology and Criminal Justice* **14** (3) 257–275.

Coogan D (2016) Listening to practitioners talking about child to parent violence and abuse: Some findings from an action research project. *The Irish Social Work Journal* 41–48.

Cottrell B (2004) *When Teens Abuse Their Parents*. Canada: Fernwood Publishing.

Department for Education (2014) *Longitudinal Study of Young People in England: cohort 2, wave 1* [online]. Available at: https://assets.publishing.service.gov.uk/government/uploads/system/uploads/attachment_data/file/374649/RR388_-_Longitudinal_study_of_young_people_in_England_cohort_2__wave_1.pdf (accessed February 2019).

Family Lives (2010) *When Family Life Hurts: Family experience of aggression in children* [online]. Available at: https://www.familylives.org.uk/media_manager/public/209/Documents/Reports/When%20family%20life%20hurts%202010.pdf (accessed February 2019).

Family Lives (2011) *When Family Life Hurts: Family experiences of aggression in children, an update to the 2010 report* [online]. Available at: https://www.familylives.org.uk/media_manager/public/209/Documents/Reports/the_aggression_report_2011_family_lives.pdf (accessed February 2019).

Fitz-Gibbon K, Maher JM and McCulloch J (2017) Long ignored, adolescent family violence needs our attention. *The Conversation*. **3 July** Available at: https://theconversation.com/long-ignored-adolescent-family-violence-needs-our-attention-78398 (accessed February 2019)

Gallagher E (2008) *Children's Violence to Parents: A critical literature review* [online]. Monash University. Available at: http://www.eddiegallagher.com.au/Child%20Parent%20Violence%20 Masters%20Thesis%20Gallagher%202008.pdf (accessed February 2019).

Galvani S (2010) *Supporting Families Affected by Substance Use and Domestic Violence*. University of Bedfordshire, Adfam and Stella Project.

Gamez-Guadix M and Calvete E (2012) Child-to-parent violence and its association with exposure to marital violence and parent-to-child violence. [Article in Spanish] *Psicothema* **24** (2) 277–283,

Gelles RJ and Straus MA (1988) *Intimate Violence*. New York: Simon and Schuster.

Government of Canada (2016) *The Chief Public Health Officer's Report on the State of Public Health in Canada 2016 – A Focus on Family Violence in Canada* [online]. Available at: https://www.canada.ca/en/public-health/services/publications/chief-public-health-officer-reports-state-public-health-canada/2016-focus-family-violence-canada.html?_ga=2.215246743.1220107877.1521538106-1093218896.1521538106 (accessed February 2019).

Holt A (2009) Parent abuse: some reflections on the adequacy of a youth justice response. *Internet Journal of Criminology* 1–11.

Holt A and Retford S (2013) Practitioner accounts of responding to parent abuse – a case study in ad hoc delivery, perverse outcomes and a policy silence. *Child and Family Social Work* **18** (3) 365–374.

Hunte B (2017) Sharp rise in parents being abused by their violent children [online]. *ITV News* **29 November**. Available at: https://www.itv.com/news/london/2017-11-30/sharp-rise-in-parents-being-abused-by-their-violent-children/ (accessed February 2019).

Hunter C, Nixon J and Parr S (2010) Mother abuse: a matter of youth justice, child welfare or domestic violence. *Journal of Law and Society* **37** (2) 264–284.

Ibabe I, Arnoso A & Elgorriaga E (2014) The clinical profile of adolescent offenders of child-to-parent violence. *Procedia – Social and Behavioural Sciences* **131** 377–381.

Ibabe I, Jaureguizar J & Bentler P (2013) Risk factors for child-to-parent violence. *Journal of Family Violence* **28** (5) 523–534.

Laurent A and Derry A (1999) Violence of French adolescents toward their parents: Characteristics and contexts. *Journal of Adolescent Health* **25** (1) 21–26.

Marjoribanks D (2016) *Happy Families? Family relationships in the UK today. The Way We Are Now – The State of the UK's relationships* [online]. Available at: https://www.relationships-scotland.org.uk/wp-content/uploads/The-Way-We-Are-Now-Happy-families.pdf (accessed February 2019).

Mills T (2017) Quarter of all youths committing family violence are boys bashing their mums. *The Age* **8 December.** Available at: https://www.theage.com.au/national/victoria/family-violence-treated-same-as-terrorism-under-new-police-strategy-20171207-h00lvl.html (accessed February 2019).

Nandy S and Selwyn J (2011) *Spotlight on Kinship Care* [online]. University of Bristol. Available at: https://www.bristol.ac.uk/media-library/sites/sps/migrated/documents/execsum.pdf (accessed February 2019).

NSPCC (2018) *What is Domestic Abuse* [online]. Available at: https://www.nspcc.org.uk/preventing-abuse/child-abuse-and-neglect/domestic-abuse/ (accessed February 2019).

Public Health England (2016) *The Mental Health of Children and Young People in England* [online]. Available at: https://assets.publishing.service.gov.uk/government/uploads/system/uploads/attachment_data/file/575632/Mental_health_of_children_in_England.pdf (accessed February 2019).

Routt G and Anderson L (2014) *Adolescent Violence in the Home, Restorative Approaches to Building Healthy, Respectful Family Relationships*. Oxford: Routledge.

Royal Commission into Family Violence (2016) *Summary and Recommendations* [online]. Available at: http://files.rcfv.com.au/Reports/Final/RCFV-All-Volumes.pdf (accessed February 2019).

Schroer S (2018) *Findings of a Peer-led Survey into the Stress, Health and Wellbeing of Adopters and Special Guardians, Interim Report*. Special Guardians and Adopters Together. Available at: https://campaignforadoptionpermanence.files.wordpress.com/2018/04/special-guardians-and-adopters-together-interim-report-6th-march-2018.pdf (accessed February 2019).

Selwyn J, Wijedasa D & Meakings S (2014) *Beyond the Adoption Order: Challenges, interventions and adoption disruption*. Department for Education.

Sporer K and Toller PW (2017) Family identity disrupted by mental illness and violence: an application of relational dialectics theory. *Southern Communication Journal* **82** (2) 85–101.

Straus MA, Gelles RJ & Steinmetz S (1980) *Behind Closed Doors: Violence in the American Family*. Garden City, NY: Anchor Press/Doubleday.

The Children's Society (2016) *Understanding Adolescent Neglect: Troubled teens* [online]. Available at: https://www.childrenssociety.org.uk/sites/default/files/troubled-teens-full-report-final.pdf accessed February 2019).

The Children's Society (2018) *Good Childhood Report 2018* [online]. Available at: https://www.childrenssociety.org.uk/sites/default/files/thegood_childhood_report_2018_0.pdf (accessed February 2019).

Thorley W and Coates A (2017) *Child Parent Violence (CPV): Grappling with an Enigma* [online]. Available at: https://helenbonnick.files.wordpress.com/2017/04/cpv-grappling-with-an-enigma.pdf (accessed February 2019).

Thorley W and Coates A (2018) *Let's Talk About: Child-parent violence and aggression (CPVA)* [online]. Extended summary available at: https://www.academia.edu/37078253/Lets_Talk_About_Child_to_Parent_Violence_2018_Summary (accessed February 2019).

YoungMinds (2014) *YoungMinds Trust Annual Report 2013-14* [online]. Available at: https://youngminds.org.uk/media/1235/ym_annual_report_2013-14.pdf (accessed February 2019).

YoungMinds (2018) *Fighting for Young People's Mental Health* [online]. Available at: https://youngminds.org.uk/media/2258/youngminds-fightingfor-report.pdf (accessed February 2019).

Wilcox P, Pooley M, Ferrando M, Coogan D, Lauster E, Assenova A, Mortenson A & Christoffersson I (2015) *Responding to Child to Parent Violence: Executive summary* [online]. Available at: http://www.rcpv.eu/78-rcpv-executive-summary-may-2015-english/file (accessed February 2019).

Williams J (2014) Today's 13-year-olds are not as bad as we're led to believe [online]. *The Conversation* **24 March**. Available at: https://theconversation.com/todays-13-year-olds-are-not-as-bad-as-were-led-to-believe-34380 (accessed February 2019).

Chapter 2: It could happen to anyone

'Maybe if someone had come to me at the end of nursery and said, he really should have settled by now. We need to be looking at … maybe people are too frightened. If they think they know you. They think they know your situation and so it can't be happening to you. Because it's S and G so there isn't anything going on there. And you know what? We've all got a bit of baggage!'
(Interview with Stephanie)

So who do we think is affected, and why?

It was not long after people started counting incidents of child to parent violence, that the attempts to determine and isolate a profile of those affected began.

Whether it is to identify those most at risk in order to better provide support, or a crude attempt at persuading ourselves that 'it couldn't happen to me', there have been consistent efforts to establish what combination of family models, parenting styles, personality traits or particular circumstances have brought about this challenging behaviour. Two things become clearer. Firstly, there is a danger, in seeking to locate the causes of CPVA within the family itself, that we blame individuals without reference to wider community and societal issues; and secondly, no parent is able to say categorically that it could never happen to them.

Over the years, researchers have considered multiple factors in attempting to answer this question. Race and culture, gender, age, social class, individual personality and diagnosis, family experience, and parenting style of course – amongst other things – have all come under the microscope.

Race

Is this something that affects some races or cultures disproportionately? Early (American) research tended towards the view that this was essentially a problem of the white community, since it was believed that African or Hispanic families would be likely to utilise more strict parenting strategies, and at that time parenting style in particular was assumed to be a key feature (Charles, 1986). As awareness has increased however, through research, and in newspaper articles, we have come to hear about examples of CPVA across the globe, which have painted a different picture.

> *'At home, he doesn't take no for an answer. One violent tantrum gives way to another. He has started smashing the crockery and breaking mobile phones … our son has turned more aggressive. He is still years away from getting a valid driving license, but our Honda City car has become his. He drinks and drives. My husband can smell alcohol in the car.'*
> (Hindustan Times, 2018)
>
> *'Saudi parents face abuse from "disobedient sons".'*
> (Khaleej Times, 2005)
>
> *'Violence, like charity, begins at home.'*
> (Shanghai Daily, 2005)
>
> In 2009 the Straits Times reported that 720 youths had been referred to the Singapore Children's Society as beyond parental control, almost half of these using violence towards their parents.
> (Straits Times, 2009)

Back in the UK, Condry and Miles (2013), looking at Metropolitan Police records in London, found that Afro-Caribbean families were over-represented in their sample, making up nearly 30% of suspects by ethnicity, in contrast to the 2011 census figures for London which give a figure of 13.3% for people of black ethnicity.

What conclusions can we draw from all of this? Have parenting styles become less strict than they were for some groups? We always need to be careful in interpreting statistics. The particular population we sample may be skewed by many factors. We know that Afro-Caribbean youth are over-represented in the criminal justice system generally, and that the population of London is very different to the UK as a whole (ONS, 2018). But it also suggests that this is not an issue that is mostly confined to one section of the population; that the issue of CPVA is more widespread than originally assumed. Indeed, Simmons *et al* (2018) suggest that the level of industrialisation of a nation is more significant than the race of an individual. The issue may not be which racial or cultural group you belong to, or whereabouts in the world you live, but how is your society organised, what hierarchies are in place, what pressures, stresses and expectations do you face?

Gender

The data around gender is far from straightforward and can also be contentious. Surveys – quantitative studies – which have asked individuals for their experience of CPVA, whether as parents or young people, have tended to suggest that there is a roughly even spread between the genders (Gallagher, 2008). However, clinical and legal samples, which are thought to give a more accurate picture of the more extreme end of the spectrum, generally give a breakdown of approximately 75% of abuse coming from young men, and 75% of parents affected being women. For instance, in Condry and Miles' (2013) research, 77% of all parent victims in their sample were female; of young people using violence, 87% were male; and 66% involved son to mother violence.

Some of this balance is undoubtedly accounted for by women being the main, or only, carer in many households. Where there are two parents in a heterosexual couple, or indeed in a two-male parent household, or where men are the main carers, men also experience abuse and violence, whether from sons or daughters. It is suggested that male and female youth may engage in different types of violence and abuse (Simmons *et al*, 2018), with boys utilising more physical violence, and girls adopting a more psychological campaign of abuse. It is important however to always remember that these figures are subject to all sorts of bias; and that they give at best an overall picture. Once we look at the circumstances of a child or young person's life, we may find that individual accounts from families give a very different story.

Age

A number of studies have addressed the question of the peak age for CPVA. Once again there is a degree of discrepancy among the data, and as always, this is a reflection of the known incidence, and – of course – the breadth of the definition in use.

A focus on adolescence, omitting younger children from the equation, gives a peak age variously of around 13-15 years (Family Lives, 2011), or 15-17 (Safe Lives, 2014). Like other forms of delinquency, within criminal justice statistics it seems to decline in older teenagers (Simmons *et al*, 2018). Notably it does not cease as a young person moves into adulthood, and this is a more recent focus of research into family violence throughout the life course.

Gallagher (2008) argues that data suggesting a peak age in the early teens may tell us more about the propensity of parents to report and seek help when a child becomes too big to manhandle, but still small enough to persuade to attend counselling. It may be that parents disengage from interacting with older teens as a means to avoid conflict. I would suggest that it also reflects the fact that specialist services are only recently accepting referrals of younger children, who have not previously featured in the statistics. More and more agencies now report multiple referrals from primary schools, and parents seeking help with their younger children.

The research from Selwyn *et al* (2014) found two significantly different groups of children in their study of adoption breakdown. One group appeared to be managing relatively well until early adolescence – the age of school transfer, puberty, and brain development all coming together in a perfect storm; while a separate group of children demonstrated violence and aggression to an extreme from a very early age. When Thorley and Coates (2018) asked parents about the age at which CPVA became a problem, they were also surprised at responses suggesting a much earlier concern, with the highest prevalence between six and nine years old. We have long assumed that a younger child cannot have the same intent to harm, or the physical strength to do significant damage, yet Al Coates (2017) attests to the fear experienced in the face of the behaviour of his own four year old.

'Early the next morning it started. "Stupid daddy". Then fighting, hitting and biting. Rages that would last hour after hour with me standing between her and the rest of the family. I tried to hold her to keep her safe but that would prolong the rages but if I let go she'd come back to start again. We knew all the standard techniques, time out, appropriate consequences, carrots not sticks. She was four-years-old and I'd become afraid of her, nervous of when the next assault would come, I was covered in bites, scratches and bruises. I couldn't sleep, laying awake waiting for the inevitable screams that would start our day at 4am.'
(Coates, 2017)

Like Selwyn, Simmons *et al* (2018) note a split between adolescence-linked (AL) violence and life-course persistent (LCP) violence (starting earlier), the former appearing to be more likely to be resolved over time. They suggest that distinctions other than the age of the one causing harm are more helpful in understanding the issue of violence within the family across the lifespan. It is perhaps time to revisit the theories about peak age.

Socio-economic status

You will not be surprised to learn that this is also a contested area. Over time, some clinicians and academics have suggested that more middle class families are represented than might be expected. Gallagher (2018) expands on this, suggesting that educated parents in the helping professions, are disproportionately represented as victims – perhaps, he suggests, because of a more indulgent parenting style. However, Condry and Miles (2013) found that almost 50% of the families in their sample were unemployed or in lower paid work. It would not be surprising to learn that families experiencing the stresses of poverty would also have higher levels of intra-family conflict. However, it may be that what we see is a difference in where families of different SES appear in the data, or receive help, with different groups disproportionately seen in different places. Certainly, families with high status are unlikely to want to attract attention in their time of need, and will be able to afford private, discrete therapies, well away from the prying eyes of the public and the number crunchers.

Individual characteristics and behaviours

Various researchers have examined whether personality style, and behaviour such as substance use or general delinquency are predictive for CPVA. From the start of interest in this area, there has been a focus on a possible overlap with mental illness such as depression or psychosis; and more recently thinking about diagnosis of autism spectrum disorders, and other behavioural diagnoses. All of these factors have been found to be relevant in research at one time or another. Calvete *et al* (2012) suggested that a personality that combines internalising problems, and an instrumental use of violence, is predictive for CPVA. Retford (2016) and Galvani (2010) found strong links between substance use and aggressive behaviour towards parents. Simmons *et al* (2016) point to high rates of depressive illness, self-harm and suicidal ideation in populations of young people using CPVA across the field of research. Routt and Anderson (2014) found consistent diagnosis of ADHD in the young people they worked with; a feature recognised also by Gallagher (2018) in his sample.

So what do we make of this? We must be careful in considering what these links mean. There may be separate factors that mediate substance use and CPVA for instance, or depression and CPVA, rather than a direct link between the two; and the mechanism of the connection may be as, or more, important than the direct link. For instance, parents reported that young people were using aggressive behaviour because of drug debts and threats if payment wasn't made, rather than a straightforward effect of intoxication (Galvani, 2010). Simmons *et al* (2016) argue that findings about behavioural disorders may be tautological, as the violence itself becomes part of the diagnosis for conditions that are more descriptive. And there is concern that expressions of ADHD may be confused with the effects of trauma, leading to over diagnosis in either direction. Finally, none of these factors are necessarily stand-alone issues. Some children may experience multiple difficulties in their life, each contributing to aggressive behaviour, and all showing separately in research studies.

Life experiences

With a focus on the transmission of violence through the generations, there has been consideration of the impact of experiencing either child abuse or domestic violence between adults in the family, with mixed results. With a vast amount of literature exploring this issue, it is worthwhile going to Simmons *et al* (2018) for an overview and review of the available research. Overall, it seems that experiencing IPV is a high predictor for later use of violence and abuse within the family by young people, with as many as 50% having lived with this. In terms of abuse of a child by a parent, there is differential evidence in terms of physical and verbal retaliation and of damage to property, depending on the type of abuse experienced, and on the time scale in question.

Parenting style

What about parenting style – the go-to explanation for so many people? How important an issue is it, and how might that connection work? Parenting style and practice is often assumed to be a major factor by professionals seeking to support families; and featured strongly as an explanation in early work in this field. An over-indulgent, 'let's be friends', lots of praise for everything parenting style might be one caricature; or a parent unable to lay down rules and boundaries now because they started too late and the kids already run rings round them; or a parent who has left the children in the care of grandparents in order to work long hours to cover the bills. Alternatively, it has been suggested that some children react against a too strict regime by using violence themselves – answering aggression in kind.

The categorisation of three parenting styles: 'authoritarian', 'authoritative', and 'permissive', was first developed by Baumrind (1966) in America and later expanded to include a fourth type, 'neglectful', by Maccoby and Martin (1983). It refers to the combination of discipline style, communication, warmth, and expectations adopted by parents. Trends in parenting come and go. The promotion of an authoritative approach as being the most nurturing and supportive style, with positive outcomes all round, is a relatively recent trend, since the middle of the last century.

Research in Spain, in particular, has focused on correlations between individual characteristics, parental situation and parenting style, while reinforcing the importance of authoritative parenting in protecting against child to parent violence (for example Calvete *et al*, 2015; Contreras and Cano, 2014; Ibabe *et al*, 2013. Yet, interestingly, other research (Garcia & Gracia, 2009), has pointed to the need to think about optimum parenting style in the wider context of societal organisation, so that what is most appropriate in one culture may be less so in another. It is easy to imagine a range of cultures where the models of family, of authority, and of community, are very different. Indeed, research into Asian parenting styles (Chao, 1994), or Latino families (Domenech Rodriguez *et al*, 2009), found that the qualities being measured in Baumrind's grid were not directly transferable, and that a different typology was needed. This suggests that whether a parenting style is protective or predictive of CPVA needs to be understood as one of a range of factors.

Gallagher (2008) reminds us that it is important to take into consideration the temperament and individual characteristics of a child, and not simply the parenting style adopted, suggesting '*what may be the optimal child-rearing environment for many children may be detrimental to children with particular temperaments*'; and also that for older children particularly, the influences within the family can be marginal. It is important to look beyond straightforward parenting style; this is certainly not the whole story.

Parents in the adoption community and those with children with diagnoses of autism, for instance, would want to reinforce the value of a therapeutic parenting style, which may superficially look like a much weaker, more indulgent version, for their families. Adoptive parents may score strongly on a measure of authoritativeness, and the children they care for (who are sometimes using extreme levels of violence and aggression), are likely responding to an earlier experience of being parented. Cottrell (2004) has also pointed out that in her experience, parents who seem to be neglectful in their parenting are more likely to be demonstrating the effects of CPVA than generating the circumstances for it to flourish. I will not argue that parenting practice is never an issue, but rather that we should be careful about starting from this position. With so many other issues involved, often overlapping, it would seem important not to rush to conclusions about the style of parenting apparently in play.

What conclusions can we draw?

In the end – examining research, auditing caseloads, and listening to families – it seems that there is no common thread or single causal factor.

Within a family affected by CPVA, a parent might be a head teacher, or a teaching assistant, a nurse, a builder, a record producer, a member of the houses of parliament, a firefighter, a social worker. They might be retired, stay-at-home, unemployed, working nights, full time, part time or two jobs. They might be male or female. There might be only one child using violence in a family, or two, or more.

There are many diverse expressions of 'family': nuclear, single parent, same sex, blended, extended, kinship, adoptive, fostering, residential and more, and none of these are necessarily immune. There are different cultural practices or expectations around the world concerning parental authority, care, responsibility and role. Parents have differential access to resources, whether material or people based, to support families, and to make families more or less publicly visible. There is differential pressure from societies: stresses and expectations, materialism, consumerism, peer activities; which might have far more influence on young people than the family itself.

Perhaps, as Coogan (2014) has said: *'The only thing they have in common is that it happens'*.

'Getting their needs met'

In order to thrive, children need to form secure attachments, they need their basic needs to be met, they need clear boundaries to offer a structure and security, they need adults they can rely on to provide these things. For all sorts of reasons, some of these essentials may not be available to some children. Other children may bring with them their own difficulties of personality or difference, neo-natal experiences, or injury. Circumstances may cause a family to move around, to flee, to be cut off from support. There may be secrets. I like the expression, 'Children are in the business of getting their needs met'. It can be helpful to think in this way, to understand behaviour as communication, and to try to work out what a child is trying to say to us at any given time.

What has happened to you?

We are encouraged these days to ask, not 'what is wrong with you', but rather 'what has happened to you?' as theories and understanding of the effects of trauma come to the forefront of our thinking. I would suggest that incorporating this into our model, while not offering a complete explanation, can bring helpful additions to our thinking. There may be no one thing that causes child to parent violence and abuse, but there are a number of indicators that appear often enough to allow us to suggest that they might be risk factors. I would like to offer the following typology, as a way of thinking about these vulnerabilities.

Children who have experienced difficulties pre- and perinatally

For instance foetal alcohol spectrum disorders (FASD), congenital conditions, or brain injury. Children with FASD may have issues around concentration, processing and retaining information, regulating mood, making friends, and in expressing their needs. Extreme anxiety or frustration may be behind their behaviour. It is suggested by the FASD Network UK that FASD, the most common non-genetic cause of learning disability in the UK, may affect at least 7000 babies born here every year. Research published in the UK in 2018 (McQuire *et al*) attempted to establish prevalence, through examination of a large body of data, and suggests a figure potentially as high as 17%. Coverage in the media, and promotion of a policy of no alcohol during pregnancy has met with fierce opposition from those who believe the state already interferes too much in private life, but has been embraced by those campaigning on behalf of their children.

> 'You see, I know what it's like to parent a child who was exposed to alcohol in utero. I have seen a young toddler unable to process the sights and sounds of daily life, looked into the eyes of a distressed young one whose brain can't handle too much input without kicking into the fight and flight mode. I have literally held with a mamma-bear hug a dysregulated child who was lashing out in distress – while neither he nor I could understand why. I've been in the schools, working with teachers who were frustrated that he couldn't focus, sit still, remember. I've spent hundreds if not thousands of hours in waiting rooms, doctors' offices, talking with therapists, trying to understand why he has trouble eating, why some bones are fused together, why he can't grasp abstract concepts. Gathering diagnosis after diagnosis until at the age of 10 we finally learned our adopted child has a Foetal Alcohol Spectrum Disorder.'
> (FASD: Learning with Hope blog, 2018)

Children and young people with neurological conditions such as autism or ADHD

> 'Imagine yourself as a bottle of pop. Your ingredients include autism, sensory processing difficulties, ADHD and a hidden speech and language delay. The world's a confusing place, and your difficulties are largely hidden to the wider world, so not many people understand things from your perspective … I knew there was something my child was struggling with, and all I had to do was understand what his behavior was telling me. My child explodes at home with me because I'm his safe place. I am predictable and calm, and he can really be himself at home. He is fully accepted at home.'
> (A Slice of Autism blog, 2018)

The BBC recently explored the problems families have in obtaining a diagnosis of pathological demand avoidance (PDA), and then in accessing help and support, in an episode of the Victoria Derbyshire Show, (November 2018). The programme included a film from Noel Phillips, in which he spoke to children about their own fears, as well as parents.

Jamie is only 7, but says, *'I get very, very mad and smash stuff'*. His PDA means that he goes to great lengths to avoid situations that cause him to be anxious. Knives, curtain poles – he has threatened his mother with both. Mum's concern is the risk to himself at those times, because he is not in control at all.

Ten year old Kierney has multiple diagnoses including PDA. *'I feel really bad when I hurt my mum and I don't want to hurt her … It's just what I do'*.

As we learn more about these conditions we are increasingly aware of the issues around over-stimulation, responses to stressful situations, sensory needs, mood regulation etc. Children may go in to freeze, fight or flight mode, and may respond to stress with the use of violence, whether as an explosive loss of control, or in an effort to control and manipulate the environment.

> Issues around violence from this group of children were brought to wider attention by Yvonne Newbold, who prefers the term 'violent and challenging behaviour' (VCB).
>
> *'When a child has a neurodevelopmental condition, violent and challenging behaviour is very common. Around one in four of all children with a diagnosis of autism or a learning disability, will develop behaviour which is both violent and challenging, also called VCB. Children with other conditions such as ADHD and PDA can also present with these behaviours.'*
> (See Interactive Autism Network, Kennedy Krieger Institute, quoted on http://yvonnenewbold.com)
>
> Yvonne blogs extensively and offers advice and training for parents, based on her own experience and study. She points to extreme anxiety as the root of such behaviour, which may include physical attacks on parents, the use of weapons, intimidatory language, insults, and destruction of property.
>
> *'They aren't hitting you because they hate you … they're hitting you because their world has just fallen apart.'*
> (Yvonne Newbold speaking on Woman's Hour, 2017)
>
> With the right intervention, she believes a child can turn their behaviour around completely.

Children with other diagnoses, for instance conduct disorder (CD), oppositional defiant disorder (ODD), or obsessive compulsive disorder (OCD), may also experience similar difficulties in regulation of mood, the need to control their environment, coping with stress, and communicating needs.

Children with developmental trauma

'Trauma wires kids to feel and respond according to a precedent, rather than to the present. They follow emotional tracks laid down in the past – when they were victims of deeply painful experiences, from which they continue to have pessimistic expectations.'
(Tweet from TraumaInformedPBS, @ti_pbs, 2008)

Children may have experienced severe neglect, physical, emotional or sexual abuse early in their lives, or may have been exposed to violence between adults in the home. As a result they may have been compromised in their brain development. They may have a small 'window of tolerance', attachment disorders, and problems responding to stress. Looking at the outworking of this, research by Selwyn *et al* (2014) into adoption breakdown, found that child to parent violence was a huge issue, being implicated in 80% of families where the young person had to leave home. It should be noted that this violence was used in families other than those where violence and abuse was first experienced by the child. Indeed, a child may have experienced multiple moves, unsuccessful return to birth parents, or even breakdown of foster care by this time, each adding to the early experience of trauma. Children in foster care will have experienced many similar life events, and yet there is less written about the plight of foster parents to remind us of their situation. Kirstie Maclean, writing in 2016 in an analysis of the death of a foster carer at the hands of the child for whom she was caring, explored the adequacy of the training of foster carers, and the sharing of information about previous experiences likely to suggest child to parent violence and abuse, amongst other issues.

Children and young people who have experiences of later loss and trauma

There are many levels of loss that a child or young person might experience, whether through bereavement, incarceration of a parent, migration, removal or movement between homes. Physical injury and abuse, bullying, child sexual exploitation, gang involvement, parental conflict or domestic violence in the home will all have an impact on how a child feels about themselves, about relationships and about life, and how they respond to stress, triggering or anxiety-provoking situations.

> 'James started out like any other little boy – mischievous, sweet, caring. But at age five, he witnessed an ordeal that would scar him for life. Four months after Kirsty became a single parent, James saw her get physically assaulted by her brothers. She was so badly beaten, she wound up in hospital. As James grew older, a dark streak emerged. And by age 13, the verbal, psychological and physical abuse against his mother was already getting "out of control".'
> (Aubrey, 2018)

The transfer from event to thoughts, feelings and actions is not straightforward, but might include an outplaying of anger and emotion towards a parent perceived as unable to offer protection or emotional connection. A child may have learnt that violence is the way to solve problems; or there may be a simple instruction from another individual through coaching, blackmail or other coercion.

> Speaking on the BBC2 Victoria Derbyshire Show in 2015, Ann Ramsden opened up about her experience as a child, both of abusing her father and her mother's new partner:
>
> 'I thought nothing of pulling a knife on my Dad … I had no intention of hurting him. I just needed what I wanted. Mentally I destroyed him I think … plus me mum at the time had met another guy who was quite abusive to her. So I needed in a sense to be violent as well, because her new partner, if he was violent, she'd ring me to go sort him out … It's only our family, children, to keep me mum alive, so I'll do whatever it takes to keep her alive … It was normal.'

Thought to be the single biggest factor in CPVA, a child's experience of family violence, most usually inflicted by the father, can have long lasting consequences. Price (1996) and Pereira (2016) both offer an explanation of the way in which family conflict generally can bring about the conditions for CPVA to develop, through the creation of alliances, and moves towards independence. Not just post-separation, conflict between parents at any time is a powerful factor in creating circumstances where power within the family is offered and taken, and where young people may find themselves needing to 'speak louder' to have their needs met.

A report for the Children's Commissioner (Cossar *et al*, 2013) into what is needed to enable children to open up and seek help for abuse and neglect, pointed to the difficulties children have in using words to convey their distress, often falling back on behaviour, *'Young people most often came to the attention of services through their behaviour and demeanour rather than through explicitly disclosing abuse'*.

Children and young people living in families where parents are not able to meet their physical and emotional needs, or provide structure and security, for a variety of reasons

For example, poor mental or physical health, parental substance use, parenting skills, poverty, or an absent parent can all affect the level of care and nurture a parent can provide. Children may act out of anger or frustration, they may simply have no sense of what is appropriate, they may try to provide their own version of leadership in a household where it feels as if this is lacking, or indeed they may be specifically placed in this role when a parent (father perhaps) goes travelling.

> Twelve year old Shah was the oldest remaining male in the family when his father returned to Bangladesh for a protracted visit. With high expectations on him to be 'in charge' of his mother, four sisters and grandmother, Shah struggled to rise to the challenge. School work, friendships and siblings with their own opinions laid pressure onto pressure. In the end he fell back on brute force when the family didn't fall into line, copying the behaviour of other men he saw around him.

The organisation Family Based Solutions, formerly known as PAARS (Parent Abuse and Reconciliation Service) found that, of families they had worked with, 42% of parents had issues of poor mental health or drug misuse, and 78% had prior experience of domestic violence within the home (conference presentation, March 2018).

Children and young people whose expectations have been raised to unreasonable levels concerning their rights and entitlement

This might look very different in different situations. Children might live in a home or community with staff or servants. They may have parents who are trying to compensate for previous lack or loss. Parents may be trying to give them as rich an education and experience as possible, while also protecting them from failure and disappointment. They may exist in a social world very different to that at home and to the one their parents experienced. They may be a desperately wanted or much needed child within the family. Within some communities they may be an oldest son. Gallagher (2018) writes that families such as these form the second largest grouping of those with whom he has worked.

Children and young people with poor mental health

Report after report draws attention to the poor mental health of young people in the UK these days, whether because of school pressures and exam stress, body image, technology, bullying, or the impact of austerity affecting their life chances. Not all of these young people will go on to be abusive in the home, but children who do so may be exhibiting responses to such stresses, with evidence, or threats, of self-harming, and depression. Families also report violence and abuse from children with psychosis, and real difficulties in accessing help from mental health services, meaning that they and their child may be living in a state of poor health, heightened anxiety, stress and fear, for months or even years.

Research into psychopathy and psychopathic traits in children and young people has linked an absence of fear and of empathy to damage to the amygdala. Without a normally functioning amygdala, adolescents have little appreciation of another's fear, or of why it might be wrong to behave in certain ways; and may use threats and violence because they have found it to be effective in getting what they want (Marsh, 2017). Interestingly, an article about CPVA and 'callous unemotional traits' on the BBC News (2017) was met with significant criticism from parents, concerned that the child might be displaying symptoms of trauma instead, which would have suggested a greater hope for the future.

Children and young people with poor physical health

We have heard earlier from both Stephanie and Jenny about their experiences of life with young men with physical health problems. Stephanie's son's glue ear remained undiagnosed for many years, giving him significant pain, as well as leading to difficulties keeping up in class once he started school. He seems to have responded both out of pain, and frustration at his situation, in a pattern of behaviour, which became embedded over time. Jenny's son felt embarrassed by his condition, angry and helpless about the bullying he experienced at school; and blamed his parents, particularly taking his anger out on his mother, as the main carer.

Children and young people with an addiction

For example alcohol, drugs or gaming. Violence may come about through the withdrawal of whatever activity is problematic – an absence of the substance, time for dinner, time for bed. Under the influence, they may act without self-control, or experience a psychotic episode. There may be bills to pay, and threats of violence from others if they are not met – threats to kill, to burn down a home, to rape a sister – which are then passed onto the family in the behaviour of the young person concerned. The work of Galvani (2010) looking into support for families affected by substance use and domestic violence was ground breaking in revealing the amount of abuse directed from children to parents, and the part that alcohol or drugs played in this.

'With drugs, it's more wanting money for drugs because they need them. And that spurs them on. It's the need for drugs that will spur them on to abuse, and you know, create, so they can get the money. I think it is more financial with drugs. I think with alcohol, it's the after effects of alcohol, and the violence that comes with that.'
(Adult interviewed, Galvani, 2010)

Interestingly, Price (1996) argues that a focus on substance use detracts from other issues such as depression, bullying or abuse, which may have contributed to a decision to self-medicate, and may actually themselves be the real cause of the violence.

Some random thing

Sometimes people have struggled to find a definitive link with anything, but it doesn't stop people looking for answers. Indeed, there are plenty of other suggestions for issues that may bring about heightened levels of aggression and abuse. Most of us can probably confirm the debilitating effects of sleep deprivation. Children with some conditions may have extreme difficulties in establishing regular sleep habits, and this should not be ruled out. The most bizarre link I have found is with a parasite in cat faeces (New Scientist, 2018). Who knows!

Changing our thinking

We should step aside from thinking about children and young people as mini-adults, making rational and informed choices and planning their lives out in organised ways. Some young people may be fully capable of this. But as we understand more about brain development in particular, and the massive changes that continue to take place in adolescence and right through to the mid-20s, we see individuals who are still immature in thinking, reasoning and impulse control, who may be further compromised in these areas by events outside their control. Adolescence is a time of significant change, a time of transitions, an opportunity to explore identity, to develop peer relationships, push boundaries, take risks – some positive, some more threatening and harmful.

Causality and directionality

It is important in any sort of research to be clear about the direction of any correlation or risk factors. While we are looking at the characteristics of those using violence and abuse towards parents, we cannot make assumptions about causality, or the direction of the link. For instance, while prior experience of domestic violence may be a factor for around 50% of children and young people using CPVA (Gallagher, 2018), only around 25% of those experiencing DV will go on to use violence and abusive behaviour themselves (Safe Lives, 2014). While mental health problems may feature prominently for young people in our cohort, the reality for those with poor mental health remains that they are more likely to be a victim of violence than to use it against others. Sporer and Toller (2017) suggest between 1% and 7% of individuals with mental illness may show a propensity to violence, with 50% to 60% of this group directing aggression towards relatives. The proportion of young people with neuro-disability using violent and aggressive behaviours may be higher (The Kennedy Krieger Institute report that 56% of children with ASD were found to be using aggressive behaviour towards parents and a further 32% towards carers (Anderson, 2012)), but there remain many other children with ASD not using violence.

ACEs and resilience

There is currently much talk about the adverse childhood experiences (ACEs) study, and about how useful this framework is for understanding levels of distress. An examination of the possible links with poor physical, mental and emotional outcomes across a large dataset can be extremely helpful, but it is not designed to be used as a diagnostic tool and it does not tell us the whole story. What about those who have experienced multiple ACEs but have gone on to lead happy and healthy lives? What made a difference for them?

How do we understand the fact that a number of children and young people experiencing some form of adversity will go on to be violent or aggressive, while a significant number of others will not, sometimes even members of the same family? There are myriad suggestions, including predisposition, and factors such as supportive individuals or networks. Children and families are often able to develop resilience that can be protective against many of the experiences that befall them in this respect. Good mental health, understanding friends and family, as well as broader community support, are all important in this field. They are not always sufficient if there are other circumstances out of someone's control, and sadly they are not always available; but they are important in prevention and protection, and can also be part of a restorative healing process. So, we go on to ask not just 'what happened to you?' but also 'who was there for you?'.

A giant Venn diagram

We still don't know enough to understand if some of these are primary links, or if they are the result themselves of different things. What we do see is that there is rarely one issue in isolation, and we can end up with a giant Venn diagram of overlapping conditions, family situations, diagnoses, and circumstances. For instance, a child who has been adopted will have experienced a primary loss and potentially multiple others; there may have been exposure to alcohol in the womb, a level of developmental trauma; they may be using substances to self-medicate, or be involved in gangs or other risky behaviours outside of the home. A young person with a parent in prison may experience bullying at school, be living with a parent who is depressed and finding it hard to pay bills. They may be left more and more to fend for themselves.

I believe that in grouping issues in this way, and in thinking about the circumstances and situations of each child separately within this framework, it is easier to step back from thinking of the child or young person as a perpetrator, or the parents as necessarily being complicit in their own victimhood; and also to start to think about the issues that might need addressing in bringing about change.

As we finish thinking about the profile of families where CPVA takes place, and the possible links to circumstances or conditions, I would like to throw another – perhaps controversial – factor into the mix. Very young children may be aggressive in their mood and behaviour, but they are far from doing the serious harm of a teenager. If we believe that prevention or change is possible then the earlier that assessment, diagnosis, and intervention can take place the better. All the evidence is that the severity of abuse is likely to increase over time, with the age and size of the child, and as patterns become fixed, potentially going forward into adulthood and future relationships. In not intervening early, whether through ignorance, misunderstanding, or funding problems, should support agencies and services be held to account for their contribution to the continuing and escalating violence and abuse displayed within families whether to parents, carers, siblings, animals or property?

Most parents, most of the time, are trying to do what is best for their kids in the circumstances they find themselves in. Basically, it could happen to anyone.

What can you do?

A different understanding of what might be happening in a family can change the way we respond. Remember, each family is unique.

- Listen.
- Put aside assumptions, and be curious.
- A full assessment, that looks at complexity.
- Look beyond the ACEs, what else is going on? What help and support is there?

Meeting families who do not meet the normal profile for our agency can be challenging. How does this work out? Is this an opportunity to revisit 'practice as usual'?

Find out more

For more information about trauma:

Beacon House is a mine of information and resources: https://beaconhouse.org.uk. This is their lovely animation explaining 'the window of tolerance' https://www.youtube.com/watch?v=Wcm-1FBrDvU.

See the **Institute of Attachment** for description of different diagnoses – what is RAD, trauma etc:
https://instituteforattachment.ong/blog/page/5/.

Interactive Autism Network:
https://iancommunity.org/cs/simons_simplex_community/aggression_and_asd.

Information about the ACEs study can be found on the **Center for Disease Control and Prevention** site: https://www.cdc.gov/violenceprevention/acestudy/about.html.

Bruce Perry has written extensively about childhood trauma, making it clear that we need to know far more about a person's life to truly understand their circumstances: http://childtrauma.org.

Danny Taggart discusses how an understanding of trauma can change the way we work, on the Research in Practice website: https://www.rip.org.uk/news-and-views/blog/trauma-informed-responses-in-relationship-based-practice/.

Karen Treisman is a specialist clinical psychologist who practices, trains and writes about trauma: http://www.safehandsthinkingminds.co.uk/about-us/.

For research about children's resilience, see **Jane Callaghan and Joanne Alexander** (2015) *Understanding Agency & Resistance Strategies: Children's experience of domestic violence*, UNARS: http://www.unars.co.uk/resources/UNARS%20Final%20Project%20Report%20(1).pdfp://www.unars.co.uk/reports.php.

For information about children living with parental conflict see the **EIF Commissioner Guide** (2017) *Reducing the Impact of Inter-Parental Conflict on Children*, EIF: https://www.eif.org.uk/resource/commissioner-guide-reducing-parental-conflict/.

For sleep deprivation https://www.sleephelp.org/autism-asd/.

For the importance of understanding the wider context of a young person's experiences, see the work of the **Contextual Safeguarding Network**: https://contextualsafeguarding.org.uk/about/what-is-contextual-safeguarding.

For information about FASD see websites such as **FASD Network UK**: http://www.fasdnetwork.org and **National Organisation for Foetal Alcohol Syndrome-UK**: http://www.nofas-uk.org.

For information about Pathological Demand Avoidance (PDA) see websites such as the **PDA Society**: https://www.pdasociety.org.uk.
National Autistic Society: https://www.autism.org.uk/about/what-is/pda.aspx.
Jane Sherwin (2015) has written a book about the challenges of bringing up a child with PDA: *Pathological Demand Avoidance Syndrome, My daughter is not naughty*.

The briefing papers from the **Oxford APV research project** are useful for an overview of the breakdown of family types, factors affecting the young people concerned, and the experience of families and practitioners: https://www.law.ox.ac.uk/content/adolescent-parent-violence/briefing-papers

For discussion about the confusion between the outworking of trauma and ASD/ADHD see **The Coventry Grid** and *Is It ADHD or Child Traumatic Stress? A guide for clinicians*, 2016, **The National Child Traumatic Stress Network** https://www.nctsn.org/sites/default/files/resources/is_it_adhd_or_child_traumatic_stress.pdf

Hanbury L (2017) ADHD, trauma and neglect, how do we prevent children who are in the child protection system from being misdiagnosed with ADHD? *Children's Research Digest* **4** (2).

The BBC have covered child to parent violence in a number of programmes, both on television and radio. They have particularly explored connections with adoption and ASD. You will find links to some of these on my website, on the sound and vision page https://holesinthewall.co.uk/sound-and-vision/.

For discussion of throughout the life course, see the work of **Hannah Bows**.

For discussion of gaming addiction, see the work of **Mark Griffiths** (2010) https://www.researchgate.net/publication/273952280_Does_video_game_addiction_really_exist.

Parental incarceration and its impact on health and behavioural outcomes has been the subject of recent research in the USA, published in the journal, *Pediatrics*, as reported in **Science Daily**, 9th July 2018 https://www.sciencedaily.com/releases/2018/07/180709101203.htm.

For Spanish research see for instance:
- **Calvete E, Orue I, Gamez-Guadix M & Bushman BJ** (2015) Predictors of child-to-parent aggression: a 3-year longitudinal study. *Developmental Psychology* **51**(5) 663–676.
- **Contreras L and Cano C** (2014) Adolescents who assault their parents: a different family profile of young offenders? *Violence and Victims* **29** (3) 393–406.
- **Ibabe I, Jaureguizar J & Bentler P** (2013) Risk factors for child-to-parent violence. *Journal of Family Violence* **28** (5) 525–534.

Sam Ross writes as *The Teenage Whisperer*, with a website and two books for parents, carers and anyone working with troubled teens, focusing on helping the individuals and their teens understand challenging behaviour and break out of negative behaviour patterns. You will find lots here about getting inside a teen's head and understanding the issues behind defiance, violence and aggression.

Thinking about parenting styles, there is an interesting critique of **Baumrind's** work, placing it very much in the culture of its age and place, on the website Positive-Parenting-Ally.com: https://www.positive-parenting-ally.com/four-basic-parenting-styles.html.

For information about the teenage brain see this TED talk from **Sarah-Jayne Blakemore** for an explanation of the workings of the teenage brain: https://www.ted.com/talks/sarah_jayne_blakemore_the_mysterious_workings_of_the_adolescent_brain?language=en.

References

Anderson C (2012) *New Research on Children with ASD and Aggression* [online]. Kennedy Krieger Institute. Available at: https://iancommunity.org/cs/simons_simplex_community/aggression_and_asd (accessed February 2019).

A Slice of Autism (2018) *Autism and the Delayed Effect* [online]. Available at: http://asliceofautism.blogspot.co.uk/2015/10/autism-and-delayed-effect.html (accessed February 2019).

Aubrey S (2018) When your child is your abuser: The family violence women don't want to talk about [online]. *Mamamia* **8th September**. Available at: (https://www.mamamia.com.au/adolescent-violence/ (accessed February 2019).

Baumrind D (1966) Effects of authoritative parental control on child behavior. *Child Development* **37** (4) 887–907.

BBC News (2017) *'We're Scared of our Adopted Son'* [online]. Available at: https://www.bbc.co.uk/news/magazine-41332662 (accessed February 2019).

Calvete E, Orue I & Gamez-Guadix M (2012) Child-to-parent violence, emotional and behavioural predictors. *Journal of Interpersonal Violence* **28** (4).

Chao RK (1994) Beyond parental control and authoritarian parenting style: understanding Chinese parenting through the cultural notion of training. *Child Development* **65** (4) 1111–1119.

Charles AV (1986) Physically abused parents. *Journal of Family Violence* **1** (4) 343–355.

Coates A (2017) *My Experience of Living with Child-on-Parent Violence* [online]. Community Care. Available at: http://www.communitycare.co.uk/2017/02/01/experience-living-child-parent-violence/ (accessed February 2019).

Condry R and Miles C (2013) Adolescent to parent violence: framing and mapping a hidden problem. *Criminology and Criminal Justice* 0 (0) 1–19.

Contreras L and Cano MC (2014) Family profile of young offenders who abuse their parents: A comparison with general offenders and non-offenders adolescents. *Journal of Family Violence* **29** 901-910.

Coogan (2014) RCPV conference, Galway.

Cossar J, Brandon M, Bailey S, Belderson P, Biggart L & Sharpe D (2013) *'It Takes a Lot to Build Trust.' Recognition and Telling: Developing earlier routes to help for children and young people* [online]. A report for the Office of the Children's Commissioner for England, CRCF and UEA. Available at: https://www.uea.ac.uk/documents/13885566/13886757/Recognition+and+telling+report/de332aea-ad72-45ff-822c-612a4a78fce4 (accessed February 2019).

Cottrell B (2004) *When Teens Abuse Their Parents*. Canada: Fernwood Publishing.

Domenech Rodriguez M, Donovick M & Crowley S (2009) Parenting styles in a cultural context: observations of protective parenting in first-generation Latinos. *Family Process* **48** (2) 195–210.

Family Lives (2011) *When Family Life Hurts: Family experiences of aggression in children, an update to the 2010 report* [online]. Available at: https://www.familylives.org.uk/media_manager/public/209/Documents/Reports/the_aggression_report_2011_family_lives.pdf (accessed February 2019).

FASD: Learning with Hope (2018) *From an Open Letter to Prince Harry and Meghan (and every parent-to-be)* [online]. Available at: https://fasdlearningwithhope.wordpress.com/2018/11/03/open-letter-to-prince-harry/ (accessed February 2019).

Gallagher E (2008) *Children's Violence to Parents: A critical literature review* [online]. Monash University: http://www.eddiegallagher.com.au/Child%20Parent%20Violence%20Masters%20Thesis%20Gallagher%202008.pdf.

Gallagher E (2018) *Who's in Charge? Why children abuse parents and what you can do about it.* London: Austin Macauley Publishers.

Galvani S (2010) *Supporting Families Affected by Substance Use and Domestic Violence*. University of Bedfordshire, Adfam and Stella Project.

Garcia F and Gracia E (2009) Is always authoritative the optimum parenting style? Evidence from Spanish families. *Adolescence* **44** (173) 101-131.

Hindustan Times (2018) *Let's Talk about Teenage Violence* [online]. Available at: https://www.hindustantimes.com/india-news/my-15-year-old-son-hit-me-am-i-bad-parent-let-s-talk-about-teenage-violence/story-Ef562omxsJmawHtjPcsKBL.html (accessed February 2019).

Ibabe I, Jaureguizar J & Bentler P (2013) Risk Factors for Child-to-Parent Violence. *Journal of Family Violence* **28** (5) 523–534.

Maccoby EE and Martin JA (1983) Socialisation in the context of the family: parent-child interaction. In: P. Mussen (Ed.) *Handbook of Child Psychology, Volume 4*. Chichester: Wiley-Blackwell.

Maclean K (2016) Reflections on the non-accidental death of a foster carer, *Adoption and Fostering*. Epub ahead of print.

Marsh A (2017) *The Fear Factor: How one emotion connects altruists, psychopaths and everyone in-between*. NY: Basic Books.

McQuire C, Mukherjee R, Hurt L, Higgins A, Greene G, Farewell D, Kemp A & Paranjothy S (2018) Screening prevalence of fetal alcohol spectrum disorders in a region of the United Kingdom: a population-based birth-cohort study. *Preventive Medicine*. Epub ahead of print.

New Scientist (2018) *Business Students More Likely to Have a Brain Parasite Spread by Cats* [online]. Available at: https://www.newscientist.com/article/2175045-business-students-more-likely-to-have-a-brain-parasite-spread-by-cats/ (accessed February 2019).

ONS (2018) *Regional Ethnic Diversity* [online]. Available at: https://www.ethnicity-facts-figures.service.gov.uk/british-population/national-and-regional-populations/regional-ethnic-diversity/latest (accessed February 2019).

Pereira R (2016) Responding to filio-parental violence. In: A Holt (Ed.) *Working with Adolescent Violence and Abuse Towards Parents*. Oxford: Routledge.

Price J (1996) *Power and Compassion, Working with Difficult Adolescents and Abused Parents*. New York: Guilford Press.

Retford S (2016) *Child-against-Parent Abuse in Greater Manchester: Key themes, collaboration and preventative interventions*. Professional Doctorate in Criminal Justice, Institute of Criminal Justice Studies, University of Portsmouth.

Routt G and Anderson L (2014) *Adolescent Violence in the Home, Restorative Approaches to Building Healthy, Respectful Family Relationships*. Oxford: Routledge.

Safe Lives (2014) *In Plain Sight* [online]. Available at: http://www.safelives.org.uk/sites/default/files/resources/Final%20policy%20report%20In%20plain%20sight%20-%20effective%20help%20for%20children%20exposed%20to%20domestic%20abuse.pdf.

Selwyn J, Wijedasa D & Meakings S (2014) *Beyond the Adoption Order: Challenges, interventions and adoption disruption*. Department for Education.

Simmons, McEwan, Purcell & Ogloff (2018) Sixty years of child-to-parents abuse research: What we know and where to go. *Aggression and Violent Behaviour* **38** 31–52.

Sporer K and Toller PW (2017) Family identity disrupted by mental illness and violence: an application of relational dialectics theory. *Southern Communication Journal* **82** (2) 85–101.

Thorley W and Coates A (2018) *Let's Talk About: Child-parent violence and aggression (CPVA)* [online]. Extended summary. Available at: https://www.academia.edu/37078253/Lets_Talk_About_Child_to_Parent_Violence_2018_Summary (accessed February 2019).

Victoria Derbyshire episodes:

'I feel really bad when I hurt my Mum' (2018): https://www.bbc.co.uk/programmes/p03bcbb7

'I thought nothing of pulling knife on my dad' (2015): https://www.bbc.co.uk/programmes/p06rlt19

Chapter 3: The impact on families

The danger of starting from an assumption that this is all about dysfunctional families with no control or boundaries, is that it is a short step to assuming parents don't care, or they 'asked for it', or even that it is just one more thing in the general chaos. Even if these views are not prevalent among professionals, we still hear them all the time in general discourse, and they inevitably colour the way the issue of CPVA, and the impact of living with it, is presented to the 'outside world'. And while parents find it hard to speak up about their experience, most people will continue to have little sense either of the degree of abuse, or the way it changes the lives of those affected. We have considered how many families might be affected by CPVA, and who they might be; but what is the impact of living day-to-day with a child who spits obscenities at you, punches and throws things at you, or breaks up the home? Another 'impossible thing' to believe.

> *'There are some times when it can be all consuming and the focus is all on (your child) and it ends up destroying everything else because you're not able to do anything else.'*
> (Interview with Demetria, 2018)
>
> *'He would strangle me, punch me, and try to push me down the stairs to get rid of the baby. He would run through doors to hit me, he would scream, he would smash my house up, throw things down the stairs and destroy everything I brought him, including new computers. I was petrified, to the point that I would cry myself to sleep. I would sit in my chair shaking uncontrollably. At one point I actually wanted to end my life because of what he was doing to me. I felt completely worthless. There's nowhere for people like us to go. It took me three years to tell people that my son was abusing me. When your child threatens you and holds you against walls, it belittles you. It's embarrassing.'*
> (Parent of an 11-year-old boy, ITV News, 2017)
>
> *'Even a week living under these conditions can seem like an eternity and affects both adults and children's self-esteem, relationships and mental health.'*
> (Boorman, 2017)

It is when we start to consider the impact of CPVA on families that the scale of what we are discussing may sink in. It is not so easy to hide behind an assumption that this is all a bit of a storm in a teacup; though, to be fair, the severity of the impact can itself be hard to swallow. The remarkable thing is that so many families apparently make it through each day with little indication to those who do not know them, and that, furthermore, they have a love for their child that is overwhelming to witness. While ignorance and shame are so powerful, families will continue to hide their plight, and stumble on without outside help.

Lists cannot do justice

When I give a presentation, I have a slide that lists the areas of family life that are impacted by child to parent violence and abuse. Periodically I add something else to the list. In itself, it is a stark reminder of how all-encompassing and devastating CPVA can be, and yet simultaneously it is cold and clinical. Sometimes I have to rush through to the next slide. Sometimes I have more time to unpack what each aspect might mean, both objectively and emotionally for the parents, for brothers and sisters, and for the child themselves. Sometimes the slide looks like this:

- Physical health.
- Mental health.
- Family relationships.
- Social life.
- Financial/economic life.
- Education.
- Housing.

Depending on where I'm speaking, who the audience is that I am speaking to, or the title of the presentation; sometimes the slide looks more like this:

- Shame.
- Social isolation.
- Insecurity, poor self-esteem.
- Physical injuries.

- Loss of treasured possessions.
- Loss of home and employment.
- Suicidal ideation.
- Death.

We work in an environment that requires us all too often to take a dispassionate view and approach to an issue, or to a request for help; in part to protect ourselves, in part to establish the facts or to have time to read the literature, make an appointment, assess, complete forms with standard questions, present a case, refer to a more appropriate agency perhaps. Some time ago, both as a counter to that approach and as a way of capturing family voices, I began to draft the stories I heard as a form of poetic prose (see the box below). I came across them again when gathering documents for this book. If you know where to look, there are plenty of accounts of how it feels to be living with violence and abuse from your child. Research literature and media coverage – mainstream and social media alike – are comprised of family testimonies that are both wide-ranging and heart breaking. I have offered links to many of them at the end of this chapter, for those who would like to explore further the data and the concrete examples.

Because of the shame and secrecy, there is no 'standard' way in which we might know what is happening. Families come in many shapes, sizes and flavours. They may appear to be surviving – or being generally dysfunctional – or they may be collapsing very visibly. Violence and abuse from a child may creep up slowly, or it may come slamming into the family's life from left field; but whichever way it develops, the impact cannot be exaggerated. I offer you here the raw voices of parents as they attempt to articulate the pain and despair of a life they did not expect, and to which they see no end.

> From a sense of disbelief that this is the turn your life has taken, to a weariness from daily undermining and foul words, the grinding down of unceasing pain without apparent end, the sense of failure that there is nothing that you can do to stop it or heal the hurt for either party, the shutting down, the depression, the thoughts of suicide, the end.
>
> Physical and mental health both victims of the assault on the body and mind. Visits to A&E. Constant vigilance, lack of sleep, poor nutrition, injury, exhaustion, despair. The turmoil of loving but not loving, having to choose between children, or between child and partner, wanting to help but pushed away, the loss of what might have been.

> Late for school all the time, then returning home to cry, the wrath of teachers, threats of fines, exclusions, a child at home with you alone because no one else can manage the violence and disruption safely. But how can I?
>
> An anger that precious things have been taken, broken, that other family members are harmed. Words of retaliation – regretted – but cannot be unsaid, an arm raised in defence, an accidental bruise shown off as a badge, the knock on the door, the investigation, the separation but not in a way that would have been planned. The suspicion and lingering doubts, forever tainting the notes.
>
> No longer inviting friends for coffee, no longer invited for a play date, no willing babysitters, judgemental words at the shops, comments and looks at the school gate, a family turned inwards, others turned away, a pressure cooker waiting to blow, no support when it happens.
>
> The humiliation, the assumption that injuries must be my husband's fault, ostracisation.
>
> Pressure on relationships, a child goes to one parent but not the other, hits one but not the other, disagreements as to blame, as to response, a couple splits, where does the child go, the abuse continues.
>
> Brothers and sisters targeted, or collateral damage, copying, deprived of attention, fearful, losing sleep, missing school, broken toys, sent to live elsewhere for their own safety, and what about the pets?
>
> Meetings to attend at school and the counsellor, days off sick because of black eyes or just too tired, words from the boss – too much time taken off, eventually it is suggested you leave, goodbyes to friends and colleagues, goodbyes to the last thing that kept you going, bills to pay, debts to clear, nothing left to sell, no point in replacing things because they will all be broken.
>
> Complaints from the neighbours – the noise, the broken glass, the people hanging round, holes in the walls, a broken post on the stairs, a damaged sink, a visit, another move, a move away from everyone you know. Where else to live?
>
> Even within this situation, a determination to keep going, battling. Battling to find understanding and support; forever hoping and forever breathing the next breath, putting one foot in front of the other, loving, seeking a solution. Energies channelled into accessing advice, support, belief.

It is uncomfortable to read the impact that child to parent violence has on families. Reading back now, I am struck by the overwhelming weariness captured in the words. Small wonder that reported levels of depression are so high. McKenna (2006) found that 29% of the parents she spoke with in an Australian study had contemplated suicide, and 2% had made actual attempts to take their life. Perhaps though the words do not capture adequately the fear experienced by many: fear for the safety and life chances of their child, but also fear for a parent's own safety.

'I do not want to become another newspaper headline that screams, "Mother killed by son".'
(Hindustan Times, 2018)

Criticism of a lack of help early on may make practitioners jumpy – if you'd only told us, we want to help but there's no money, that's not the way we see it … Listening to families is not easy, but we cannot deny their truth.

And the young person themselves?

How does it feel to be the child or young person in this situation? It is too easy to assume there are gains to them in a cost-benefit analysis, but they too have become trapped. A need for control, when everything else in their life seems very much uncontrollable. Escaping one experience of chaos perhaps, they create another around them. A lack of personal safety, of emotional integrity, no sense of who they are themselves. A mind set on survival above all else. They need boundaries to feel safe, but push against these when they are in place. Then, when the boundaries collapse, they too fall.

Eventually the child moves out…

Such a bland statement, but so different to the projected gradual move to independence that the family dreamt of so long ago. They may have gone missing, sofa surfing with friends or worse. A best case scenario may be grandparents, or an understanding relative. A home with an absent parent may be a mixed blessing. Or into care, a hostel, supported lodgings. Young people may struggle to manage in their new circumstances: living in an empty room, with few skills; an angry child, so vulnerable to more abuse themselves.

It would be disingenuous to suggest that, despite their catastrophic experiences, all families remain committed to staying together.

'I long for her to be 16 so I don't feel so responsible.'
'I am just waiting for his 18th birthday then I will ask him to leave.'
(Comments on message boards, posted anonymously)

There are times when we hear parents express their loathing of a child, or a desperation that they might reach an age soon when they can be allowed to fend more for themselves. How sad though that matters have reached this point! Maybe there is one significant trigger, at which point a line is drawn, but often all concerned have reached this place after many years, where it is no longer in their best interests to struggle on.

When parents ask for help or removal in this situation, we need to understand the unspoken and unsupported time of trauma that has brought the family to this state. This is not necessarily the response to a one-off incident that might be easily patched up. Are families asking for respite or permanent separation; for term-time accommodation, or full-time; for a different way to remain together as a family, or for a clean break? Is reunification and an adolescent's return home always in the family's best interest? Is this what is wanted? We are well advised to listen closely to the story and to the injury suffered.

'I don't know how you have managed to keep going for so long.'
'I don't know how one person is doing this. Ten people would struggle.'
(From Twitter, undated)

But placing a child elsewhere also carries responsibilities. It may be the best solution, but parents report feeling let down, even at this stage, by the perceived lack of support for their child, or an apparent carelessness in the attitude to needy and vulnerable youngsters. And we should beware an assumption that this is the end, with little attempt to heal the pain or to allow relationships to carry on. Does more need to be done to support parents in dealing with the emotional fall out of a child's removal?

Families may continue to 'parent at a distance', ensuring a young person's needs are met on a daily basis, while still facing abuse for their efforts. Do we genuinely need to up our game in the support a young person receives to live independently? What is our understanding of the emotional maturity, or the vulnerability of young people in this situation?

With real understanding of the issues, and good support, families can be helped to reunite, to reach a point of greater safety, and a restoration of healthy family relationships. With so much damage done, it will not be a quick fix. It may take years. But we need to understand the extent of the impact on the family in the first place, in order to put in place the full range of support that will be needed.

Other types of family and home

A word at this stage about those caring for children outside of home, whether in foster or residential care, hospital, or secure settings, remembering that children may be placed here precisely because of their behaviour and the danger they have posed. In England, the majority of children in care are not in residential establishments, but this differs around the world. Indeed, where there is extreme violence and distress, a secure residential placement may be the best option. Sir Martin Narey writes (2016), *'During my most recent visit to a secure children's home … I was struck by the exceptional challenge of the children there, the extent to which they were a grave danger to themselves and others, and the conscientiousness and dedication of the staff who cared for them'.*

While adults in each of those situations may also experience abuse and violence from those in their care, the relationship between young person and carer is a different one. How does that play out in terms of impact? Do we assume a lower level of tolerance, or a 'harder' attitude of mind? Or do we assume greater levels of patience, commitment and skills honed over the years? Adults will be conscious of the competing needs of others in their care – and their safety. There may be protocols around violence which mean they have to respond in particular ways. A fostered child may be moved on because of the risks to other family members from their violence and abuse. Staff in residential care have often been criticised for calling the police too quickly, yet at other times are praised for the level of therapeutic care offered over long periods of time to children in their care. In some therapeutic establishments, staff will be privileged to have received specialist training. The disruption, the damage, the financial costs, the concerns about vulnerability: these do not change, because of the type of 'home'. Perhaps the main difference is the emotional bond, but that feels a risky generalisation to make. Each young person is different, each carer is different.

What can you do?

As always, listening to families in crisis in a real and compassionate way is an important starting place.

Putting down the pen and focusing on the words is of immeasurable worth to a parent who feels no one takes them seriously.

Asking gentle supplementary questions:
What might be behind the anxiety, sleeplessness, panic attacks, depression, for which a parent is seeking help?

When someone says they cannot get their child to come to school, what does this experience actually look and feel like?
How long has this been going on?
What has been tried so far?
Does this change our understanding of why a family might be seeking help, or how we might need to be involved?

Undertaking a risk assessment:
What do we know about the mental health of members of the family?
What are the physical risks to all concerned?
Are there any support mechanisms in place?
What would the family do if there was an immediate risk?
Are there other agencies already involved?

Can we help the family identify and build a support structure specific to their situation – to help re-build parental authority in the home, to reinforce a message, or in an emergency?
Who would it include? Which agencies, which friends or family members?

If we have a new understanding of the impact of living with CPVA, how might this alter our emotional, policy or agency response?
What can we offer to make it possible for the family to keep going? What resources locally might be able to offer practical support?

Understanding more of the impact for one family, can we extrapolate about the costs for families in our area more generally?

Can we find a way of intervening earlier to prevent some of the damage, and to permit some of the family's own vital support structures to be strengthened and remain in place?
How would this impact on costs and benefits for our local agency and services?

Find out more

Part novel, part personal family story, **Julie Myerson's** book, *The Lost Child* (2009) brings to life her family's experience of gradually realising the enormity of her son's behaviour, and coming to terms with the need for him to live elsewhere.

In a rare analysis, **Thorley and Coates's** book *Let's Talk About: Child-parent violence and aggression* (2018) discuss the economic costs of child to parent violence or aggression, in addition to the direct impact, for both family and society, in their response to a survey of birth and second families experiencing child to parent violence and abuse. This impressive compilation of data and discussion dissects the experiences of different family types. https://www.academia.edu/37078253/Lets_Talk_About_Child_to_Parent_Violence_2018_Summary

The campaigning group, **Special Guardians and Adopters Together** have also reported on the mental health of families affected by child to parent violence following an in depth survey in 2018: https://specialguardiansandadopterstogether.com https://campaignforadoptionpermanence.files.wordpress.com/2018/04/special-guardians-and-adopters-together-interim-report-6th-march-2018.pdf.

A special edition of the **Adoption UK magazine**: *Trauma-fuelled Violence*, addressed the impact of CPV and families' experiences of seeking help: https://www.adoptionuk.org/shop/adoption-today-supplement-trauma-fuelled-violence.

For an illustration of secondary trauma – the experience of parents as they take on the trauma of their child in their own life – read the eBook, *Side by Side*, from **Beacon House**: http://beaconhouse.org.uk/wp-content/uploads/Side-By-Side-Ebook.pdf as well as other material on the Beacon House website, https://beaconhouse.org.uk.

Also a blog from **Amy Sugeno** about adoptive parents' experience of secondary trauma: https://www.amysugenocounseling.com/secondary-trauma-in-adoptive-parents/.

There are so many blog and websites documenting family experiences, it is hard to know where to start.
Amanda Boorman (https://allaboardthetraumatrain.com)
Al Coates (http://www.alcoates.co.uk)
Mumdrah (http://mumdrah.co.uk) and
Herding Chickens (https://heardingchickens.wordpress.com)
All write as adopters and give valuable insight into that experience.

For life as a family, specifically with a child with special educational needs, try **The Institute for Attachment and Child Development** blogs (for example: https://instituteforattachment.org/what-it-feels-like-to-be-a-parent-of-that-kid-the-one-with-reactive-attachment-disorder/).

Websites such as **Uniting**, in Australia, offer information to parents and practitioners alongside illustrations of the impact of abuse and violence: https://www.kildonan.org.au/programs-and-services/child-youth-and-family-support/family-violence/adolescent-violence/support-for-parents-and-carers/.

For more academic work, see *Beyond the Adoption Order: Challenges, interventions and adoption disruption*, by **Selwyn, Wijedasa and Meakings** (2014), published by the Department for Education. This was a ground breaking report, bringing to public awareness the issues faced by adoptive families living with violence and abuse.

Also, a paper in the journal, *Child & Family Social Work*, from **Clarke K, Holt A, Norris C and Nel PW** (2017) Adolescent-to-parent violence and abuse: parents' management of tension and ambiguity – an interpretative phenomenological analysis *Child & Family Social Work* **22** (4) 1423–1430.

Galvani authored the 2010 report into the impact of living with a family member using alcohol or drugs: *Supporting Families Affected by Substance Use and Domestic Violence*, The Tilda Goldberg Centre for Social Work and Social Care: University of Bedfordshire. Available from: https://www.adfam.org.uk/files/docs/adfam_dvreport.pdf.

References

Boorman A (2017) CPV: *Help is at Hand* [online]. The Open Nest. Available at: https://www.theopennest.co.uk/single-post/2017/04/27/CPV-Help-Is-At-Hand (accessed February 2019).

Hindustan Times (2018) *Let's Talk about Teenage Violence* [online]. Available at: https://www.hindustantimes.com/india-news/my-15-year-old-son-hit-me-am-i-bad-parent-let-s-talk-about-teenage-violence/story-Ef562omxsJmawHtjPcsKBL.html (accessed February 2019).

Hunte B (2017) Sharp rise in parents being abused by their violent children [online]. *ITV News* **30 November**. Available at: http://www.itv.com/news/london/2017-11-30/sharp-rise-in-parents-being-abused-by-their-violent-children/ (accessed February 2019).

McKenna M (2006) *Adolescent Abuse of Parents* [online]. Radio interview with Richard Aedy on ABC Radio National (Australia). Available at: https://www.abc.net.au/radionational/programs/lifematters/adolescent-abuse-of-parents/3328416 (accessed February 2019).

Narey M (2016) *Residential Care in England: Report of Sir Martin Narey's independent review of children's residential care*. Available at: https://assets.publishing.service.gov.uk/government/uploads/system/uploads/attachment_data/file/534560/Residential-Care-in-England-Sir-Martin-Narey-July-2016.pdf (accessed February 2019).

Chapter 4: Punished for being a victim

'Don't be ridiculous!' was a common response when I first started raising CPVA as an issue. But of course it happens in other arenas. We are used to the notion of women being held to account for their appearance or behaviour in cases of domestic violence and sexual assault for instance, so why not here? In the case of violence and abuse from their children, many parents report that the treatment they receive goes way beyond simple blaming, to actual punishment, for being a victim of abuse. There are indeed many different layers of experience.

Parents are ridiculed for allowing this to happen

You had one job: to raise a charming and respectful member of the next generation; you couldn't even do that successfully! We have only to think of the disapproving glances thrown at a parent in a supermarket when their child is disobedient; or the tutting from bystanders when a toddler throws a tantrum and is carried away screaming and kicking to know that parent shaming is a very real issue. The number of people coming forward to offer to help will likely be far outweighed by those whose criticism reinforces their own sense of superiority.

Mothers are typically assumed to have the main caring role and so come off worse. Gallagher (2018) points to the dual effect of blaming mothers first for having raised such an aggressive child, and secondly for not being able to protect themselves.

Parents are assumed to have been to blame

They must be the protagonist in this situation; 'What did you do to wind him up?' Perhaps there is a suspicion of 'heavy handed' parenting, or they are simply too weak and inconsistent in their parenting style. Blaming feels very much like punishment, when there is no help or support on offer. In the ground breaking examination of adoption disruption, Selwyn *et al* (2014) reference the combination of lack of support and sense of blame that many parents reported:

'My daughter was only put back into care as the Local Authority would not give her a full psychiatric assessment after ... taking and hiding knives around our family home where I had two birth children ... The Local Authority never accepted the aggression my daughter displayed and failed to take on how destructive this behaviour can be to herself and especially to the family ... The Local Authority seemed far more interested in blaming the family than ever looking at the possible issues.'
(Selwyn *et al*, 2014)

The experience of feeling blamed may be more important than whether it is a reality, but when so many parents report this experience, it cannot be written off.

The *assumption* of blame is the problem. Undoubtedly some children *are* responding to levels of neglect and abuse, which they experience within the home. One of the early explanations for CPVA was that children were responding to being abused themselves. Yet, while some young people will attack a parent to protect themselves or others from violence, it is often the case that the violence is directed towards a different parent to the one causing the original injury (for instance post-domestic abuse, or post-adoption). Some styles of parenting are more likely than others to be associated with violence. A number of studies have looked at this, suggesting that very strict, or very permissive parenting practices, are closely linked with their child's abusive behaviour (see Simmons *et al*, 2018 for discussion). Others, for instance Gallagher (2018), have pointed to the strong sense of entitlement which many young people demonstrate as having originated in the style of parenting offered them. But there are strong caveats around a correlation between abuse and 'weak' parenting, where the link may be in the opposite direction to the one expected.

Parents are humiliated in meetings with professionals

If it was hard persuading one practitioner that you weren't to blame, now you're in a room with what feels like scores of them, all inclined to believe each other rather than you because they're, well ... professionals. We need to be wary of a tendency to assume expertise on the basis of training and qualification, whether or not there is actual prior understanding or experience of child to parent violence. Where professionals have listened to parents' suggestions of what works, and have been open-minded in their attitude, the difference is immeasurable: time is saved, respect gives hope to families, people work together, and lessons are learnt.

'We asked you to come over for a meeting because Ben's behaviour during the last few months has been very aggressive towards other children and staff'" … The school staff seemed open to help, but they didn't know how. They were asking me what to do, and if I had any idea. This was a first for their little school. I asked them to give me a couple of days to come up with a plan … When I came back to the school with my plan to help my son managing his emotions, all the professionals were really impressed. They didn't have anything to add to it. They also took notes and said they'll implement some aspects of my plan with some other challenging kids. Thank God for the professionals!' (Boccaleone, 2018)

Parents are investigated for allegations of abuse BY them

'I called the police and I was the one that they arrested. My Son is so good at lying that I can actually understand why the police believed him over me. I am extremely depressed and feel like I have to give in to whatever he wants so I don't get hurt anymore because the last time he pushed me so hard that I can barely walk.' (Comment by 'Linda' on the We Have Kids website, 2018)

A recent survey (Schroer, 2018) of special guardians and adopters found that 20% of the 398 who responded had had to deal with false allegations made by their children against them, or a family member, necessitating an investigation by Children's Services. There are numerous stories from parents of investigations from Children's Services simply because a crisis point has been reached, and it is assumed there must be a failure of parenting involved. And of course there are the counter-allegations by children, when the police turn up to deal with a report to them by parents and carers.

Candice had cared for her granddaughter, Alicia, on and off for a number of years before she came to live with her full time. Alicia had a difficult relationship with her mother who had poor physical and mental health, and was frequently in hospital. Now 18, she was attending college but lacking the stability to enable her to learn, and so Candice was keen to take her in to offer a safe home. Alicia was less tidy and organised than Candice was used to, but it was the demands for lifts, and financial expectations that were most exhausting. When she found that Alicia had been buying clothes and a phone online using her grandmother's name and bank account details, Candice finally found the courage to confront her granddaughter about her behaviour. A struggle ensued, before Alicia ran off into the night. When she did not return, Candice reported her missing, but when the police caught up with Alicia she showed them the bruises on her arm where her grandmother had 'grabbed her', and alleged systematic abuse as her reason for running away. The police took Candice to the station, where she was kept for the night in a cell and later charged with assault, being advised to accept a caution.

It is worth remembering that parents may be simply defending themselves from attack, or a child may make a mischievous allegation as part of a system of control. It is particularly ironic that this should be an issue, when the usual concern in the past has been that children have not been believed in the claims that they have made; and it is right and proper that all allegations are investigated thoroughly. Nevertheless, where parents assert that they are themselves a victim, this must be part of the investigation process. Parents are well advised to make schools, or other agencies with whom they are involved, aware of abusive behaviour patterns as a matter of course, if not for support, then at least for evidence. A criminal record, or even an investigation, may preclude a parent from being able to practice their profession, or to obtain work in many areas of life.

Parents may have other children removed

This may be by protective services because of a perceived failure to keep them safe. Again, this is a tricky area to consider. Other children in the family may well be facing levels of stress on a daily basis, through the actions of a sibling, whether directed towards them or their parents. They may face actual danger. They are almost certainly losing out in terms of time and attention. They may be missing school, they may be unable to have friends round to play or to visit other homes. They may be called upon to respond in a manner way beyond their years to acts of violence and abuse. But why do we consider removing them, rather than the child demonstrating the behaviour, or instead of putting in other support?

Parents are expected to comply with requirements not suited to their circumstances, or sent on inappropriate generic courses

If we start off by assuming that the problem is one of ineffective parenting, then the 'obvious' response is to send parents on a course, of which there are numerous, to improve their skills. If this is the first level response, then parents may not be offered any other support until they have complied with this expectation. Yet, there are many and varied reasons why a generic parenting course may not be appropriate to all. If a child has additional needs because of a particular diagnosis or history, then a different style of parenting may be required. Parents with children adopted from care in particular find that a style of nurture known as 'therapeutic parenting' is a pre-requisite to overcoming previous harms and securing future well-being. Standard parenting courses, aimed at whichever age or community, tend to share an expectation view that boundaries, consistency, rewards and consequences will be sufficient to the need when applied over time. The experience of parents experiencing actual abuse, is first that they feel unable to share stores of their home life with the group, because of shame or the complete incongruity of it all. But then that the methods proposed may be actively damaging in their situation, encouraging further assault and alienation. A different understanding, and a different approach is needed. Frequently, parents speak of being sent on multiple such courses, with little imagination apparent as to whether they might not be working, generating a wry suggestion, 'What, you want us to teach it?'. To refuse to attend risks being viewed as non-compliant (Adoption and Fostering podcast, 2018).

Parents, and the whole family, may lose their home

'I have the Housing Association coming to the house for a property inspection shortly and they have mentioned eviction in meetings if my son continues to damage the property and I am unable to maintain the property so that's more stress.'
(Personal correspondence with Jocelyn, 2018)

When parents are unable to work because of the abuse, and so unable to continue with mortgage payments, there is a real risk that they might lose their home. They may be unable to afford essential repairs to damage in the property and are therefore asked to leave by a landlord. Their child's behaviour may lead to complaints from the neighbourhood, placing a tenancy at risk. As training is rolled out to housing providers in the recognition of, and response to, domestic abuse, it is important that this awareness should include the possibility that the abuse is from a child rather than an adult, with consideration given to appropriate support.

And finally, families may choose to move from an area with significant support, to a new home away from 'bad influences' – a so-called new start, but without the support of friends and understanding services.

Parents are punished further through the judicial system

'Found out I have to pay for public defender for my daughter for her to be charged with felony assault with a deadly weapon.'
(Personal correspondence from a parent in USA, the victim of the assault, 2016)

If a child is prosecuted for criminal damage or for offences against a parent, depending on the country where they live, a parent may be required to fund their child's legal representation. They may be required (or choose) to pay fines for damage to the home, or other punishments. They may be required to attend courses, which question their parenting skills and suggest strategies which may even make the abuse worse. Holt (2009) discusses this in her paper, *Parent Abuse: Some reflections on the adequacy of a youth justice response*, in which she questions the appropriateness of issuing parenting orders when a young person has also been abusive towards their parents; and of using a youth justice model in understanding this phenomenon.

Parents are re-traumatised by the helping professions

The combined effect of asking for help, and then receiving a less than positive response, makes some families reluctant to seek further help in future. They now find themselves in a worse position, emotionally and practically; their integrity has been called into question; and the young person's power within the family has been raised further by the ineffective response, leading potentially not simply to continued abuse, but to a raised level of violence and aggression.

> 'My son was abusing me well before he was a teenager. He is adopted with a whole host of emotional and psychological issues. I have called the police so many times. I have brought him to hospitals for psych evals. One time I brought him and he looked so small and cute that they sent the psych/social worker out for me. I have even had him arrested for assaulting me with my own bed. Of course, he got off. He is now emboldened. I can recall me driving him to the hospital and him saying, "They'll never believe you, mom. I know just what to say. They will think you are crazy". I did think at that point that I would lose my mind.'
> (Comment by 'Marley Carroll' on the We Have Kids website, 2018)

What can be done to bring about change?

- **Awareness and training for all** is a requisite for change. Without this, there is no reason to believe that current practices would change.
- **Proper assessment**. This is not about asking for blind acceptance of a parent's version of events, just a proper enquiry, built on the understanding of the full range of issues that might make a child and family vulnerable to the use of abuse and violence.

- **Respect for parents as part of the solution**, not necessarily as all of the problem; working as partners to bring about hope and change. They may have great expertise in their child's behaviour, triggers and means of de-escalation. Parents may be the most important resource we have as practitioners, to be built up and not crushed down. Where it is necessary to instigate a full investigation, this should be done in a respectful way, thinking about how the need to do so is communicated, and parents are made aware of, and kept informed at, every step of the process.

- **Professionals to be aware of the wholes range of parenting styles, techniques, approaches, and courses available** that might be more appropriate than a standard parenting course.

- **Campaigning to bring about change in the legal and judicial system.** Each country and jurisdiction will need to take their own steps, but it has been extremely encouraging that, in Britain, courts are now directed not to require parenting course attendance in cases of child to parent violence and abuse. Within the United States, parent abuse is now legally recognised in the state of Florida, following intense campaigning by those affected.

Things to think about

- What can be done to raise awareness among colleagues?
- Are there additional questions that can be added to an assessment to elicit more information about CPVA?
- In a rushed, overstretched environment, what can be done to ensure all individuals receive a respectful response?
- In multi-agency, professional-heavy meetings, what can be done to help parents feel more comfortable, as accepted partners?

Find out more

Laura Boccaleone blogs about her experiences as a foster and adoptive parent. In this post, 'The Kindness of Strangers', she describes an unexpected positive and affirming response from the school her son attends: https://fulltimetired.com/2018/02/03/the-kindness-of-strangers/.

In this YouTube video, parent **Heather Willis** has documented her family's desperation in the face of violence from her daughter. She decries the focus of helping agencies on abuse AGAINST the child, and seeks legislative changes to permit and prescribe more effective responses than are currently available. 'Our Story of Parental Abuse': https://www.youtube.com/watch?time_continue=316&v=y1GYAhw2EAQ.

The Silent Suffering of Parents is a hub on the **We Have Kids** website, moderated by Lou Purplefairy, offering parents a chance to share their experiences of abuse, with some resources also listed: https://wehavekids.com/family-relationships/The-Silent-Suffering-of-Parent-Abuse-When-Children-Abuse-Parents.

References

Adoption and Fostering Podcast (2018) *An interview with Carrie Grant*. Episode 35. Available at: https://adoptionandfostering.podbean.com/e/episode-35-an-interview-with-carrie-grant/ (accessed February 2019).

Boccaleone L (2018) *The Kindness of Strangers* [online] Fulltime Tired blog. Available at: https://fulltimetired.com/2018/02/03/the-kindness-of-strangers/ (accessed February 2019).

Carroll M (2018) *The Silent Suffering of Parents* [online]. Available at: https://wehavekids.com/family-relationships/The-Silent-Suffering-of-Parent-Abuse-When-Children-Abuse-Parents (accessed February 2019).

Gallagher E (2018) *Who's in Charge? Why children abuse parents and what you can do about it*. London: Austin Macauley Publishers.

Holt A (2009) Parent abuse: some reflections on the adequacy of a youth justice response. *Internet Journal of Criminology* 1–11.

Schroer S (2018) *Findings of a Peer-led Survey into the Stress, Health and Wellbeing of Adopters and Special Guardians, Interim Report* [online]. Special Guardians and Adopters Together. Available at: https://campaignforadoptionpermanence.files.wordpress.com/2018/04/special-guardians-and-adopters-together-interim-report-6th-march-2018.pdf (accessed February 2019)

Selwyn J, Wijedasa D & Meakings S (2014) *Beyond the Adoption Order: Challenges, interventions and adoption disruption*. Department for Education.

Simmons M, McEwan TE, Purcell R & Ogloff JRP (2018) Sixty years of child-to-parent abuse research: what we know and where to go. *Aggression and Violent Behaviour* **38** 31–52.

We Have Kids (2018) *The Silent Suffering of Parent Abuse: When children abuse parents* [online]. Available at: https://wehavekids.com/family-relationships/The-Silent-Suffering-of-Parent-Abuse-When-Children-Abuse-Parents (accessed February 2019).

Chapter 5: Nobody's problem

'Where are the signs on the back of toilet doors? How are people supposed to know where to go for help?'
(Booker, 2018)

'They all assume it is my husband. If it was, there would be help and support available, both immediately and in the longer term. Then I tell them something nobody wants to hear. There is silence at the end of the phone line, followed by a whispered, "Sorry, in that case there is nothing we can do". He is a seven-year-old boy. This is severe non-verbal autism.'
(Anonymous comment on the Autism Awareness website, 2016)

When I was doing my own small piece of research in 2005 into how parents were able to access help, it was interesting to see that my experience mirrored what families report happens when they seek help for themselves. Most often the agencies I approached – generally small local charities – had not heard of what I described, or were clear that I needed to go somewhere else to find the help I sought. While there are now towns or cities where a clearly articulated, adequately resourced, proven effective, and easily accessed response to child to parent violence exists; sadly then, and still to a lesser extent now, there are many places where families are brushed off, sent away, directed elsewhere over and over again, and where practitioners ask, at best, 'what are we supposed to do?'.

Holt and Retford, writing eight years later in 2013, stated, *'Parents' accounts of experiences of parent abuse suggest that they have frequently sought help and support from a range of front-line services, and in the main have been disappointed by the response'*. They go on to suggest there is evidence of failings right across the board, by police, judiciary, youth offending, social care services, education and health, as well as voluntary and community services, and that in some cases, a misinformed response has actually made things worse and left parents more at risk, triggering further violence, or leaving parents feeling blamed. Harsh words perhaps, and difficult to hear when most practitioners are trying to do an effective job; yet unless we are able to acknowledge that we have not got this right in the past, we will be unable to move forward now with an effective and supportive response.

Writing now, in 2019, it is hopeful to see that the situation is gradually improving, yet I continue to hear of parents finding it difficult to access help, not knowing where to go, having no local services, trying lots of places but without much success; and practitioners still left without the tools for the job.

The Family Lives report (2011), which analysed an online survey and calls to their helpline, shows the sorts of places parents and carers had approached for help with their children's behaviour. While 44% of parents had not previously sought help at all, a third of these because they did not know where to go, others had approached multiple agencies and individuals, ranging from school (54.2%), their GP (51.4%), friends and family (34.6%), CAMHS (30.8%), social services (28%) and police (11.2%) through psychologists, other therapists, online support, and charities. Six percent of survey respondents reported that *'they made initial enquiries and then hit a brick wall'*. The Family Lives report is now comparatively old, and yet Thorley and Coates (2018) found a similar scattering of services in their more recent survey of parents experiencing CPVA. While the most frequently approached agency was social services, voluntary groups, education and CAMHS followed closely behind, with police and other health staff also featuring prominently. Thorley and Coates report *'families are involved with a myriad of service provision and often with more than one provision simultaneously. This indication demonstrates that the majority of families are receiving support from 4-5 different professional services'*. This finding is replicated time and time again in different reports. However, while it might be hoped that this would indicate a positive outcome for the families concerned, Thorley and Coates suggest instead that multiple approaches are a result of a lack of responsiveness or knowledge and understanding.

'No one helped for about seven years, then everyone got involved, but no one actually did anything to help. We just went round in circles from agency to agency; police to GP to CAMHs to hospital to social services to education, back to charity/voluntary agency, the police, GP, CAMHS etc. This happened repeated [sic] *for years and years. They were so proud of the inter-agency approach, but we got no actual help.'*
(Parent quoted in Thorley and Coates, 2018)

Sometimes parents seeking help report being simply shrugged off. Sometimes they are passed from one agency to the next without a satisfactory outcome.

'Where are the resources for abused parents? Where is THEIR help? I spoke with a national abuse hotline and even the operator told me she wasn't sure what could be done. I tried several times to communicate my worries to the police, and they were shrugged off.'
(Rushing, 2010)

A similar situation continues today for many parents:

'Just called the police about CPV. They refused to come out because J is 9 and told me to call Children's Services… who always tell me to call the police. She's currently outside trying to break the windows. My parents are coming from half an hour away to help. This is horrible.'
(Tweet by Hannah Meadows, 2018)

There is, of course, work of a high quality with families experiencing CPVA taking place around the country, in Britain and elsewhere, in a multitude of different agencies. Sometimes one-to-one work, sometimes group programmes; whether individually designed or using an 'off the shelf' curriculum; delivered by professionals and groups as diverse as youth offending teams, social workers, school mentors, domestic abuse charities, youth workers, education attendance officers, adoption support agencies, police officers, child psychiatrists, counsellors - and parents who have given up searching and started their own networks. In one town there might be multiple groups operating. Down the road there might be nothing, or there might be a six-month waiting list, or longer. Where a response has developed it has often come as a result of specific campaigning and training in the face of a locally recognised need. One person's awareness perhaps, or a caseload audit, shows this up as an issue demanding attention. But the very fact that the work is taking place in so many different agencies emphasises our difficulty in locating whose responsibility this might be.

Where there is experience of intimate partner violence, carefully coordinated multi-agency groups meet regularly and work together to ensure there is proper risk assessment and response. Yet with child to parent violence, the distinct absence of such coordination can mean that the family falls through the gap, as Galvani (2012) found in interviews with family members supporting someone with drug or alcohol problems.

'A clear message from parents was that in many cases they did not believe the services that supported them and their family talked to each other or approached problems in a strategic way. The clear sense that CPV is somehow falling through the gaps of support indicates that this lack of communication and shared strategy is having a seriously detrimental effect on the overall support provided to parents.'
(Galvani, 2012)

Why is it nobody's problem?

I would suggest that there are multiple factors at play here. Some may sound familiar. Some you may balk at. But read on, and consider whether any chime with you, bearing in mind that this grouping is suggested after listening to, and speaking with, a whole range of professional and parents over the years.

Lack of training and awareness

It still comes as a shock to know that there may be as little as one day given over to domestic abuse training on a social work degree (in Britain), and child to parent violence and abuse may not warrant a single mention. Thankfully we do not hear so often, 'Who says it's abuse?' or, 'You mean abuse BY parents?' yet there remain professionals who are still woefully unprepared for an approach by a family experiencing CPVA, and may simply not understand what they are being told, or asked. In such situations practitioners understandably fall back on long standing constructions of 'challenging young people' and of 'weak and ineffectual parenting'.

Normative constructions of family relationships

This may be an issue for individuals trying to navigate an approach from a family for help, based on traditional understandings of power within the family; or for practitioners as representatives of agencies, which have developed services based on a particular understanding of family roles, to which child to parent violence presents a serious challenge. Depending on professional background, an individual may well 'hear' a different version of events to a colleague from another agency, and can certainly 'hear' a different version to the one the family is trying to convey. Once again, there may be an assumption that the parenting offered is at fault.

Agency mandate

Without protocols or policies, there is no action, no framework for response – it's somebody else's responsibility. Holt (2012) suggests that the policy understanding of domestic abuse as being perpetrated by adults over the age of 18, and of abuse within families being meted out by adults *towards* children, impacts on our abilities to frame this as an issue, or to offer a meaningful response. In the same way, if the only response in your town is within the youth offending service, but your child has not come to the attention of services because of vulnerability in terms of offending; or if you need a diagnosis of mental health problems before you can access help, but this is not relevant in your situation, then you are likely to be frustrated in your efforts to obtain help.

So long as we continue to adopt a binary understanding of family relationships or difficulties: children as vulnerable/victims, adults as caregiver/threat, there may indeed be no room for a service for families where these roles are reversed. Whose social worker are you? Yet listening to a family we may learn that there are multiple issues involved, many of which do fall within a particular mandate, and ultimately all agencies have a responsibility to support the safeguarding and welfare of children. The Home Office's information guide, *Adolescent to Parent Violence and Abuse* (2015) makes this clear.

Asking for the wrong thing

Sometimes people go to the wrong agency. Sometimes individuals go to the 'right place' but ask for the 'wrong thing'. There is a world of difference between tantrums and rages, between being disobedient and beyond control. We see that many parents do not name what they experience as abuse. They may not have heard the term child to parent violence and abuse. They may minimise the issue themselves because it is too frightening to contemplate. Typically a parent might seek help with depression or anxiety from a doctor; they might be referred to a child and adolescent mental health service about a child with conduct disorder, or ADHD; or they might be approached by a school because of a young person's non-attendance. Each may be a genuine problem, but they mask the real issue and the underlying need for help. Where people go for help matters – if you ask for the wrong sort of thing from an agency and they cannot help because it is not their mandate, or the help is superficial and does not tackle the root cause, or because your request is misconstrued, then the lack of response can appear to give more power to the young person, or make everyone more helpless.

Not yet ready

'We don't want to start asking questions, because we don't have the infrastructure in place as yet to respond'. A project may be in developmental stages, training still to carry out, posts to fill, a programme to write. A reluctance to delve too deep may seem understandable, yet 'not being quite ready' suggests that there is at least an awareness which could be used to promote an interim strategy: listening, suggesting emergency responses, developing a waiting list…

Not bad enough

At any time when requests for help outstrip resources, rationing prevails, but what must it be like to be told as a parent, 'Come back when he actually comes at you with a knife', or, 'Until she is suicidal there is nothing we can do for you'? The evidence for rising thresholds is understandably questioned by those with responsibility for the provision of services. Nevertheless, the All Party Parliamentary Group for Children, reporting in 2018, stated clearly:

'The Inquiry heard of cases not being taken on until families reached more complex levels of need, and children already receiving support subsequently being deemed to no longer reach the threshold for help.'

Responding in a press release, Alison Michalska, then President of the Association of Directors of Children's Services, commented:

'This report raises some important questions worthy of further debate, not least in relation to the cumulative impact of wider government policies, exacerbated by financial austerity, on our most vulnerable children and families. Since 2010 local government budgets have been reduced by almost half, at the same time demand for costly child protection service has risen significantly. Cuts to vital early help and preventative services have been necessary in order to balance the books which has reduced our ability to work with families at the earliest opportunity to help them build resilience and prevent family breakdowns.'

Similar reports have been received in relation to children's and adolescent's mental health services. The state of the nation report into children and young people's mental health (Frith, 2016) found that 23% of children referred to children and adolescent mental health services (CAMHS) were turned away, often because their condition was not deemed serious enough, or not suitable or specialist mental health treatment; with many children waiting six months for a first appointment, and some up to 42 weeks for the start of treatment.

Austerity

With budgets cut, and services sliced to the bone again and again, workers stressed and overstretched, why would you look to take on new issues? Child to parent violence and abuse is by no means the only 'new' issue vying for attention in these austere times. Whether it is county lines, rising knife crime, child sexual exploitation, or almost any other issue hitting the news, there will be campaigners, researchers, and practitioners all making a case for their own particular priority. Clearly it makes more sense to pass another new problem on to someone else. But when the issue is having a huge impact on individual and family lives now, and ultimately even more so on agency budgets further down the line, it is hard to accept this as a civilised, humane, or even sensible economic response. Indeed, this was a specific focus of the All Party Parliamentary Group for Children report (2018) *Storing up Trouble*.

So whose problem is it?

Hunter *et al* (2010) emphasise how difficult it is to frame CPVA within one particular agency framework. Despite many similarities with other issues, this is a 'new thing' and needs to be understood as a unique problem. At the moment it tends to be defined by what it is NOT – not domestic violence, not child protection, not a mental health issue, not anti-social behaviour …

The very complexity of the issue, cutting across adults' and children's services, with a multitude of potential co-existing diagnoses or difficulties, all to be addressed, suggests that a multi-agency understanding and response is imperative, wherever help might be actually sited. In some areas, families experiencing CPVA are now brought to Multi-Agency Risk Assessment Conferences (MARACs); and with a plethora of innovative programmes springing up in response to particular pots of money, we see services for families experiencing CPVA situated within 'troubled families' programmes, multi-agency domestic abuse consortia, and – interestingly – individual charities specifically conceived and funded to work with this issue. Early help services too would be ideally suited to the provision of cross-discipline intervention, were they not being culled in the name of austerity.

Finally, in Holt and Retford's words (2013); there is a need for training first, but *'this would enable a coherent cross-agency risk assessment strategy for use by all practitioners who work with children and families, and would enable the development of good practice around how parent abuse might be presented to families to avoid blaming individuals and risking their disengagement from intervention work'*. With so many separate factors involved for each family, what matters is less the particular named profession of the individual offering support, and more, perhaps, an overarching awareness, coupled with individual personal skills: compassion, perseverance – and a belief in the impossible!

No wrong door

Whose problem is this? Everyone's. All need awareness at the very least, and at best a working model of useful intervention. With effective training, all can respond.

What can you do?

- As a team, can you come up with a clear policy on how to respond when families approach you for help, so that parents are given a reliable and consistent message?

- Do you understand why other agencies, or indeed your own, are not responding – so that you can explain this clearly to families who may be distressed or frustrated?

- Even if you cannot help with all aspects of CPVA, are there elements of children's violent and aggressive behaviour, or of the family's situation, which your team does recognise and for which you can offer support?

- If your agency does offer a distinct response to CPVA, how well is this publicised? Would families be able to find your service easily? Are there posters in community spaces, or leaflets available?

- Can you join with other agencies to agree a co-ordinated response if families seek help?

- Are there aspects of a family's experience, which would allow you to refer them to a specialist agency offering help with CPVA (such as adoption support)?

- Are you familiar with the numbers for confidential helplines, to give details to families if you feel there is nothing else appropriate available locally?

Find out more

The **Family Lives** reports from 2010 and 2011 give a good indication of the experiences of families in accessing help:

- **Family Lives** (2010) *When Family Life Hurts: Family experience of aggression in children*: https://www.familylives.org.uk/media_manager/public/209/Documents/Reports/When%20family%20life%20hurts%202010.pdf.

- **Family Lives** (2011) *When Family Life Hurts: Family experiences of aggression in children, an update to Family Lives' October 2010 report*: https://app.pelorous.com/public/cms/209/432/256/391/the_aggression_report_2011_family_lives.pdf?realName=2xCtiO.pdf.

The **All Party Parliamentary Group for Children** reports, 2017 and 2018, are interesting for a review of children's social care and the issues impacting on provision and delivery around the country:

- **All Party Parliamentary Group for Children** (2017) *No Good Options: Report of the inquiry into children's social care in England*. National Children's Bureau: https://www.ncb.org.uk/sites/default/files/field/attachment/No%20Good%20Options%20Report%20final.pdf.

- **All Party Parliamentary Group for Children** (2018) *Storing up Trouble: A postcode lottery of children's social care*. National Children's Bureau: https://www.ncb.org.uk/sites/default/files/field/attachment/NCB%20Storing%20Up%20Trouble%20%5BAugust%20Update%5D.pdf.

Reports from **Galvani**, investigating the experiences of families where there is alcohol and substance use, shed light on what families found helpful, and what not:

- **Galvani S** (2010) *Supporting Families Affected by Substance Use and Domestic Violence*. University of Bedfordshire, Adfam and Stella: https://www.adfam.org.uk/files/docs/adfam_dvreport.pdf.

- **Galvani S** (2012) *Between a Rock and a Hard Place: How parents deal with children who use substances and perpetrate abuse*. Adfam and AVA https://www.adfam.org.uk/files/docs/Between_a_rock_and_a_hard_place_-_Project_report.pdf.

4Children (2016) *Britain's Families: Thriving or Surviving? An inquiry into family life in Britain today*: http://cdn.basw.co.uk/upload/basw_30725-10.pdf
Recommendations that there should be more help for parents of teenagers (advice and support) and that this should be designed to meet the needs of modern family life – open at weekends, and combining parent and child support in one place.

Home Office (2015) *Information Guide: Adolescent to parent violence and abuse (APVA)*: https://assets.publishing.service.gov.uk/government/uploads/system/uploads/attachment_data/file/732573/APVA.pdf.
For professionals across different agencies, with useful resources and links at the end.

The Context Report (2017) from a recent Australian research project provides a wealth of background to the issue as a whole, as well as this specific project. There is useful information pertinent to the situation in Australia, and discussion of the need for an approach that encompasses disciplines across the board:
Elliott K, McGowan J, Benier K, Maher J & Fitz-Gibbon K (2017) *Investigating Adolescent Family Violence: Background, research and directions*. Program on Gender and Family Violence, Monash University: https://arts.monash.edu/__data/assets/pdf_file/0007/1532275/investigating-adolescent-family-violence-background-research-and-directions.pdf

Coogan describes an action research project conducted in Ireland, listening to practitioners' accounts of working with families experiencing CPVA and introducing one particular response:

- **Coogan D** (2016) Listening to practitioners talking about child to parent violence and abuse: some findings from an action research project. *The Irish Social Work Journal* **Winter** 41–48.

Home Office (2014) *Multi Agency Working and Information Sharing Project: Final report*: https://assets.publishing.service.gov.uk/government/uploads/system/uploads/attachment_data/file/338875/MASH.pdf.
Findings from a project to better understand the various multi-agency information sharing models in place; with case studies from around the country.

Examples of leaflets for parents can be found on the resources pages of the website, **Holes in the Wall**: https://holesinthewall.co.uk/resources/.

Some, including **Thorley and Coates,** and **Family Lives**, have suggested that many, or all, aspects of CPVA can be understood best as 'conduct disorder'. This is certainly an avenue worth exploring further, but to understand all CPVA in this way risks leaving those children without a diagnosis (or with very clear alternative risk factors) without support or understanding.

Thorley W and Coates A (2018) *Let's Talk About: Child-parent violence and aggression* (CPVA). Extended summary available at: https://www.academia.edu/37078253/Lets_Talk_About_Child_to_Parent_Violence_2018_Summary.

References

All Party Parliamentary Group for Children (2018) *Storing Up Trouble – A Postcode Lottery of Children's Social Care*. National Children's Bureau.

Autism Awareness (2016) *The Fragments of My Heart* [online]. Available at: https://autismawareness.com/the-fragments-of-my-heart/ (accessed February 2019).

Booker L (2018) Conference presentation at an Adfam training day.

Family Lives (2011) *When Family Life Hurts: Family experiences of aggression in children, an update to the 2010 report* [online]. Available at: https://www.familylives.org.uk/media_manager/public/209/Documents/Reports/the_aggression_report_2011_family_lives.pdf (accessed February 2019).

Frith E (2016) *CentreForum Commission on Children and Young People's Mental Health: State of the nation* [online]. Available at: https://epi.org.uk/wp-content/uploads/2018/01/State-of-the-Nation-report-web.pdf (accessed February 2019).

Galvani S (2012) *Between a Rock and a Hard Place: How parents deal with children who use substances and perpetrate abuse* [online]. Adfam and AVA. Available at: https://www.adfam.org.uk/files/docs/Between_a_rock_and_a_hard_place_-_Project_report.pdf (accessed February 2019).

Holt A (2012) Adolescent-to-parent abuse and frontline service responses: does Munro Matter? In: M Blyth and E Solomon (Eds) *Effective Safeguarding for Children and Young People: Responding to the Munro Review* (p91-106). Bristol: Policy Press.

Holt A and Retford S (2013) Practitioner accounts of responding to parent abuse – a case study in ad hoc delivery, perverse outcomes and a policy silence. *Child and Family Social Work* **18** (3) 365–374.

Home Office (2015) *Information Guide: Adolescent to parent violence and abuse*. Available at: https://assets.publishing.service.gov.uk/government/uploads/system/uploads/attachment_data/file/418400/Final-APVA.pdf (accessed February 2019).

Hunter C, Nixon J & Parr S (2010) Mother abuse: a matter of youth justice, child welfare or domestic violence. *Journal of Law and Society* **37** (2) 264–284.

Rushing R (2010) Parent abuse. *The Record Live* **29th September**.

Thorley W and Coates A (2018) *Let's Talk About: Child-parent violence and aggression (CPVA)* [online]. Extended summary available at: https://www.academia.edu/37078253/Lets_Talk_About_Child_to_Parent_Violence_2018_Summary (accessed February 2019).

Part 2: Four traps to avoid

Chapter 6: The difficult parent

'I'm NOT a hero. Nor a warrior.
I'm a worrier, a botherer.
I'm an incessant annoyance like a wasp at a party.
An itch you cannot reach.
A questionner, a critic.
A loving parent.'
(Tweet from Bethany's Dad @JeremyH09406697, 2018)

How do we, as practitioners, think about, and respond to, individuals who question our practice and assumptions, who trip us up in our thinking, and keep us awake at night? As I write this, I find myself reflecting on my own response to a number of individuals. It is true, I find them immensely frustrating. I interpret their actions and campaigning as too strident and likely to annoy people rather than achieving their desired ends; or, conversely, I think they are not doing as much as they could do to bring about change. So is there a 'correct' level of annoyance that we will tolerate? How 'difficult' are parents allowed to be? If it were my child I am sure I would go to any lengths to find help and support, and use all means available to me to do so. Who are we to suggest otherwise?

If you google 'difficult parents', there are pages and pages of advice as to how to 'deal with' people who don't engage with the service you offer in the manner that you think they should. Use this phrase, and people think they know exactly who you mean. At the end of 2017, an employment agency advertised for a practitioner to work in the field of special educational needs 'with difficult families'. Short hand, the detail is assumed and we all nod along. On this occasion though, people responded critically to the advertisement and its underlying message, rejecting the interpretation of behaviour as problematic, and the 'othering' of certain groups.

Thinking about parents in this way can make it possible to ignore their experiences and requests for help, to minimise their plight, and even to dismiss their stories and genuine need. When we see it written so starkly we might already be reacting, perhaps finding justifications as we remember a particular individual; or starting to reflect on how we might think about a family differently in future.

Or difficult practitioners?

It used to be commonplace to describe some individuals as 'hard to reach'. These were members of communities who were thought of as on the margins of society, or naturally antagonistic to professional intervention. Times change, and we now recognise rather that it may be the services that are 'hard to access', and that we need to do more to reach out to people, to build trust, and to find better ways to engage.

> I was interested to read the suggestion in a response to an article about 'challenging parents', that we should consider that families might think of some professionals as 'challenging', and how we would respond to this.
>
> 'We would like to invite Gemma Corby to talk to "challenging" parents like us and to engage in a meaningful dialogue with us rather than to put a name on our attitudes in order to dismiss or "manage" our concerns. We would also like her to consider how SENDCOs may feel about an article about 'how to work with challenging SENDCOs'. At Learning Disability England, families have come together with adults with learning difficulties, service providers and commissioners to find a way to work together based on common ground, we would suggest that this is an approach that needs to be taken in the SEN sector if we are to find the best ways to support our children.'
>
> (Open letter from Learning Disability England, to the editor of the TES, tweeted by Lucy Burke, @lucyburke23, 2018 in response to TES article https://www.tes.com/news/send-working-challenging-parents)

Where did it all go wrong?

What has happened between our original intention as practitioners when we came into this work, to bring about change, and fight for social justice, and the position in which we now find ourselves, a place where we apparently routinely think of some parents as difficult, obstructive, or confrontational?

Working in large organisations, or any bureaucracy, can bring its problems:

- Issues about power, knowledge and authority.
- Concerns about risk and safety.
- Budgetary constraints which impact on the help available.
- Time issues because of short staffing or large caseloads.

- A shortage of good reflective supervision, which can help us overcome such a way of thinking.

Some services and some practitioners lend themselves to an adversarial or confrontational relationship, but any time there is an imbalance of power we can slip into disagreements and 'them and us' scenarios; or anything other than quiet acquiescence can start to be interpreted as a threat to our position and authority. Depending on how confident you feel yourself about the facts of the situation, that can be quite challenging. For instance I belong to a generation who were encouraged to understand their GP as the holder of all wisdom and knowledge about our bodies and their workings, and I was seriously discouraged from having any opinion about what my symptoms might mean. Thankfully it seems, this notion no longer prevails, but we have a long history of a model of work across the field whereby those in need plead for help from a powerful master who allocates meagre resources to the most deserving; a model which still sadly lingers at an unconscious level in the minds of some.

We may have a certain model in our heads of the type of people who need our help and generally use our services. We may not imagine that they might have greater knowledge or experiences in some fields than we do ourselves, that they might themselves be professionals, that their level of training may outweigh our own. We might be used to working with families where we fear they are obstructing our investigations, or we believe their parenting practices are a cause for concern, generating anxieties about risk and danger. Meeting people who do not conform to that assumption is challenging. They do not 'behave' as we expect. More importantly, it should challenge our baseline assumptions about the way we relate to all individuals, and how we develop a relationship upon which we can base our work with all. David Wilkins (2018) suggests that services and social workers should take criticism and feedback as constructive rather than an attack:

'When parents feel able to disagree with social workers and have high expectations of children's services, this sounds to me not like the actions of affluent, over-entitled parents, so much as engaged and capable parents who, critically, have sufficient social capital and resources to do what they think is best for their child. If only all parents were so fortunate.'

When budgetary constraints can mean that responses are resource-led rather than needs-led, individuals who keep coming back for more, or who seem to need and demand what we cannot give, will inevitably cause turmoil in our thinking – whether about the specific task or about how we feel about the job as a whole. There will be rightful questions, which demand proper consideration in an environment that nurtures personal and professional development.

Pushed for time, it can be too easy to fall back on ideas and understanding about the way this relationship works, and about entitlement to the service we are able to offer. Alex Clapson (2018), writing about the benefits of sharing power with service users, says of the old ways: *'people who used services had to conform and comply or face the consequences'*. Where time is in short supply it makes even more sense to use it profitably for all concerned. Learning alongside families and working to resolve issues in partnership maximises time, knowledge, understanding, authority, resources – and relationships – all round.

Within social work training there has always been much focus on the ethics and values underpinning practice. Students are required to demonstrate their understanding and practice around concepts such as empowerment, partnership and respect. In my experience, the depth of that understanding can vary tremendously from one individual to another, and yet in general there is an acceptance that working 'with' people will achieve better outcomes; that respect is a basic human entitlement. Despite this, research continues to demonstrate ways in which practitioners 'other' those seeking help on a regular basis. Gupta and Blumhardt (2017) examined the exclusion of families impacted by poverty in particular, but commented on the importance of lessons learned across all of social work:

'Strengths-based practice that recognises an individual or family's abilities and supports them to rebuild their lives after difficult circumstances have worn them down is crucial. Social workers must be alive to how unconscious bias and disrespectful treatment can promote deficit-based thinking, which undermines recognition of an individual's potential and precludes effective capacity-building. More broadly, social workers must avoid inadvertently replicating the dismissive attitudes that many disadvantaged individuals experience in society.'

Who is the difficult parent?

- Someone who keeps phoning up and asking for visits or meetings?
- Someone who is not happy with the assessment or the recommendations you made?
- Someone who gives the impression of a lack of insight into their situation?
- Someone who argues with you?
- Someone who refuses to follow the recommendations you made, or to engage with your plan of action?
- Someone who challenges your practice, who asks to speak to a supervisor or makes a complaint?

- Someone whose behaviour might eventually lead to an escalation of intervention (removal of children) or at the other end, case closure?

Time after time, parents have written and spoken about being perceived, and treated, by professionals as 'difficult'.

> 'Parents, and carers of children/yp with #SEND are literally expected to become a combination of legal professional, educational professional, Psychologist, advocate, inclusion specialist, and report writer and PA. To then be told "they're demanding".'
> (Tweet from SEND Supermum @sen_supermum, 2018)
>
> 'At times, in fact most of the time, the spotlight seemed to be firmly pointed on me as the problem. The more I read Dan Hughes, Caroline Archer etc the more I turned down advice to do behavioural charts, send her away from me on respite and all the other inappropriate responses to grief, displacement and trauma. The more I turned this "support" down the more hostile those attempting to help us became. It really was a very difficult situation for us both to be in psychologically and especially against a backdrop of school exclusion and regular violence in the home.'
> (Boorman, 2015)
>
> 'The problems we faced as a family were still not understood and his school refusal was attributed to my inadequate parenting, which was compared unfavourably with foster care throughout the care proceedings, even though there were no suitable foster carers to be found. It felt as if what was wanted of me was compliance, but I wanted an understanding of our needs as a family. There was a mismatch and my frustration was so easily misinterpreted as my being 'difficult' to deal with, which is how I was viewed and presented by the local authority. This meant anyone new to the case made judgements about my character.'
> (Special Guardians and Adopters Together blogpost)

Parents feel caught in a double bind: they want to get the best help they can for their child, but when they try to do so, they are accused of being part of the problem itself.

This business of not believing a parent's account of events

Child to parent violence and abuse lends itself magnificently to this problem. Parents describe being told the behaviour they complained about was normal, that all children do this, that it's just a phase, or that they should try harder, parent better. It must be hard for any practitioner coming across this for the first time. Perhaps they have their own children, perhaps not. What has been their past exposure to family conflict and violence? How open-minded are they? How easy to assume that parents must be exaggerating, weak, attention seeking, irresponsible, neglectful, hysterical. Sally Donovan (2016) writes here about a familiar response from helping agencies:

'Many families describe a strange dystopian world where their child's trauma is considered a figment of their imagination and dark forces are employed against them to prove that the problem is their hysteria, their neediness and their poor parenting.'

What's it like to be a difficult parent?

Think of difficult parents as just like regular parents but with thicker skins. They feel the same hurts, hold the same hopes and fears, get tired, get sick, but they have had to deal with more setbacks, more criticism, more disappointment. Some people have even embraced the term, as a badge of honour.

'Most people want to be liked. But the difficult parent is willing to take the risk of not being liked because their child needs them to, however uncomfortable that makes them feel. If they make a suggestion, check something out or follow something up, they are not trying to undermine professionals. They are trying to ensure their child gets what they need … Most of us hate having to intervene at any level. The worry about how to approach a professional may keep us awake at night. We do not raise issues lightly and there is no handbook. We have to learn from our mistakes. This sometimes upsets professionals and makes them dislike us.'
(Hooper, 2018)

'Fighting the "support services" for help we desperately need, week after week, month after month, is stressful, exhausting, and very hard on my mental health. I am often overwhelmed and cannot cope. Today is one of those days. #TimetoTalk'
(Tweet from Hannah Meadows, @HLMeadows, 2018)

Parents seeking help may be desperate. They may be terrified – for themselves and for their child. They may present in ways we associate more usually with anger and threat to ourselves. Parents seeking help when they are experiencing violence and abuse from children already feel very unsafe. They may be showing signs of trauma themselves.

Asking for help is often difficult; more so when reports from friends or acquaintances – or prior experience – have inclined someone to be anxious about the response of those you approach. I believe it is important that we acknowledge that training in this field is still far behind what could and should be expected; that the parents we are working with most probably know far more than we do about the issues; that they are indeed living with the reality on a daily basis while we may have no personal experience and may find it difficult to grasp the enormity of it all. Furthermore, we likely have no specific resources to offer. When we do not, it is small wonder parents talk about being re-traumatised by the very services they go to for help.

We should first stop, and check our attitudes. For any support to be effective, it is arguably important that parents and practitioners work together; even more so when the practitioner may be learning as they go, and from the parent as expert in this situation. It takes humility to admit to not knowing what to offer or how to help. We deceive ourselves if we assume that our task is always to have an answer, always to come up with a plan, always to be proactive and dynamic, always to save the day. To work in partnership, to seek for answers together, to listen and to learn is a more realistic journey.

Particular issues around children in care

This is worthy of a specific mention, as the end of the road may sadly be that a child is accommodated because the violence and abuse eventually becomes too great to be safely managed in a normal family environment. It would be a mistake however to see families as having given up on their children. Undoubtedly there are some for whom this cannot come soon enough and who wish for no further contact, but for many families, particularly where children are accommodated under a voluntary arrangement, many parents would like to be thought of, and understood as, 'parenting from a distance', with a hope that the situation may be bettered at some point in the future. Where this is not fully understood or accepted it is all too easy for bad feelings to arise as continued parental input is perceived as inappropriate, unwelcome, hyper-critical, or contravening a child or young person's wish for independence. There is a wish and a hope that corporate parents will have the same care and ambition for children as the families they come from, and while younger children within the fostering system may meet with such care, there is understandable anxiety around the extent to which older children in supported lodgings or residential care are monitored, supervised and supported appropriately. Parents of these children do not wish to be routinely thought of as being awkward, demanding, or over-involved. They continue to fight for the health and well-being of the children and young people they have most decidedly not given up on.

Be careful what you write, be careful what you read, be careful what you believe

Once we commit our opinions to paper, or technology, the effect ripples outwards. I know how this feels. In one particular job, someone wrote in a family's file – a family about whom I had quite serious child protection concerns – that everything I said should be ignored, as I didn't know what I was talking about. It came to light quite by accident too.

In a different situation, Jenny Kitzinger, writing about the terrible experience of watching her sister kept in a vegetative state following a traffic accident, said:

'Several people have asked how family could be ignored, especially when we were so persistent and documented everything? Well, when lawyer got Polly's notes we found us sisters labeled "difficult, obsessed" "vociferous" & "writing letters+++" to consultant. Mmmmm, part of answer?'
(Tweet from Jenny Kitzinger @JennyKitzinger, 2018)

But what if we think of this parent in a different way?

Someone who has perhaps successfully raised other children; someone who has invested time, money and energy in enabling this child to thrive and contribute; someone who has become an expert in their child's condition in order to access the help they will need; someone who has read every book and tried every programme they can find; someone who is scared about the future for themselves and their child; someone who is sleep deprived and financially stretched; someone without a support network because they are ostracised by other families; someone intimidated and exasperated by a system which apparently seeks to confound every attempt to access help for their child; someone angry beyond compare that no one believes their account or seems willing or able to help; someone who believes this may be all their own fault. Someone who is determined, highly motivated, keen, advocating, ambitious.

There is surely much to learn from an individual such as this, and there is indeed a growing movement to involve parents and carers in the training of professionals at all levels. Listening to 'real people' rather than reading something, or being told second-hand, can be more meaningful for many students.

'And having service users more involved in the learning ... We had one guy, I still remember the session with him as clear as day, but it would have been nice to hear more from parents. Those involved in child in need, in child protection – what helped them, what did they get from their social worker that I could learn from, what helped them move on ... People value that as well.'
(Interview with Sandi, a social worker, 2018)

When parents were asked to encapsulate in a single request what they wanted from professionals, researchers found they had plenty to say (Galvani, 2012). This was chosen as the one that best represented the views and wishes of the majority:

'For all the multi-agency services to come together rather than try and exclude me. If my son is in rehab then they don't want to talk to the family, probation don't want to talk to me, but they want information from me, you know? We need a little bit of a two-way street rather than an avenue that suits them, we need that little bit of respect, and our experience and our input. We know that person – they don't. We live with that person – they go home at night. Come to us a bit more, don't exclude us.'
(Galvani, 2012)

Difficult parents or difficult situations?

So less of the difficult parents, and more acknowledgement that it is perhaps rather the situation that is difficult: lack of knowledge, resources, time, answers, energy – for practitioners maybe, but certainly for parents and families. The writers of the blog in response to the employment agency advert at the start of this discussion suggest:

'We don't know difficult families, but difficult situations are something we see plenty of – mainly caused by shrinking resources that neither family nor services can control ... we know families who simply want what other families want – for their children to be healthy, happy, fulfilling their potential and surrounded by love and laughter. Let's stop the stereotyping, cut out the labels, and be brave enough to meet the people and real lives behind the scare stories.'
(Wilson and Selby-Boothroyd, 2017)

A parent fighting on behalf of their child does not want much – and they want everything. There is much to be gained by all when we start to understand parents in a different, compassionate way: as people who want to work in partnership, who are a valuable, onsite, 24-hour resource, who can be thought of as genuine experts in their children's lives. They may come across as shouty because they are used to being ignored. They would like to be respected, to be listened to, and to be included in conversations and plans.

When it goes right

'The behaviour therapist had so much knowledge, but even she would say, "We're going to try this. We don't know if this will work or not" ... everything was trial and error, but because of the way she came at things it made you feel she wasn't the expert, up there on a pedestal and you've got to bow down because she knows everything and you know nothing. She really made me feel comfortable and I do find a lot of meetings I go to, a lot of people are now saying – you're the mum, you know him best. Which is really nice.'
(Interview with Rachel, 2018)

It needn't – and it certainly doesn't always – go wrong. Within his ethnographic research into child protection social work, Harry Ferguson has witnessed both the negativity of social workers towards those with whom they practice, but also great creativity, helpfulness, and 'transformative relationship-based practice' time after time:

'[This] occurred when spirited, creative, resourceful #socialwork connected with the spirit, creativity & resourcefulness of service users to overcome any organisational problems. And it was a great privilege to be present to be present to see it.'
(Tweet from Harry Ferguson, @Harr_Ferguson, 2018)

More words of comfort here from Annie, who blogs at 'Safeguarding Survivor':

'I know you are not always gifted the tools you need to help families in need as a result of lack of resources, I know these same families can be hostile and you can sometimes work within a climate of fear. I know sometimes we tell you where to go and just what to stick where. But you also change the course of people's lives, you reach the unreachable, you help those cast out by society, you empower the vulnerable, you keep children safe, you support families in need, you believe in them. For that, I thank you.'
(From World Social Work Day, quoted in PSW Magazine, 2018)

Things to think about

Do I need to change the way I think about some families?

What might be stopping this parent engaging with what you are offering?

- The time of day is inconvenient.
- The day itself does not work with other commitments.

- No childcare provided.
- Too far to travel.
- Too expensive.
- They already took this course before.
- They tried it already and it didn't work/made things worse.
- Their parenting may already be above and beyond 'good enough'.
- They don't understand the offer.
- You are both talking about different things.
- They feel disrespected.
- They find it difficult to trust workers because of previous experiences.
- They may be fearful of the actions you might take.
- Language or cultural difficulties.
- They are exhausted/unwell.
- Disability access issues.
- You are making it difficult for them to engage by your attitude, words or actions.

What is going on for this parent that means they believe they need to fight so hard for their child? How can I help this parent to believe they have been heard?

Have I stopped to listen to what this family is actually asking for?
What can I do or say to change things around?

How can I use the expertise available? Can parents offer me recommendations for reading or viewing, to help me better understand their situation?

Good supervision should include helping us to check out assumptions. If this isn't happening right now for you, what can you do to bring about a change?

Find out more

The blog post about the advert, from **Liz Wilson and Marianne Selby-Boothroyd**, *Difficult Families? A blog from two parent carers*: https://www.dimensions-uk.org/families-post/difficult-families-parent-carer-blog/

Judith Hooper writing about being a difficult parent for a child with special educational needs:
https://senmagazine.co.uk/articles/articles/senarticles/the-difficult-parent

In this blog, *Bridging the Gap – Expert to Alongsider*, on the site Nurture Development, **Rashid Mhar and Cormac Russell** have an excellent graphic outlining different models of intervention, 'To, for, with and by', and how they have traditionally been linked with particular approaches:
https://www.nurturedevelopment.org/blog/abcd-approach/bridging-the-gap-expert-to-alongsider/.

The Family Rights Group has drawn up a charter addressing how families and practitioners might better relate and work together: *The Family Rights Group Mutual Expectations Charter*:
https://www.frg.org.uk/images/YFYV/Mutual-Expectations---Parents-Charter.pdf.

Yvonne Newbold's blog: www.yvonnenewbold.com.
Yvonne is a parent of a child with physical and learning difficulties, who spoke bravely about her son's violent behaviour first – and without having planned to do so – on the radio, before building resources and arranging conferences to raise awareness and campaign for better support.

Surviving Safeguarding: blog: http://survivingsafeguarding.co.uk.
Annie blogs about her own experience through the child protection processes, and her fight to have her children returned to her care. She works to promote a more collaborative and humane relationship between social workers and service users.

Amanda Boorman's blog, **All Aboard the Trauma Train**:
https://allaboardthetraumatrain.com.
Amanda is a social worker and adopter who has developed expertise around children and young people using violent and abusive behaviour following early trauma. She blogs about her own experience (including input from her daughter) and about the support network she has built for other adoptive families.

Special Guardians and Adopters Together website:
https://specialguardiansandadopterstogether.com.
This is a campaigning group seeking to bring about a more empathetic and supportive response from practitioners, and in law, for special guardians and adopters, when a child or young person's needs are not easily met under the present situation. The site includes testimony from families about confrontational situations with the authorities, particularly when situations have not been fully understood.

The POTATO group: https://thepotatogroup.org.uk.
Parents of traumatised adopted teens organisation, a group of parents supporting each other and raising awareness of their needs, often around child to parent violence and abuse and parenting from a distance.

References

Boorman A (2015) *Actions Speak Louder than Words* [online]. All Aboard the Trauma Train. Available at: https://allaboardthetraumatrain.com/2015/11/08/actions-speak-louder-than-words/ (accessed February 2019).

Clapson A (2018) *Sharing Power and Interests is a Win-Win* [online]. Professional Social Work Magazine. Available at: https://www.slideshare.net/AlexClapson/professional-social-work-psw-article-february-2018 (accessed February 2019).

Donovan S (2016) *Adoption Services Should Work With, Not Against, Parents to Learn From 'Near Misses'* [online]. Community Care. Available at: http://www.communitycare.co.uk/2016/03/02/sally-donovan-adoption-services-work-parents-learn-near-misses-failures/ (accessed February 2019).

Galvani S (2012) *Between a Rock and a Hard Place: How parents deal with children who use substances and perpetrate abuse* [online]. Adfam and AVA. Available at: https://www.adfam.org.uk/files/docs/Between_a_rock_and_a_hard_place_-_Project_report.pdf (accessed February 2019).

Gupta A and Blumhardt H (2017) Poverty, exclusion and child protection practice: the contribution of 'the politics of recognition & respect'. *European Journal of Social Work* **21** (2) 247–259.

Hooper J (2018) *The Difficult Parent* [online]. SEN Magazine. Available at: https://senmagazine.co.uk/articles/articles/senarticles/the-difficult-parent (accessed February 2019).

Special Guardians and Adopters Together (undated) *When Help Seeking Leads to Blame and Removal Instead of Help* [online]. Available at: https://specialguardiansandadopterstogether.com/when-help-seeking-leads-to-blame-and-removal-instead-of-help/ (accessed February 2019).

Wilkins D (2018) *Why we Should Want More Parents to Challenge Social Workers* [online]. Community Care. Available at: https://www.communitycare.co.uk/2018/06/15/want-parents-challenge-social-workers/ (accessed February 2019).

Wilson L and Selby-Boothroyd M (2017) *Difficult Families? A blog from two parent carers* [online]. Available at:
https://www.dimensions-uk.org/families-post/difficult-families-parent-carer-blog/ (accessed February 2019).

Chapter 7: I blame the parents

Who is to blame? This is the question I think I found hardest to grapple with when I was first learning about violence and abuse from children towards their parents. I would think I'd understood, and then someone would ask me a question and when I tried to answer, all the doubts and confusion came flooding back. When a child as young as five years old is routinely hitting a parent, throwing things at them, threatening to kill them, our first thought can easily be 'what have they done to bring it on?'. We like to have a sense that things don't happen randomly. We look for a sense of reason, of cause and effect, of fairness in events. There is a need to understand; but this becomes more problematic when we move on to needing to apportion blame.

> 'Very sad how mothers were blamed for so long. It still happens. Maybe it's human nature to try & make sense of complex issues, & also to "fix" things, but a lot of damage is done when assumptions are made & conclusions jumped to. Real understanding is often in very short supply.'
> (Tweet from Yvonne Newbold, @YvonneNewbold, 2018)
>
> 'It seems like as a teenager it was really kind of tough because the behaviour she was displaying, people would look at me and think, "Well, why can't you control your daughter?" There was one meeting, a TAC meeting, and the head teacher of her school said "Elixia needs to have a stable loving home".'
> (Interview with Demetria, 2018)
>
> 'When you are seen through a lens as "the problem" then ALL your behaviour is recalibrated as part of the problem. I accept this is a real and serious issue.
> (Tweet from Sarah Phillimore, @SVPhillimore, 2018)

Within Britain, the strong messages of the Respect agenda developed under Tony Blair's government continue to permeate our thinking. *'Tough on crime, tough on the causes of crime'* was a phrase coined by him even earlier, and as they came to power in 1997, the Labour party manifesto focused on the family as *'the core of our society'*, and the place in which right from wrong should be taught, with a 'zero tolerance' approach to neglectful parents.

Holding parents to account for their children's actions was a philosophy and movement which reached across the board, from anti-social and criminal behaviour on the streets, through educational commitment and attendance, to relationships within the home. This was a period that saw parents punished in the courts for their children's violence, even towards the parents themselves (Holt, 2009). What is more, we see that mothers are held more accountable than fathers, in that gendered expectations continue to colour the way we imagine families to operate.

While in Britain, there has been pressure to move away from this victim-blaming response in the courts, you don't have to look too hard, when CPVA is in the news or on our screens, to hear the same attitudes elsewhere.

> *'All these mums left it too late to become disciplinarians… should've happened when the kids were toddlers… any how any of my kids put their hand on me (they're grown now) they knew they'd be six feet under!!… seems like all the kids in this programme have whatless fathers.'*
>
> *'I can't believe my eyes!! I mean these parents are so passive……! All of them wants a good hard whopping! Unbelievable!'*
> (Comments under the My Violent Child video on YouTube, https://www.youtube.com/watch?v=F9nmZbvlvuM)
>
> *'Thank heavens someone sees the situation from the parents side. We have been dragged through courts, social services and youth offenders for the past 3 years!! But all the law wants to do is support the child and blame the parents.'*
> (Comment by Sam on *The Silent Suffering of Parent Abuse* post on the We Have Kids website, 2018)
>
> *'Children become abusive towards their parents when they feel entitled to receive whatever they want … Parents should take parenting classes and learn how to give their child consequences after they misbehave.'*
> (Counsellor Russ Talbot talking to abc4, 2014)

How do we read these sorts of comments? The first responses contain enough vitriol to encourage us to question them. But even when a parent speaks more calmly having found someone who apparently understands, maybe we want to say, 'well yes, but I want to hear the other side too'. And then a counsellor – a fellow professional – speaks, and surely we need to give their opinions weight? Because parents are the adults in this situation, right? So they should know better?

One thing you can be sure of is that parents have absorbed this way of thinking too, and their own first response may well be to question how they have brought this on themselves. The general presumption is that children can be 'trained' through good parenting practices. Therefore, if I have a child who is clearly not 'trained', then it must be my fault.

What we are learning – and we've been learning this quite fast – is that things are not always what they first appear. Yes, the parents are the adults, and in a normal environment they would hopefully hold more authority, be shown more respect, have more guidance to give and certainly more strength and patience. There are, of course, some families where a chaotic or lax approach to discipline and structure, and family priorities and influences have left children without boundaries and structure, and have even encouraged violence. But what we read, and what we often see in families in crisis, are parents who are struggling with their own demons; or who have worked hard to put boundaries in place, have attended course after meeting after course; who may have successfully raised any number of other children; who have asked for help time after time; and who are now ground down after perhaps many years of battling with a child who does not seem to understand the rules of the game. We need to be open to the possibility that other things are going on here that need to be considered too.

So if it's not the parents' fault, it must be the child?

Oh, how we love a binary model of life! And in countries with a low age of criminal responsibility, the belief in quite young children's powers of choice and self-determination, of personal agency, is played out on a daily basis. Our youth justice models swing one way over the years, in response to growing knowledge, and political inclination, from punishment and retribution to more welfare-orientated delivery, and back again. The prevalent thinking at the time we did our training may well continue to influence how we unconsciously view the world and understand concepts such as responsibility – criminal or otherwise. We are unlikely in this day and age to find ourselves thinking of some children as monsters, as tyrannical, as evil even; yet views such as these do continue and undoubtedly impact how much people feel able to hold them accountable for their behaviour within the family and within society as a whole. The reports into child sexual exploitation in Britain over the last few years have underlined how relatively recently we have assumed children to have quite complex self-determination and power over the direction their lives have taken (Jay, 2014).

A medical model may also seek to locate a problem 'within' the child, through diagnosis for instance. Some parents may find a diagnosis reassuring in 'explaining' the issues they see, particularly when explosive behaviours may be part of the diagnostic criteria themselves. But diagnosis and violence do not map directly on to each other. Within CPVA discourse we need to remain particularly vigilant around confusing correlation and cause when we start talking about mental health difficulties, autism spectrum disorders, or learning difficulties – to name just a few. There is not necessarily an inevitability to the situation.

We may be mocked in some circles for refusing to pin blame on a child for their violent and abusive behaviour. But to refuse to apportion blame in this way is to acknowledge that there are more complicated and complex histories, more complicated and complex environments, more complicated and complex dynamics and relationships than might first seem to be the case. This may look like a dance between two parties, but there are other players in the wings too, some off stage and some who have long ago left the theatre.

It's complicated then!

What we may see as practitioners is a tiny snap shot on one occasion of a child's response to something said, or to an event. And it is worth stating here that parents often say that children behave beautifully when in the company of others, which is in itself part of the controlling and abusive behaviour. Social workers, counsellors, friends, have most likely never witnessed a 'meltdown' lasting several hours, or days even, and involving the smashing of windows, or the destruction of furniture, as well as the hurling of hateful and abusive language. They were probably not in the car at that time that the child seized the wheel to drive the car into a tree. But if you do see a small event, then it is important not to simply interpret what happens as in that moment. The trigger is part of the event, but only a small part, and there may be many more people involved than the two we see at this time.

Blame vs. responsibility

Once parents and young people are able to access help, we can start to see a gradual reclaiming of authority, and an acceptance of responsibility in moving things forward. Blame and responsibility may look like the same thing, but the differences are important. Something may not be my fault, or not wholly my fault, but I can accept responsibility for the part I have played in aggravating it. I can take responsibility for my choices in the situation, or in changing the circumstances now.

> Sue's story demonstrates how complicated family life can prove to be. She moves from a position of trying to find out who was to blame for her situation, through a more nuanced understanding of the contributory factors in her family's life, to one of accepting responsibility for her part and for the changes only she can make.
>
> 'It is different now. I used to think I've got a rat of a kid and then I realised my kid's got a rat of a parent. So I'm working on the bits I can and I keep picking myself up and remembering that I'm the only person responsible for myself. I can't blame anyone anymore. What I realise now is that what I can work on is me. It's no good blaming the kids or anyone else. I've always thought Susan was responsible for her behaviour and now the challenge for me is to see her as a 13 year old rather than a monster. Now I want to give a positive message. I think it is beginning to change. We certainly have better days. Susan still doesn't talk to me but she does talk to other people, to family members and she says life is a lot happier at home which is a very positive message.'
> (*Breaking the Cycle: Sue's Story*, Anglicare Victoria)

But it would be wrong to leave it just there

The quest for causation and reasons is not limited to the media or to individual members of society. The proliferation of theories regarding human behaviour across the world and throughout history is a very rich field. Over time, in the arena of child to parent violence and abuse, different approaches and understandings have held sway. Some of these have seemed to perpetuate the practice of blaming – or at least holding parents and families responsible for the abuse, looking particularly at parenting style or patterns of family interaction. Others have looked at wider societal factors. I will not attempt to give an in depth critique of each of these theories. This has been done elsewhere and by people better qualified than me. If you are interested to know more, I have included links at the end of this chapter. What I will offer though, is a brief overview of some, and then, lastly, my preferred all-encompassing proposal.

Social learning theory

Much of the CPVA literature explores the helpfulness or limits to Bandura's (1977) explanation of the transmission and development of behaviours through observation, imitation and modelling. Certainly, in many families, children have been witness to abusive and violent behaviour from fathers towards mothers, leading them to believe that this is not just an acceptable and normal way to behave, but also effective as a model of problem solving. Similarly some young people have themselves been victims of violence within the family and may then go on to perpetuate violence themselves. Some children are involved in violence in their peer groups as well as their family; others not. We know from testimony that in some families, children may be actively coached by absent fathers to continue the abuse. However, we also see families that have experienced violence where a child has not gone on to be abusive themselves; and that CPVA may manifest in families where there has been no history of violence; and so we must caution against too simplistic or overarching an explanation.

Feminist theory

The impact of living in societies that routinely exploit, undermine or dismiss women cannot be underestimated. Even when the education system or families themselves are offering a challenge to such positions, young people are surrounded by media, friendships, and structures, which may serve to reinforce the message that women are somehow lesser. When it looks as if significantly more women are abused by their children than men, and that those using violence are apparently more often male than female, this understanding holds considerable appeal. We need to be aware though that the data with respect to CPVA is not clear-cut and, while these beliefs undoubtedly contribute to some violence and abuse from children towards their parents, there are certainly also large numbers of girls and young women using violence at home and large numbers of fathers experiencing violence and abuse.

Attachment theory

Building on the work of John Bowlby (1969) in developing a theory of attachment, and of Mary Ainsworth (1978) in identifying a range of 'styles' of attachment, 'attachment theory' has also been much used in recent years to offer an explanation for child to parent abuse. Where, for instance, fathers seemed to be often absent, where children had experienced traumatic early childhoods through abuse and neglect, or through prolonged hospitalisation, or where a 'difficult child to love' – perhaps because of a learning disability or awkward temperament – had made bonding with the infant harder than expected, some practitioners have found this to be a helpful understanding. Arguably, this has been particularly prevalent in television documentary programmes pitting therapists against hapless families. Holt (2013) discusses the use of attachment indicators in large-scale quantitative studies of parent abuse, which have been used to support a link, somewhat misleadingly she argues, between parent abuse and attachment.

I find this a tricky area for consideration. The term 'attachment' is often used in common parlance to mean something other than its closely defined origins; and sadly, the general evidence is perhaps more strongly supportive of the theory being misunderstood and misused, than of its usefulness as the go-to explanation for difficult parent-child relationships.

However, there are many circumstances in which knowledge about attachment may be crucial to understanding a child's behaviour. Those parenting children who have experienced separation and trauma will attest to the impact of attachment disorders – as well as the difficulty in obtaining a diagnosis. But it is important to remember that the attachment behaviours observed may have developed in a previous relationship. Over time therapeutic parenting practices can help repair the trauma and encourage more positive attachment behaviours. Listening to adoptive parents, it is discouraging to hear how often their therapeutic parenting style is interpreted as the cause of the behaviour in the first place.

Nested ecological theory

This manner of understanding child to parent violence and abuse has grown over the last few years, and certainly holds an attraction in bringing in a wider series of influences and contributory agents, as well as acknowledging their interaction with each other. Originally developed by Bronfenbrenner (1977), and later explored in relation to CPVA by Cottrell and Monk (2004), and other authors, 'nested ecological theory' considers the reciprocal interaction of different levels of systemic influence, from the ontogenic, micro, meso, exo, macro systems. As such, it recognises the validity of other theories in giving meaning to human behaviour even where they cannot in themselves offer a complete explanation.

So, for example, at an ontogenic level, a child may bring an attachment style, a congenital condition, mental health diagnosis, particular skills of communication or even a personality type, while a parent may also be experiencing poor mental health, or may have drug or alcohol dependency. They also bring their own experiences of being parented. The micro-system is the most immediate circle in which the child exists, and includes communication and parenting styles and all interaction within the family, day care, or school setting where a child primarily exists. It might include experience of abuse or neglect, as well as the experience of witnessing violence, but also the possibility of strong nurturing relationships. At a meso-systemic level there is recognition of the inter-relationship between the individual and the immediate neighbourhood or circle of support, so this might include support structures available to a parent, or peers with whom a child interacts on a day-to-day basis. The exo-system draws in wider individual and family functioning, considering the part played by employment or poverty for instance in creating stress, and organised support services in alleviating it (or making it worse). At a macro-systemic level, we start to recognise the effects of the cultural norms of the society in which the child and family exist, and the larger societal structures such as housing, education, health, and law. Here we bring in feminist theory, as well as practices of parent blaming prevalent in wider society.

In expanding the possible influences, rather than closing them down and seeking one explanation, the nested ecological theory offers the most comprehensive and, in my opinion, realistic understanding of the dynamics at work in child to parent violence and abuse, for now. Since we now see so many different families affected, with vastly differing backgrounds and circumstances, it is unrealistic to expect one clean, simple explanation. We are complex beings and live in a messy world. The nested ecological model leaves room for individual explanations for individual families.

Who is to blame?

So long as we try to find someone to blame, we narrow our gaze and our understanding of this issue, alienating ourselves from those who seek our help, and potentially closing down the possibilities of change for families. In moving away from an inclination to apportion blame, we open up the possibility of considering wider influences, risk factors and vulnerabilities, as we saw in earlier chapters. In thinking about responsibility, rather than blame, we can start to move forward, and find ways to bring about hope and change.

Things to think about

- Particular disciplines, agencies, or training schemes may focus more on some theories of behaviour than others. When working with families experiencing CPVA it can be important to lift our gaze to consider new or complementary ideas in helping to understand the family dynamics.

- Whether or not we believe one party may be more at fault in a situation, it is always better to avoid language that reinforces a blaming attitude. Parents may blame themselves anyway. They do not need to be made to feel even worse. Moving beyond blame makes it easier to find ways through to more healthy and happy family relationships.

- When very young children are involved, what other things have happened in their life in the past that may be having an impact now?

- Who else is this child in contact with, or who has an influence in their life?

Find out more

Eddie Gallagher has produced a 'quiz sheet' which he has used for many years with parents, helping them to understand the many different influences in a young person's life and to help them feel less self-blaming, particularly as a child ages. The quiz sheet can be found as an exercise about parental influences in his book *Who's in Charge? Why children abuse parents, and what you can do about it* (2018).

Amanda Holt's book, *Adolescent-to-Parent Abuse, Current Understandings in Research, Policy and Practice*, published in 2013 was the first academic book to address child to parent violence. Examining intrapersonal, interpersonal, intra-familial and structural explanations, she gives a thorough analysis of different approaches to understanding parent abuse, both at a theoretical level and from the families themselves, noting that parents' understandings and conceptualisation of the roots of the abuse go on to shape how they then go on to seek help.

Declan Coogan addresses the nested-ecological theory in Chapter 2 of his book, *Child to Parent Violence and Abuse* (2018), considering its particular relevance in discussing child to parent violence.

Simmons, McEwan, Purcell & Ogloff use the nested ecological model to analyse existing work on CPVA since the 1960s, in Simmons M, McEwan TE, Purcell R and Ogloff JRP (2018) Sixty years of child-to-parent abuse research: What we know and where to go. *Aggression and Violent Behaviour* **38** (1) 31–52.

Barbara Cottrell interviewed a number of young people for her book, *When Teens Abuse Their Parents* (2004). She found great variation in their honesty, reflective skills and preparedness to change, with a propensity to blame their parents for provoking their behaviour; and she also notes the complexity of many young people's lives.

Community Care offers tips in practice guides about using attachment theory. You will find excerpts here: https://www.communitycare.co.uk/2018/01/22/using-attachment-theory-practice-top-tips/.

References

Abc4.com (2014) Son goes to jail for abuse to mother and grandfather [online]. *Abc4* **19 December**. Available at: https://www.abc4.com/news/local-utah-state-news-/son-goes-to-jail-for-abuse-to-mother-and-grandfather/205002343 (accessed February 2019)

Ainsworth M, Blehar M, Waters E & Wall S (1978) *Patterns of Attachment: A psychological study of the strange situation*. Oxford: Psychology Press.

Anglicare Victoria (2019) *Breaking the Cycle: Sue's Story* [online]. Available at: https://www.anglicarevic.org.au/news/breaking-cycle-sues-story/ (accessed February 2019).

Bandura A (1977) *Social Learning Theory*. General Learning Press.

Bowlby J (1969) *Attachment and Loss*. New York: Basic Books.

Bronfenbrenner U (1977) Toward an experimental ecology of human development. *American Psychologist* **32** 513–531.

Cottrell B and Monk P (2004) Adolescent-to-parent abuse, a qualitative overview of common themes. *Journal of Family Issues* **25** (8) 1072–1095.

Holt A (2009) Parent abuse: some reflections on the adequacy of a youth justice response. *Internet Journal of Criminology* 1–9.

Holt A (2013) *Adolescent to Parent Abuse, Current Understandings in Research, Policy and Practice*. Brighton: Policy Press.

Jay A (2014) *Independent Inquiry into Child Sexual Exploitation in Rotherham (1997-2013)* [online]. Available at: https://www.rotherham.gov.uk/downloads/file/1407/independent_inquiry_cse_in_rotherham (accessed February 2019).

Chapter 8: We need the young person to engage

A teenager being rude and uncooperative – that is literally part of the job description!

It is interesting to reflect perhaps that, when working with women experiencing violence and abusers from adult partners, the focus has generally been on engaging with the victim, on looking for changes that they can make, on placing responsibility on them for bringing about a safer future. This approach now faces a challenge as the sense of responsibility shifts and evidence builds up of the importance and effectiveness of engaging with the perpetrators themselves. In work with young people using abusive behaviours, the sense of who is the 'client' will differ from agency to agency, so some may continue to focus on the 'victim' as the one who needs to change – parenting programmes for instance – while others will locate the problem within the child themselves, perhaps with a mental health diagnosis, and insist that their compliance is intrinsic to any offer of support. If change can only come about when the young person engages with the process, but they refuse to do so, what then?

'At an earlier stage, he (the judge) noted the CFA (Child and Family Agency) had found that the teenager was not cooperative, but the judge has pointed out that this was one of the reasons the boy was before the court. The teenager was also involved in some levels of violence "way beyond his years, and that is a significant issue", the judge had said.'
(Teen who attacked his father and absconded from residential care home remanded in custody, *Sunday World*, 2015)

When a child or young person apparently refuses to accept the help on offer and to 'engage' in work there are clearly a number of possible reasons, for instance:

- They may not identify their behaviour as a problem.
- They may be too heavily invested in the current situation – too much to lose by changing their behaviour.

- They may be being used as a puppet by a third party.
- They may not understand the work at all – what is being asked of them or what the outcomes might be.
- They may not have significant control over their behaviour for a range of reasons.
- It may be difficult for them to work with particular individuals because of past history.
- The style of work, or content, may not be appropriate for their age (chronological but also emotional age).
- They may be physically unable to get to the appointment time and place.

You may well be able to suggest others from your own experience. Once identified, some of these issues can be fixed relatively easily where there is the will to do so. Others may demand more innovative thinking.

This mother is blogging about issues in accessing help for her neuro-atypical teen, but the issues are remarkably similar, and her deep frustration will resonate with others.

'We can't help if he won't engage…

What does that really mean?

It means that if you can fit into the one-size-fits-all service that was designed for neurotypical people with an ordinary upbringing and a lifestyle that means you can drop everything and travel to a destination of our choice…

Then, and only then, will we consider you engaged enough to help you.

To everyone else, well, you should have engaged.

That is, of course, only the first step to satisfying the rules of engagement. The next step is that you must interact with us in a way that we would like you to. In a way that we can understand and relate to. In a way that fits our rigid models and frameworks that have been designed around the needs of people like us. That you will be able to cooperate and receive help in a way that suits our narrow outlook and "one-size-fits-all" service.

If you deviate from that, well, that's not our fault, you should have engaged better.

I wonder if sometimes these rules of engagement are simply another way of rationing services? If you have 100 referrals in a month, and 20 people can't make it to your clinic you only have to see 80 and your waiting list will be shorter.'

(It Must Be Mum blog, 2018)

Where an agency exists to support young people, and their engagement in the process is an actual objective criteria for work, or the particular programme on offer demands the involvement of the young person as well as the parents, then every attempt needs to be taken to resolve the issue. These parents, and indeed their children, may be extremely vulnerable; it is not sufficient to simply close the case and move on to the next person. The question remains, where time is at a premium, how many attempts is it reasonable to expect a worker to make to establish engagement before moving on to the next person on the list?

In some instances attendance might be mandated as part of a court order. Youth offending teams in Britain have developed significant practice around work with young people using violence in the home, as part of their wider mission. Mandatory attendance, avoiding sanctions, does not of course necessarily equate to engagement in a programme – that will still be down to the skills of the practitioner alongside the design of the programme itself, although it may be important to the young person as a clear and official indicator that their behaviour is not acceptable. In the US, a programme which originated as a diversion from custody – 'Step Up' – is now offered frequently as a voluntary programme and with good attendance, so it should never be assumed that a young person would be unlikely to want to address their behaviour. There is an interesting discussion to be had around the benefits of mandatory or voluntary attendance. It would be easy to make assumptions either way.

Break4Change

Break4Change is a programme developed in Britain, offering parallel sessions for parents and young people which from its inception included strategies to encourage young people's involvement. The 'creative element' will vary from venue to venue, but might involve an art project, song writing, rapping, or film-making. Not simply a 'bribe', the work completed becomes a reminder of the journey, and a powerful force for reinforcement and communication. The creative part of the offer needs to be delivered by those with youth work experience as well as specific artistic skills, otherwise the benefits are lost! Even so, it may take a while for a young person to feel comfortable to join the group. It may be necessary for a single person to work alongside them for a number of weeks before this can be achieved. The relationship formed in this time itself further facilitates the therapeutic intervention.

When we think, or suggest, that we cannot help a family's situation if the young person is refusing to accept support, what does this say about the way we are framing the difficulties, or about our imagination and creativity in moving things forward? How can we adapt our approach to help the young person engage? Or, alternatively, is there another way of addressing the problem?

We need the adults to engage!

In contrast to the young people, we do need the adults – the parents or carers – to actively engage in the process. Since the rationale for involvement is to re-establish parental authority, it is essential to work with the adults to explore ways of effecting this, and to eventually bring this about. Excluding parents from the process potentially reinforces the notion that the problem is entirely the fault of the child (although the effect for the young person may be to confirm that the parent is entirely the problem!). While many parents will be on board from the start with the importance of a relational adjustment, there will be some who find it difficult to accept a need for change themselves, and so they might be reluctant to accept help without bringing in the young person being violent. Surely though the majority of families, when reflecting on their current situation, will accept, at the very least, a chance to talk about how they envisage the future, and the sort of parent they would like to be.

There are also good reasons from a therapeutic point of view to work with the parents and to have them on board. Price (1996) suggests, *'Individual therapy with aggressive young people is associated with notoriously poor outcomes'*. Routt and Anderson (2015) talk about the difficulties in achieving change using traditional methods of counselling with families of aggressive and abusive children. *'Parents reported that their teens seldom disclosed their abusive behaviour during individual counselling sessions. When teens did disclose it, they either minimised the violence or blamed it on their parents' overreaction and exaggeration'*. Gallagher (2018) similarly discusses the problems inherent in working therapeutically with a young person to the exclusion of their parents: the unlikelihood that the full picture will be revealed, either of the young person's own anxieties or the degree of abuse; the collusive nature of holding 'secrets' with a child; and the additional distancing effect which this has on the parents' relationship with their child. Some change may come about in a young person's sense of self, but it is suggested that there is unlikely to be a lessening in the use of violence and abuse, solely though this work.

Is there another way?

Although we understand child to parent violence and abuse as a relational issue, and one to be resolved through changes to the relationship, ultimately each individual can only directly change the way they themselves behave. Taking this as a starting point, accepting that it is not always possible to work with the young people concerned, and recognising that if I change how I react to a situation, then that can contribute to the disruption of established patterns of confrontation, a number of CPVA interventions have been developed which seek to work solely with the adults in a family. This is not about helping parents to feel more okay about living with the situation as it is, but rather about bringing about dynamic change through intervening in the relationship patterns that have developed. After all, if I have failed to change something despite working on it for a considerable time, maybe I need to try a different method!

What does this look like?

Who's in Charge? program

Eddie Gallagher developed the Who's in Charge? programme in Australia as he identified a growing group of parents in his caseload, all with experience of violence and abuse from their children. A nine-week programme in three parts, plus a follow up session, Who's in Charge? aims firstly to empower parents through understanding causes of behaviour, and reducing shame and guilt; secondly to encourage practical changes through exploring the use of rules and consequences; and thirdly to reinforce the changes made, while also addressing topics such as anger, assertiveness and self-care. Typically parents will gain encouragement from meeting with others in a similar situation, and often go on to remain in contact in the long term, providing ongoing mutual support. While he is very careful to say that there are no guarantees of improvement, sufficient years of data collection now exist to demonstrate happier, safer family relationships and behaviour following parents' participation in the programme and at follow-up six months later. The programme is now available in other countries, and has been rolled out in parts of Britain, under licence.

Non-violent resistance

Non-violent resistance (NVR) has its roots in the work and teachings of Gandhi, Nelson Mandela and Martin Luther King. Used widely around the world as an approach to conflict resolution, a particular programme has been developed for use with young people using violence towards parents, and further adapted to include trauma-informed practice. The four main areas in which parents become skilled are: de-escalation, breaking taboos, taking non-violent action, and reconciliation gestures. Parents might meet a practitioner alone, or as part of a group, initially over a period of twelve weeks, but ultimately NVR is a lifelong commitment to a different way of relating; not so much a programme as a philosophy which can impact on every aspect of life. That can make it sound like a cult of some sort. Rather, it is a choice to behave in a way that promotes peace in every aspect of one's relationships. NVR is often used alongside other therapies and approaches, as a means of bringing a young person to a place where they are better able to access and accept other support.

> 'You have probably made the same attempts to improve things over and over again. You will often find yourself in a situation that is utterly predictable – e.g. when you are trying to reason with your child, part of you already knows that this will merely lead to a heated argument, with smashed objects in the house, shouting, and maybe even physical violence. You have become locked in a repetitive, unhelpful pattern. Using NVR, you will carefully develop "strategies" to respond to the controlling behaviour, that at first may appear strange and counterintuitive, but that are very different from the reactions you have shown before. However, this is not "behaviour management" – these are strategies for making peace in the family and changing relationships. Making peace requires constructively challenging harmful behaviour, refusing to be controlled by harmful behaviour, and reaching out and reconciling with the young person – to again become the parent who can look after their child's needs."
> (Partnership Projects, 2019)

As different methods of support become more established, evidence of their efficacy emerges. You can read more about the effectiveness of the practice of NVR in reducing conflict in families, and in restoring healthy relationships, in the work of Weinblatt and Omer (2008) and of Gleniusz (2014), for instance.

Peer support networks

Around Britain, and elsewhere, there is a growing network of peer group support around child to parent violence. Some of these groups exist online – Facebook or WhatsApp for instance; others meet in real life to share stories and support one another on the journey. Some groups have come about through previous engagement in a programme; others are a response by a parent to the specific absence of professional help when it was needed. That anyone could have the strength, time and tenacity to organise such groups is witness not only to the hidden reserves of some people under immense pressure, but also to their sheer desperation in achieving some element of recognition and support in times of crisis. Within the UK, such groups have formed around specific issues facing adoptive families, or those where a young person is using drug or alcohol, as well as groups that welcome all comers.

Confidential helplines

A number of national charities have confidential helplines (as well as online chat facilities), which now provide a degree of expertise and long-standing experience. Many of the people answering calls have been specifically trained in practices such as NVR and may offer a regular service to parents as well as one-off advice.

If not us, who?

When we turn a family away because a young person doesn't engage, what do we understand happens next? Is this of any concern to us? Should it be? Ultimately, we cannot work with everyone who comes to the door – there are simply not enough hours in the day, so it is inevitable that some form of rationing will occur, generally through the referral criteria established by the particular agency we work with. So it may be that, once we have exhausted all approaches and attempts within a specified time frame, the family needs to seek help from a different agency. We cross our fingers perhaps and hope the next agency will have space to take them. But if our agency allows it, and our skills and experience support alternatives, then we can explore other ways of working which can still bring about change within families, just from a different perspective or from an unexpected angle.

Things to think about

- What do you believe are the reasons for the young person's refusal to engage? How can these be overcome?

- If the work you offer demands a young person's involvement, how long are you allowed to persevere? What activities are possible to build a relationship?

- Can you work with other members of the family first, while the young person works out if they can trust you?

- How can you work to ensure a young person (or indeed a parent) is giving more than lip service to engagement in change?

Find out more

For more information about both the Who's in Charge? programme and non-violent resistance, see Appendix 2.

In his 2004 paper, **Eddie Gallagher** discusses ways to engage young people, specifically around CPVA, looking at ways to avoid collusion and styles of work that can encourage meaningful dialogue. He also argues that the engagement of parents is far more useful than that of the young person, and it is always important to work with them as well.
Gallagher E (2004) Youth who victimise their parents. *Australia and New Zealand Journal of Family Therapy* **25** (2) 94–105.

The website **Teenage Whisperer** offers interesting comment and advice on engagement from a young person's perspective: http://www.teenagewhisperer.co.uk The author, Sam Ross, has many years' experience of work with young people and uses this site to encourage parents and practitioners to relate better, understand teens more, and help them break out of negative behaviour cycles.

The Youth Justice Board carried out an engagement exercise with children and young people in England and Wales between April and May 2016, to inform their work with young people. There were 382 respondents. Asked what the three most important qualities were for adults working in the youth justice system, 62% chose *'knowing how to deal with difficult behaviour'*, 62% chose *'being non-judgemental'* and 52%, *'being able to talk to children and young people'*: https://www.gov.uk/government/uploads/system/uploads/attachment_data/file/548440/Summary_YJB_CYP_Engagement_Exercise_160608.pdf.

Peer group support
- **Adfam:** https://www.adfam.org.uk/families/find_a_local_support_group.
- **Adoption UK/PAC:** https://www.adoptionuk.org/auk-and-pac-uk-joint-support-services.
- **Everybody Hurts:** https://community21.org/partners/cpv/.
- **POTATO:** https://thepotatogroup.org.uk.

Confidential helplines include:
- **Family Lives** (and their other international equivalents).
- **YoungMinds**
- **Samaritans.**

References

Gallagher E (2018) *Who's in Charge? Why children abuse parents and what you can do about it*. London: Austin Macauley Publishers.

Gleniusz B (2014) Examining the evidence for the non-violent resistance approach as an effective treatment for adolescents with conduct disorder. *Context* **132** 42–44.

It Must Be Mum (2018) *We Can't Help If He Won't Engage* [online]. Available at: https://itmustbemum.wordpress.com/2018/02/24/we-cant-help-if-he-wont-engage/ (accessed February 2019).

Partnership Projects (2019) *Parents* [online]. Available at: http://www.partnershipprojectsuk.com/non-violent-resistance-nvr/parents/ (accessed February 2019).

Price J (1996) *Power and Compassion, Working with Difficult Adolescents and Abused Parents*. New York: Guilford Press.

Routt G and Anderson L (2015) *Adolescent Violence in the Home, Restorative Approaches to Building Healthy Respectful Family Relationships*. Oxford: Routledge.

Weinblatt U and Omer H (2008) Non-violent resistance: a treatment for parents of children with acute behavior problems. *Journal of Marital and Family Therapy* **34** 75–92.

Chapter 9: Just like domestic violence

I am frequently asked to present about child to parent violence and abuse at conferences, by domestic abuse (DA) organisations. As part of the general rising awareness, such groups are keen to include CPVA in the programme, to consider how this fits into a broader understanding about violence within the family, as well as thinking about ways of developing their response to meet the wider needs of those accessing their services. Indeed, many DA groups now include an offer to parents experiencing violence from their children, whether as a bespoke service, or in a more ad hoc manner. Often the title I am given reflects a positioning of CPVA as 'like domestic violence'.

But what does this mean? Are we talking about how people experience CPVA, how we should understand it in a wider framework, or how we respond to it?

> 'And she went mad! She pushed me up against the wall and she was banging me against the hallway wall, and then she threw me out into the hallway and was banging my head against the hallway wall and then she slapped me down onto the toilet floor and I couldn't believe it.'
> (Interview with Demetria, 2018)
>
> 'Boy aged FIVE could be Britain's youngest domestic violence offender.'
> (Brown, 2018)
>
> 'I feel CPV is similar to how IPV used to be 20+ years ago and that it is only just starting to be spoken about. More courses, training, resources and programmes across the country are desperately needed so professionals know how to respond appropriately safely and feel they can help or signpost to help.'
> (Feedback from a conference participant, 2017)

The experience

Certainly many parents will make the comparison. They might use similar language when they talk of their experience, or describe the same sorts of abuse, the same level of fear. There is talk of 'walking on eggshells', of living with 'a Jekyll and Hyde character'. Many parents will have previously experienced violence and abuse from an intimate partner, and see their child 'stepping up to the plate' as the original perpetrator leaves.

Young people may use the same types of violence and abuse within the family as adults, and we may recognise many of the same features. Verbal abuse, physical violence, emotional abuse, financial abuse and damage to property are all frequent aspects. Though sexual abuse is thought to be less common, and there are fewer examples in the literature, this has also been known.

The abuse may 'creep up' on a parent, so that it takes a while to recognise the relationship as unhealthy. Adults may find their parenting compromised by continual stresses. They may find themselves isolated within the home as well as outside it; and may be confined to one space, or denied use of resources. Young people may use threats to harm themselves or to run away as means of coercion and control.

A young person may present with violent and abusive behaviour only in the home, and so friends or family may falsely believe them to be well behaved and the parent to be exaggerating, or blameworthy, 'Oh but he's an angel when he's with me!'. Outsiders (teachers for instance) may see all the evidence but assume the abuse is from a partner, or that the parents are not trying hard enough, or even that they must have somehow provoked the attack.

Faced with disbelief or a lack of sympathy, parents feel even less empowered and struggle further to discuss the shameful situation or seek help. By the time they do so, the violence may be deeply entrenched, and the impact on the family wider and more damaging. Parents may have been forced to give up work to look after a child excluded from school, or because it becomes increasingly difficult to take time off with injuries or depression. The young person themselves, and siblings, may miss out on education. Damage to property may incur fines, or even the possibility of eviction. Loss of employment may make it hard to keep up with mortgage payments, leading to the loss of the home. Other children may be removed by the child protection services. Poor mental health is frequently reported by parents, with suicidal thoughts; and death at the hands of the young person is not unheard of.

> 'My daughter's violent behaviour started when her father and I broke up. She had seen her dad being aggressive and seemed to slip seamlessly into the role of aggressor. I was so low and physically exhausted that my self-esteem allowed her to treat me as she saw fit.
>
> At first it was insults and put-downs. The violence escalated when I told her she was not allowed to go to a party – her unprovoked attack left me physically injured and scared. After that she would hit, kick punch, push and spit at me. On the internet I found little to suggest there were parents like me...I realised this was something parents didn't discuss openly.
>
> I was terrified about disclosing it, because I thought I'd be seen as an unfit mother and my child would be taken away from me.'
>
> (Cassidy, 2012)

So, plenty of reasons exist why someone might think of CPVA as 'like domestic violence'. There are indeed some objective links with the experience of intimate partner violence.

The domestic abuse organisation, CAADA (2014) reports that as many as 25% of children who have witnessed domestic violence may go on to use violence themselves in the home; and, from the other angle, Gallagher (2018), amongst others, suggests that around 50% of young people using violence, may have experienced previous DV.

We need to be careful about how we understand these statistics. If 25% of young people are going on to use violence themselves, then presumably 75% are not – and recent research has pointed to the many different ways that children experience adult domestic abuse, and to the role of relationships and resilience in determining outcomes. The notion of the cycle of violence, which held sway in the '80s, is less favoured. While it is important not to minimise the impact of experiencing domestic violence on children, we must be careful not to make assumptions and predictions about the inevitability of future behaviour.

Likewise, if around 50% of those using abuse towards their parents have previously experienced abuse at home, another half have not. We have already seen the myriad of different vulnerabilities that may be linked with CPVA. And, I might add that even where there has been past DV, this may not in itself be the relevant issue. In our giant Venn diagram, many other factors may be more prominent.

Archie

Now aged twelve years old, Archie has been living alone with his mother since the age of three, when she fled an abusive relationship. Archie's mother had good support at the time and they have made a new start in a different area. At primary school Archie was diagnosed with autism, but with the help of an excellent special needs team made good progress through the school. However, he has found transfer to secondary school extremely difficult, with increasing demands, frequent changes, and the loss of his familiar support workers. In class he is managing to mask his anxiety at present, but when he returns home at the end of the day everything explodes. His mother has reported that she is feeling increasingly under siege, unable to do or say anything right. He shouts, throws things at her and down the stairs, pushes past her aggressively, and has rages that last for hours.

Billie

Billie is fourteen years old. She and her mother recently moved to a small flat in a new part of town after her father was charged with abusing her mother over a long period of time. Billie frequently stood up to her father and now has taken on something of a caring role for her mother. Mum is struggling to find her feet in the new situation, and has been prescribed anti-depressants. Billie sometimes misses school. Her mother has been missing more and more time at work, and Billie knows that she is not always able to pay the rent. On the estate Billie makes new friends who hear about her troubles at home, and offer her 'work'. Keen to help at home, Billie soon finds that she has been drawn into a new and frightening life, but is unable to tell anyone because of the shame, threats and fear. At home she cannot answer her mother's questions about where she has been and lashes out in anger and despair.

How then do we understand domestic violence and abuse? What are the defining features that will help us – or not – in the way we think about child to parent violence and abuse?

The framework

Paula Wilcox (2012) argues that parent abuse, or CPVA, '*…needs to be integrated into the domestic violence framework in order for it to be properly addressed*'. By failing to recognise and articulate the links, she suggests we are contributing to the silence around the subject and thus to the possibility of finding help. The role of gender in understanding CPVA, and issues of power and control are seen as central; and she posits that the youth violence framework, more in use then, was problematic in pointing towards criminalisation as the response. Instead, inclusion within the domestic violence framework was envisaged as opening up access to pre-existing multi-agency networks with expertise in the field, and as a way of countering the prevailing narrative of mother blaming.

A word first about the way we are using the terms domestic abuse and domestic violence. Although the newly proposed legislation in Britain makes it clear that other forms of violence and abuse within the family are also included (such as elder abuse), the two terms are often used as shorthand for intimate partner violence, and it is probably fair to say that this is how the general public understand their use. Sam Lewis (presentation at the N8 PRP Conference on Improving Policing Research and Practice on Child to Parent Violence and Abuse, 2018) has suggested we might want to be more circumspect in swapping and changing, since thinking about 'domestic abuse' opens up other forms of violence against women in particular. If we conceptualise CPVA as 'like intimate partner violence (IPV)' then that potentially narrows down our thinking about responses, whereas bringing a 'domestic abuse' lens to bear offers the possibility of a broader range of understanding and response.

The legislation

In 2013, within Britain, the age band for domestic abuse was lowered to include sixteen and seventeen year olds, encompassing the issue of teen partner abuse, and coincidentally recognising adolescent to parent violence as an issue. Also in 2013, the Home Office VAWG guidance included sections on raising awareness of and responding to adolescent to parent violence and abuse (APVA), resulting in the production of an information guide for practitioners in 2015. Sadly, there has been little further acknowledgement, or follow up to this, until changes to legislation were recently proposed.

In January 2019 the government published their commitments to transforming the response to domestic abuse, with the Domestic Abuse Bill. For the first time, the definition is expanded to include economic abuse:

'Behaviour by a person ("A") towards another person ("B") is "domestic abuse" if –
a. A and B are each aged 16 or over and are personally connected, and
b. the behaviour is abusive.

Behaviour is "abusive" if it consists of any of the following –
a. physical or sexual abuse
b. violent or threatening behaviour
c. controlling or coercive behaviour
d. economic abuse
e. psychological, emotional or other abuse.'

(Home Office, 2019)

Britain is not the only country to have had this discussion. Within Australia, the Victoria state government held a Royal Commission into Family Violence, which reported in 2016, with six of the 227 recommendations specifically about adolescent use of violence in the family.

So, the UK government currently positions some adolescent to parent violence and abuse within the domestic violence framework. Are we happy with this? Is this the right road to travel?

The problems of a domestic violence framework

The gender issue

One of the key tenets of the study of domestic abuse is that of gender. While men also experience violence and abuse from partners, and women also use violence and abuse in relationships, it is understood that the overwhelming majority of abuse in relationships, as in society as a whole, is by men, towards women. We recognise the messages, subtle and less so, about masculinity, and the role of women, the long history of patriarchy and continuing inequalities, and the way these things feed into a narrative that legitimises the way some men feel entitled to behave. Some research into CPVA has seemed to suggest that CPVA is spread more equally: 50-50 even. While clinical practice and justice statistics continue to confirm a bias towards a gendered understanding and expression, this is considerably less strong than with adult perpetrated violence.

Also for consideration here is the main driver of the violence or abuse, whether retaliatory, trauma related, anxiety-based, or deliberately harmful and controlling. For some children there may be a conscious singling out of a mother or female caregiver. For others it may be down to who is available and nearby at the time. It may simply be that the person who is the main caregiver is the one who cops it.

Coercion and control

These important elements of adult perpetrated domestic violence have long received little recognition, a situation which is now changing with additions to legislation and increased awareness. Young people may also be said to use coercion and control within the family – perhaps by threatening harm to themselves or others, by 'looks' which suggest that something else might happen if they are ignored, or through long established expectations of a parent's behaviour. However, Routt and Anderson (2015) suggest that, in their experience, the motives are somewhat different. An adult may act to control a partner's life, simply because they can, whereas adolescents may be using controlling tactics in order to get something that they want.

Language

The way we conceptualise an issue can determine the way we think and talk about it, and importantly, the response we put in place. As soon as we start to think about CPVA as like domestic violence, there is a tendency to start using language that we might otherwise want to avoid. While we think about adults, we are generally comfortable with terminology such as 'perpetrators' and 'victims'. In labelling young people as perpetrators, as abusers, we can fix a mind set which then closes down other options and questions the possibility of change. Baker (2012), talks about the 'problematising' of young men. Not only this, but we risk missing other important factors in the home which may require intervention and support.

Response

In aligning CPVA with IPV there is concern that we risk drawing young people, particularly at the older end of the age spectrum, into the criminal justice system or into programmes designed with adult perpetrators in mind. There is a significant anxiety among those uneasy about the inclusion of younger people within the domestic abuse legislation about such an unforeseen consequence. In terms of the types of response offered, the use of restorative justice remains controversial with adult perpetrators for instance, but is a central component of work with young people; and many programmes designed specifically for young people bring parents and young people together for at least part of the work, something that would be considered inappropriate and dangerous with adult partner violence.

Intent

I have already discussed intent, and do not plan to rehearse the issues again here, other than to reiterate that it remains a contentious issue amongst many of those living with violence from their children.

Perhaps we feel comfortable thinking about domestic abuse in relation to a sixteen or seventeen year old, but what about an eleven year old, an eight year old, or a four year old? That might feel significantly less appropriate. How does that alter what we are saying? Do we suggest there are different frameworks for different ages? Do we reject it completely and find a completely unique framework, not borrowed from somewhere else? Or does each situation need to be judged for itself? Many people would argue that it is unhelpful in itself to conceptualise CPVA as domestic abuse; that we are looking in the wrong direction completely, and need to readjust our gaze.

Leaving home

The possibility, or not, of leaving the abusive situation is often held up as an important difference. While the focus has often been on a woman to leave an abusive partner, the possibility of separating from an abusive child is not only practically and emotionally difficult but also legally problematic. Some have completely failed to grasp the complexities of the situation with questions such as, 'why don't you just kick him out?' or 'why don't you give her back?'.

'I've had enough. If this was my husband who was being so violent and abusive I would have left him by now. If I leave her I will be failing her as a parent. If I let her run away, I still have to get her home and be her responsible parent.'
(Adopting Safe Mummy Ways blog, 2015)

At the same time, the emotional ties established over the years (whether or not a child is 'flesh and blood'), might persuade a parent that separation is far from what they seek.

'The apparently high tolerance levels of abuse experienced by parents also appear to mirror those of victims of partner abuse. However it is possible that parents have an even higher tolerance level of bad behaviour with their children given they have parented their child through childhood and adolescence and lived with the demands this often places on tolerance levels.'
(Galvani, 2010)

Described by a friend as 'like a teetering cake', Kayleigh's family and personal life was a catastrophic mix of crisis piled on crisis. In an unusual example, Kayleigh and her two daughters all moved out of the home, and out of the borough, to escape her son who had been released on bail following an assault on another individual – the final straw after years of abuse and violence towards them.

Parents may be asking for alternative accommodation for their young person, but it is more likely that they seek support to remain together and restore a healthy and happy family life. Even when separated from their children, many parents seek to remain in contact with a view to eventual reconciliation.

A different hope

It is not simply that patterns of behaviour may not yet have become so embedded, but our understanding of brain plasticity and development too persuades us that all is not lost. The brain undergoes tremendous growth and change in adolescence. There is still time for progress in terms of learning impulse control and decision making skills. This is a time when strong positive relationships can make all the difference. There is hope!

Domestic abuse agencies as a source of help

Notwithstanding concerns about the way we might think about CPVA, many families do find help within the domestic abuse field. I certainly would not want to imply that this is also a problem.

Without a clear sense of where to go, women may be encouraged by others to approach their local DV services for help with CPVA; or having received help here in the past, mothers may now return as their children appear to replicate previous experiences. Adolescent to parent violence, and child to parent violence, increasingly feature in advice and guidance on the websites of DV agencies and we see a blossoming of specific services for CPVA situated here, either by the agency alone or in conjunction with others. Break4Change in Brighton is one such service, a multi-agency offer from children's services, youth offending, domestic abuse and media organisations. Lessons from the domestic abuse field inform a wider model of work, as different perspectives and skills feed into a response that recognises a broad range of personal circumstances.

Whether or not this is the 'natural home' for services, as is sometimes claimed, it is 'a home' and while we struggle to decide not just what child to parent violence and abuse is, and how to think about it, but also how best to help, we can little afford to argue with clearly thought out programmes of help – wherever they are found.

So what about the Cambridge News article?

For those of you worrying about the newspaper article quoted at the start of the chapter: *'Boy aged FIVE could be Britain's youngest domestic violence offender'* I, likewise, find much to take issue with.

By using words such as 'offender' inappropriately in this instance (children younger than ten are below the age of criminal responsibility in Britain and so cannot be 'offenders') the article encourages a way of thinking about children using violence that sees only their behaviour and not their needs, experiences or vulnerability. In the public eye they become monsters, 'bad people' who deserve punishment. It is also factually inaccurate, in that children younger than 16 fall outside of the government's official domestic abuse definition, so further misleading the public. And finally, the reporter seems to play fast and loose with both the available statistics and the remarks of the Detective Inspector interviewed for comment. Sensationalising the issues like this serves to whip up prejudice and stigma, rather than encouraging parents to come forward earlier for help as is suggested. This is a prime example of why it may not be helpful to think of the two as similar. (Rant over!)

A different framework?

Whether or not we think of CPVA as 'just like domestic abuse' may depend ultimately on our training, background, or the sector in which we work. An understanding of the impact of gender, a focus on anti-social or criminal behaviour, the prioritising of safety for particular individuals, a mandate to work with one party rather than another: all these may be 'givens' for us, which then go on to contribute to conceptualisations, and ultimately responses. Whether it is possible to fit child to parent violence and abuse within one already existing framework of understanding, or whether we need to look for a new and unique way of understanding and responding to this phenomenon is an interesting discussion. Perhaps, as Helen Baker (2012) suggests:

'Parent abuse […], requires a specific conceptual framework of its own, similar to those conceived for other forms of violence such as child or elder abuse. This framework would provide an understanding of the commonalities of parent abuse with adult domestic violence, but also its differences from it, which include complexities such the power relations between adults and children which are implicit in such violence.'

In the end, whether we use a domestic abuse framework or not to make sense of the issue itself, likening the *experience* of CPVA to that of IPV/DV can be a useful way of hearing from parents and making sense of their story.

An afterword

What do we think happens with these children and young people after eighteen years old? Having developed a particular understanding of the risk factors or narratives for children under 18, how does this link with our understanding/ assumptions when it comes to later violence between partners, or towards other family members? Might this affect the way we frame our responses to the older age group? There is a growing body of work examining violence towards older people by adult children. If you are interested in finding out more, the work of Hannah Bows, Rachel Condry or Amanda Holt is a good place to start.

Things you can do

- In reflecting on your own conceptualisation of child to parent violence and abuse, how much is this determined by your own training or agency mandate?
- Does what you have seen and heard from families support the framework you use?
- What learning can you take from one particular framework rather than another?
- Are there colleagues in other agencies, or working from a different perspective, with whom you can discuss these ideas?

Find out more

Eddie Gallagher has drawn up a chart comparing the two forms of violence and abuse. This can be found on his website:
http://www.eddiegallagher.com.au/Comparing%20CPV%20&%20IPV.pdf
Note that this was written in 2007 and some understanding may have changed since then.

Safe Lives (UK) have produced a wealth of material around the use of violence by children and young people:
http://safelives.org.uk/sites/default/files/resources/Safe%20Young%20Lives%20web.pdf.
Other media on the website include podcasts: http://www.safelives.org.uk/knowledge-hub/spotlights/spotlight-3-young-people-and-domestic-abuse.

The **full response to the consultation**, and the Domestic Abuse Bill can be seen at: https://assets.publishing.service.gov.uk/government/uploads/system/uploads/attachment_data/file/772202/CCS1218158068-Web_Accessible.pdf (accessed February 2019)
I have written a response to the proposals, which is published on my website: https://wp.me/p1sWM6-1mI.

Lifeline, (Australia), have produced a fact sheet, *What is Family Violence?* including response advice: https://www.lifeline.org.au/static/uploads/files/what-is-family-violence1-wfyvfrnjembh.pdf.

Jo Howard and Naomi Rottem authored a report in 2008, based on interviews with ten sole mothers of young men aged 13-18 who were violent towards them. *It All Starts At Home, Male Adolescent Violence to Mothers, A Research Report*, Inner South Community Health Service, Australia: https://trove.nla.gov.au/work/25698061?q&versionId=30953049
They found that boys' experience of living with violence had a profound effect on their mental health, attitudes towards women, their own violent behaviour and future life chances; and the report describes the complicated and complex emotions expressed by mothers about their own abuse and the relationship with their sons.

For discussion about the use of restorative justice (RJ) with young people, see for instance: **Routt and Anderson** (2015) *Adolescent Violence in the Home*. Oxford: Routledge, or this short YouTube video in which **Kate Iwi** presents the work Respect have been doing to include restorative justice in their work on CPVA: https://www.youtube.com/watch?v=oeqtPBpF3l0.
Nicole Westmarland, and colleagues **Kelly Johnson and Clare McGlynn,** looked into the use of out of court settlements, including RJ, by police forces working with IPVA: **Westmarland N, Johnson K & McGlynn C** (2018) Under the radar: the widespread use of 'out of court resolutions' in policing domestic violence and abuse in the United Kingdom. *British Journal of Criminology* **58** (1) 1–16.

Hunter C, Nixon J & Parr S (2010) Mother abuse: a matter of youth justice, child welfare or domestic violence. *Journal of Law and Society* **37** (2).

Helen Baker (2012) Exploring how teenage boys are constructed in relation to parent abuse. *Criminal Justice Matters* **87** (1) 48–49

For research into the ways in which children respond to their experience of domestic abuse, see the work of **Jane Callaghan**: https://stir.academia.edu/JaneCallaghan.

The **From Boys to Men Project** also has discussion about why some young men become abusers, and others do not: http://www.boystomenproject.com.

Lambert C (2018) *Putting to Rest "Why doesn't she just leave?"* provides a useful discussion about this question: https://www.psychologytoday.com/gb/blog/:mind-games/201806/putting-rest-why-doesn't-she-just-leave.

Holt A (2015) Adolescent-to-parent abuse as a form of "domestic violence": a conceptual review. *Trauma, Violence & Abuse*. Epub ahead of print.

Karyn Sporer and Dana Radatz (2017) Mothers of violent children with mental illness: how they perceive barriers to effective help. *Journal of Family Violence* **32** (7) 683–697.

This is a discussion of similarities with IPV in the types of barriers women faced in accessing understanding and help, including not being believed, being blamed, stigma, financial concerns, availability of help, and recurring feelings of hope and hopelessness.

There are few examples in the literature of cases of sexual abuse of a parent as a form of abuse. One such case is WBC v A as reported in the judgement of HH Judge Owens: http://www.bailii.org/ew/cases/EWFC/OJ/2016/B70.html.

References

Adopting Safe Mummy Ways (2015) *Could Change be Coming?* [online]. Available at: https://adoptmum.wordpress.com/2015/03/22/could-change-be-coming/ (accessed February 2019).

Baker H (2012) Problematising the relationship between teenage boys and parent abuse: constructions of masculinity and violence. *Social Policy and Society* **11**(2) 265-276.

Brown R (2018) Boy aged FIVE could be Britain's youngest domestic violence offender. *Cambridge News* **6 June**. Available at: https://www.cambridge-news.co.uk/news/cambridge-news/boy-five-britains-youngest-domestic-14740205 (accessed February 2019).

CAADA (2014) *In Plain Sight: Effective help for children exposed to domestic abuse* [online]. Insights. Available at: http://www.safelives.org.uk/sites/default/files/resources/Final%20policy%20report%20In%20plain%20sight%20-%20effective%20help%20for%20children%20exposed%20to%20domestic%20abuse.pdf (accessed February 2019).

Cassidy S (2012) Rise in parents terrorised by their children. *Independent* **18 February**. Available at: https://www.independent.co.uk/news/uk/home-news/rise-in-parents-terrorised-by-their-children-7079798.html (accessed February 2019).

Gallagher E (2018) *Who's in Charge? Why children abuse parents and what you can do about it*. London: Austin Macauley Publishers.

Galvani S (2012) *Between a Rock and a Hard Place: How parents deal with children who use substances and perpetrate abuse* [online]. Adfam and AVA. Available at: https://www.adfam.org.uk/files/docs/Between_a_rock_and_a_hard_place_-_Project_report.pdf (accessed February 2019).

HM Government (2019) *Transforming the Response to Domestic Abuse: Government consultation* [online]. Available at: https://consult.justice.gov.uk/homeoffice-moj/domestic-abuse-consultation/supporting_documents/Transforming%20the%20response%20to%20domestic%20abuse.pdf (accessed February 2019).

Home Office (2015) *Information Guide: Adolescent to parent violence and abuse (APVA)* [online]. Available at: https://assets.publishing.service.gov.uk/government/uploads/system/uploads/attachment_data/file/418400/Final-APVA.pdf (accessed February 2019).

Routt G and Anderson L (2015) *Adolescent Violence in the Home*. Oxford: Routledge.

Royal Commission into Family Violence (2016) *Summary and Recommendations* [online]. State of Victoria. Available at: http://files.rcfv.com.au/Reports/Final/RCFV-All-Volumes.pdf (accessed February 2019). See p.123-128 for recommendations around APVA.

Safe Lives (2014) *In Plain Sight* [online]. Available at: http://www.safelives.org.uk/sites/default/files/resources/Final%20policy%20report%20In%20plain%20sight%20-%20effective%20help%20for%20children%20exposed%20to%20domestic%20abuse.pdf. (accessed February 2019).

Wilcox P (2012) Is parent abuse a form of domestic violence? *Social Policy and Society* **11** (2) 277–288.

Part 3:
Three aspects of work with families

Chapter 10: Understanding the issue of power

The next two chapters look at assessment and intervention, but in this chapter I want to consider further the issue of power, as it seems to me that this is fundamental to whether child to parent violence and abuse is seen to warrant a response, in our understanding of the experience of parents; and also in determining the nature of our intervention.

Power and authority

First, a quick word about what we mean about power and authority here – how do they differ and how are they linked. Sometimes people use the terms interchangeably, which can be misleading. 'Power' refers to the potential or ability to influence another's life. The exercising of that power is legitimised by the authority we hold. We can think of having different types of authority as practitioners. There is one type that comes from our role, our status if you like; there is authority vested in that position that comes with the lanyard and the name badge. Secondly, we have professional authority, which is about the learning and knowledge we have acquired. We are deemed competent when we qualify, and as we continue to learn. Lastly, we might have personal authority, by virtue of our individual personality and demeanour: in the way we carry ourselves and perform our work. As practitioners, when we use our authority properly, all three aspects come together to make our intervention legitimate, accountable, and considerate. We are, however, also reliant on our employer – and on the government – to provide the resources necessary to enable us to carry out our work. Without that we might have authority, but no power: a significant consideration perhaps in this work.

Within a family, power and authority would normally be held by adults – by the parents. They have the material resources to buy or withhold goods, to feed, clothe and house a family. They have the benefit of size, which allows them to pick up and physically move a smaller child. They have the experience of years, which gives knowledge and wisdom. They have the authority vested in their role by society and the particular culture in which they move. That might mean that one parent is deemed to have greater power and authority than the other, or the responsibilities may be shared in a particular way. There are situations where a child may hold relatively more power, by means of language, or because of a parent's care needs, for instance. As a child grows, the power differential changes, but the expectation would be that parents continue to hold the authority – an aspect of development particularly challenged in the teenage years! If children start to use their greater power in a way that is not legitimised by authority, then their behaviour becomes a problem and potentially abusive. Within some cultures, it may be that an older son may be deemed to hold more authority than female members of the family, by virtue of their gender. In this situation their behaviour might justifiably be thought of as abusive, when they use power to control others in an oppressive way, with or without the authority to do so. It is significant that the practice of non-violent resistance emphasises the importance of thinking about *authority* rather than power as such; avoiding the possibility of oppression, so it talks about the 'new authority', and there is a recognition that this is the more important quality to work towards.

We have already looked at the way that the balance of power is disrupted and inverted in a family where CPVA is an issue. It may be gradual, initially unrecognised, or perhaps tolerated for complicated reasons. It may be sudden and unexpected. But it is this unnatural acquisition that partly determines whether we call something child to parent violence and abuse, or whether it is more properly thought of as normal, age-appropriate behaviour – all kids do that! We can talk also in terms of harm caused, whether physical or emotional, or indeed fear, as a determining factor, but at the end of the day, the ability to cause harm or to generate fear is linked to the power invested in that person. Edenborough *et al* (2008) remind us that our assumptions about where power is held ignore extenuating features of many parent-child relationships, '*such as the power of a child who behaves recklessly, the power associated with engendering fear, and the balance of power in mother-headed households and/or reliving past roles of victimization*'. A child may have no money, no status in the eyes of wider society, no independent means; but if they can make me uneasy, afraid of them and what they might do, and cause me to make adjustments to the way I live, then they have a degree of power over me.

Families seek help because they, in turn, believe that professionals have the power to help make changes, to bring about a restoration of healthier relationships, to stop the violence, or simply to make life a little more bearable on a day-to-day basis. The power we have that comes from our access to resources and our connections, legitimised by our role and status; from our knowledge and training, and – digging down into the detail – from the actual authority we have to make life-changing decisions about a child's place within a family. But in a similar way that a lack of resources can leave us with authority but not power, a lack of knowledge and understanding of CPVA can leave us with power but little authority. This is something we would do well to bear in mind.

The power in a name

There are other ways too of thinking about power. There is power in the naming of something. The recognition of its existence, that it is 'a thing' that needs to be addressed; bringing it out of the shadows and banishing secrets. Just as parents are encouraged to name the abuse they suffer – to themselves, to friends, to the child, as a first step to reclaiming authority – it is important, if we are to get to grips with this, that we name child to parent violence and abuse for what it is, rather than hiding behind notions of 'socially unacceptable child behaviour' (Holt and Retford, 2013), or of seeing it as simply a facet of something else.

Power to change, power to design a service

Governments, national and local, wield their power in defining and legislating on an issue, in making resources available according to a philosophical and political point of view, and in prioritising one issue over another. It has been encouraging to see the recognition and take up by governments around the world, albeit a small number so far, of the issue of child to parent violence.

Within Britain, a small working group collaborated on the development of Home Office Guidance (2015) in responding to adolescent to parent violence and abuse. Knowledge and understanding has moved on since then and it may well be time for this to be updated, but there has more recently been acknowledgement of the issue in consultations on the response to domestic abuse. There is recognition too at a national level within the Youth Justice Board; and within the Department for Education where the adoption community has been instrumental in raising awareness and pressing for action. Many were excited to see the debate about child to parent violence and abuse at the Palace of Westminster in February 2018, brought by Toby Perkins, MP (Holes in the Wall, 2018a). There is, of course, a vast chasm between debating something and properly funding a response, but it's a start.

Within Australia, publication of the report of the Royal Commission into Family Violence (2016) brought greater optimism, which has been partly realised with the funding of increased work in this field (Holes in the Wall, 2018b). It is the power of campaigning that is crucial in all these instances, persuading critical individuals that this is an issue of importance and deserving of attention. Within the US, the campaigning of Alice Flowers, on behalf of her sister, Rose, who was killed by her son, was persistent, imaginative and finally successful with the passage through the Florida Senate and House of Representatives of a bill which makes mandatory the gathering of information, distribution of resources, and provision of training in the field of child to parent violence, within that state (Holes in the Wall, 2017).

As a result of campaigning and greater recognition, guidance for professionals now exists at a local level within most safeguarding boards, with an increasing sense of the needs of families in this position. Increasingly, CPVA is named on domestic abuse websites as an aspect of violence in the family; and resources and booklets are made available, for practitioners and/or families.

> ### Parent abuse: a call for action from a London Borough.
> Within the London Borough of Hillingdon, council members became aware that the abuse of parents and carers was an increasing problem, and convened a working group which went on to produce a report for the council (2010), entitled *Parent Abuse. Report of the children and young people who abuse their parents and carers working group*, with recommendations for action.
>
> It was essentially a scoping exercise, but with the aims also of raising awareness and formalising arrangements for addressing the issue across departments. Although it had originally been anticipated that it would be possible – and necessary – to reach some estimate of the extent of parent abuse in the borough before developing further services, it was concluded that this was not possible; **'As such, the focus should be placed on identifying parent abuse as a problem, raising awareness of it and putting investment in place to catch it at an early stage'**.
>
> Evidence was taken from local services and from a particular family who spoke of their own experience. The report neatly captures the safeguarding dilemma regarding responsibilities to individual members of a family, when a problem does not conform to the model of support available.
>
> It concludes that *'as parent abuse cannot be solved by a single service, department or organisation, it is important that efforts to address the issue involve a range of coordinated initiatives that 'cut-across' or span different organisations'*. The Domestic Violence Action Forum was identified as the natural place to host discussions and future planning.
>
> This report was one part of a wider strategy that included producing information for parents, and a training day for professionals.
>
> While it was seen as important not to rush things, in order to get it right first time, it was also appreciated that parent abuse is a controversial issue, and *'the Working Group resolved that doing nothing was not an option'*.

Power to oppress. Power to enable

Howard and Holt (2016) draw attention to the need to be aware of the systemic power and privilege inherent in our position as workers. Whether as a male worker with female family members, or as a member of a more powerful majority seeking to support individuals from a minority culture, we bring baggage that can impact the work we do at a subconscious level. We need to remain aware of our own assumptions about cultural practices for instance in relation to child care and discipline, to wider family support, or to authority roles; as well as to how a parent – or young person – might be responding to us as an individual member of a particular class, race or gender. Do they even understand properly what we are saying, or are the concepts we use completely alien and inappropriate? Do we need the assistance of a translator, or should we be thinking about rewriting the actual curriculum? Misunderstandings, or blatant assumptions, at this level can so easily disrupt or invalidate our intervention.

I am interested to see that one of the many debates within social work in Britain at the present time is with regard to the understanding of the relationship that we have with the families with whom we work. Through a combination of budget cuts, increased demand, organisational structures and philosophical approach, we have arrived at a position where many people feel that social work is a process which is 'done to' individuals and families. Far from the notions of advocacy and empowerment underpinning social work training, the demands of deadlines, assessments and reports have further reduced the role of the relationship within practice, despite suggestions that this is in fact a more effective, and ethically sound, way of working. In such an environment, there is a danger that practice becomes oppressive: the professional comes to hold immense power in determining the nature and priority of a 'problem', and in offering – or not - a particular response.

If a practitioner comes to this work with an assumption that it is 'all about parenting', then it is easy to see how they might end up with a relationship style which emphasises their own expertise. A parent taking a child for counselling, attending a multi-agency meeting, or simply speaking with a particular practitioner, can feel either undermined, demoralised, and re-victimised by a system which feels a need to stress its expertise and authority; or they can feel validated and supported by the attitude and approach of the various individuals present, according to the attention paid to their story and to their lived experience.

Parents would like their expertise to be valued, but what does that mean? I would suggest there are two strands to this, both about power.

Power to share

Firstly, parents would like to be offered respect, to be listened to courteously and for their accounts of violence and abuse to be believed – and as professionals this is what we would aspire to do. They would like their years of experience in supporting a young person through their difficulties to be acknowledged; and to be counted as 'co-workers', partners in the process of bringing about change. They are, after all, a crucial resource, immediately to hand and not subject to budgetary restrictions. The very aims of the intervention are for them to retake control. This might feel like handing over some of our power, and we may naturally feel some concern if a family has other issues that undermine their parenting abilities. We could equally argue that it is, rather, a correct and proper use of our power and authority in the relationship. Indeed, only if we think of power as a zero-sum equation need this mean a diminution of our own standing. Paradoxically, it is when professionals are most confident in their own authority and power: the boundaries and extent, that they are most able to empower others to use their own judgement and skills to make decisions.

Power to teach, power to learn

Secondly, it requires us as professionals, practitioners, to acknowledge that we may actually not know very much about this issue. We have probably had no input on CPVA in our initial training. We may perhaps have been privileged to attend a day's training along the way. A very few will have developed specific skills in facilitating group programmes or in supporting parents using a particular approach. An even smaller number of individuals will be specialists in the field, working in this area exclusively. But in whichever group we place ourselves, we all, always, have more that we can learn. Only the parents involved can be said to truly understand the impact and implications of child to parent violence.

'Unless you can define "dysregulated" & have experienced the impact of it at least 100 times …
Do NOT tell me
"All children do that"'
(Tweet from Emma Sutton, @emmalgsutton, 2018)

This lack of knowledge can be quite a hindrance. All the more reason to be open to listening, and to learning from the experience of parents! We do everyone an injustice if we focus on our apparent power within the relationship, and fail to take up this opportunity.

Power to access help

When I asked a friend to comment on this chapter, they pointed out that I had not considered the power some people have to access help. Information about where to go, 'contacts' – someone you can call for advice, and money may well affect how readily and easily a family can access a service. A solid bank balance will allow you to avoid a long and damaging wait if you can pay for private help. Some families may choose to go down this route even without such security, sacrificing much in desperate times.

Power to make life-changing decisions

When families come to us in desperation, feeling that they cannot continue, the way in which we respond says a lot about our own anxieties around this issue. Assuming that we accept this as an issue to which we must offer a response, do we respond out of our own position of fear about the young person's behaviour? What does our risk assessment tell us about the dangers of leaving a young person in the home? How do we balance that understanding with confidence in our own skills to bring about change? Are we controlled by the demands of the agency in which we work to respond to certain scenarios in a particular way? Is there time to work with this family? At times tremendous efforts have been put in to avoiding removing a child from the home, particularly in respect of teenagers. Families have been persuaded to take back a recalcitrant – and potentially threatening – teen after a short period of mediation or a night in the cells. Other protocols may demand that we see the dangers to siblings and take steps to protect them from harm. But do we really know what a parent is asking for here? Certain words and phrases can have power in sending a piece of work inevitably along a particular course, and if we are not careful, we may have neglected to find out what a parent wanted or was actually asking for, in order for them to make the situation safer themselves. If a child or young person is removed, is this the end of the road? Can we be sure that this was, or is, the desired option? What does this mean about a family's future relationship with a child? How can this be maintained in a way that acknowledges familyhood, whether or not return to it is possible? How can we best support a family through this, and in the aftermath? Some of these questions are discussed further in considering the nature of an intervention. It is worth parking them here too though, while we are considering the power of words, of feelings and of protocols to determine the trajectory of a family's life.

The disempowering effect of a diagnosis

Whether or not a diagnosis is helpful has been already discussed, but this is one of many issues that keeps rearing its head. Is it easier to contemplate the possibility of change if we think of a young person's actions as within their control and choice (as 'bad') or as a symptom of either a mental health problem or the experience of trauma? Offering a young person a diagnosis might be, for them, the perfect cop out: 'well, that's just how I am, I can't help it'. Similarly, Price (1996) talks about the risk that the involvement of psychiatric medical professionals immediately takes away a parent's residual power and authority: 'we are the experts here, we will fix this for you now'. A young person is hospitalised for a while, then they return home with no change in the underlying issues perhaps, but parents are now more fearful because of the generalised anxieties around danger and mental ill-health, and find themselves living an even more circumspect existence.

'When parents are disenfranchised, young children (as well as teenagers) also suffer. When experts usurp the role of parent and disregard the family as the primary healing element for children, the process becomes inhumane. Instead of packaging and labeling children as if they were aliens from outer space, professionals must help parents do the tough and tender job of loving and controlling their children.'
(Price, 1996)

Some would argue that in making such binary distinctions, we do no one a service. The field of mental health is a constantly evolving one, with new understandings developing year on year. Opinions differ between professionals and between schools of thought, but many are keen to point out that a diagnosis does not automatically take away choice. Furthermore, if the young person's behaviour is understood as communicating a deeper need or difficulty, change can come about as we start to understand this other message.

The use of power in intervention

Although I have come across a small number of projects working exclusively with young people on their use of violence in the family, and there will be other young people receiving one-to-one therapy absent of any intervention with their parents; it is a strongly and generally held belief (Price, 1996) that therapeutic involvement with the young person to the exclusion of the parents can actually work to further the young person's position of power within the family. The protocols of confidentiality can prevent any means of 'checking out' the accuracy of a version of events, and can present a strong ally for the young person in demonising their parents. A relationship that holds secrets easily becomes collusive and practitioners can find that they are further victimising the parents at a time when their work should rather be focused on restoring their authority in the home. Interestingly, Price (1996) talks about the young person's behaviour being a pointer to other issues within the wider family relationships, which will also need addressing for the violence and abuse to end.

However, we do not avoid collusion simply by working with the whole family either. A practitioner then needs to work hard to avoid being overtly critical of a parent's position, or of taking over the authority role as they come in as saviour and rescuer, and to be particularly aware of the way diagnoses can appear to remove all sense of responsibility from a young person, and power to effect change from a parent. It may well be that parents need to change – whether their attitudes or actions, in learning de-escalation or in planning more structured understandings of the consequences of a young person's actions. But how they are enabled to make this change is all-important.

Case study: Eileen and Max

Mike had been working with Eileen and Max for several weeks. His assessment pointed to the possibility that eleven-year old Max was finding things hard at school, but was unable to communicate his needs to his mother, Eileen, who was still grieving the unexpected death of both her parents over a year ago. Furthermore, she felt completely isolated having fallen out with her sister over the family inheritance. As she felt increasingly helpless and shut down more and more, Max used greater and greater forcefulness in his attempts to attract attention to himself and his own needs, shouting, throwing things, damaging furniture forcefully, and generally refusing to cooperate; and he was now also refusing to attend school.

Mike wanted to convey his ideas and test out his hypothesis, but he needed to do so in a way that did not heap further blame on Eileen, or confirm her inability to act in Max's eyes. It was important too to separate out Max's genuine need for help from the impact of the family bereavement.

Mike helped Eileen reflect on her strength in having come so far despite feeling so isolated. He worked with her to help her identify long standing friends she could call on for support in emergencies as well as for her own sense of worth. Rather than suggesting specific things to try with Max, Mike helped Eileen formulate her own responses as they brainstormed what had worked in the past and what might need some adjustment. He agreed to accompany her to a meeting at the school,

> but made sure she made all the arrangements, and he acted as an observer and note taker. Mike helped Max to work on his own grief at the loss of two special people in his life, and to draw on their example and hopes for him to help him find more appropriate ways to express his needs and fears.
>
> Eileen and Max had felt in a dark place, but because they were able to access help before Max's behaviour had become actually dangerous, Mike was able to help them to find a way through relatively quickly, and to restore a more healthy relationship. In using his own power and authority – his learning, skills and experience – Mike helped Eileen assume greater authority in the home; and the power of Max's proper anxieties within the relationship was lessened.

A parent's voice

As with so many things, the most powerful statements about the sort of help needed, the attitudes of those involved, and the usefulness of an intervention come from those who have the real, lived experience.

'I tell my kids that if I go for a walk with someone and it starts to rain, then I stop to put up an umbrella. I don't do it because I want the walk to stop, but because I want the walk to continue. When I 'stopped' to ask for respite, it was because I wanted the walk to continue but I needed some resources to make that happen. I don't think the umbrella shop should make me feel bad for asking for an umbrella. It's not particularly helpful to be handed a small umbrella that only covers my kids. (And if you hand the umbrella straight to my kids then they'll almost certainly refuse to carry it themselves.) I have yet to find a shop that sells big golf umbrellas. I don't want critical comment on how I've been walking up to now (I'll be criticising myself for walking into this storm anyway). If you have suggestions on a better route to help me, then let me know; but please put up an umbrella first so we can be dry while we look at your map.'
(Parent on The Adoption Social Blog, 2017)

And the relief of finally hearing your experience validated by those in power:

'I'm listening now. And crying. Listening and crying that this is being spoke about in that room.
When she said "The devastating impact on the families concerned" is perhaps the most recognition I have ever felt.'
(Tweet from @Mumdrah, 2018, following the discussion at parliament of the issue of child to parent violence)

The gradual shift of power in a relationship from parent to child might be unsettling or shocking, but is undoubtedly damaging to all concerned. The power which we hold as professionals can be as damaging, if we fail to understand and reflect on its place and use in the relationship we have with families. When we do understand the dynamics involved, we can begin to be more effective in the way we respond, in the way we bring hope.

The power of supervision

I make no apologies for talking about supervision before we have properly started to think about intervention. It is worrying to hear of so many practitioners working without the benefit of regular, quality supervision, whether at clinical or case management level. All of us need space to stop, to stand back, and to reflect on what might be going on and what that might mean. Without such a space, there will always be a risk that we follow a formulaic response – 'it worked in the past' – which denies the individual nature and needs of families, quite apart from the possibility of developing and changing knowledge and understanding of an issue. Within the field of CPVA we have the added complications of power and abuse – and of the difficulty in believing this in the first place.

'The unique details of a case are hard to see when anger, fear and distaste compromise the therapist's ability to think clearly. It's hard to tell, for example, if a teenage boy who's swearing at his parents is trying to dominate everyone or to get his parents to take charge of a family that's out of control.'
(Price, 1996)

Despite being immersed in this work for many years, there will still be occasions when I hear something that is too hard to comprehend. Doubts flood in. Have I just understood this completely wrongly? Surely there is a simple explanation and a clear reason; a straightforward solution? Time to go back to basics, to listen with humility and grace to a story from a family that is individual to them.

Secondly, we need all the help we can get to avoid being drawn into the power battle going on in a family: how to build relationships as a means of change without 'getting down with the kids', or taking over the authority of the parents and making work with the young people nigh on impossible. There are times when we might need to take a more directive stance in ensuring safety for all; but while our role is to support members to identify the particular issues, to encourage family members to think about the consequences of their actions, and even to advocate for individuals, we need the benefit of reflective space to avoid issues of transference, of being sucked in to the fear and drama, and to continue to be able to provide a safe environment for all to think, learn and change.

Lastly, this is about abuse. The chances of a practitioner having personal experience of abuse are high, whether within wider family, friendships, or personal relationships. Often this is the very motivator for this sort of work. We have seen that CPVA is no respecter of individuals, and yet it may only be as we start to work in this field that we make connections with our own childhood, or even our current experience. We may need to be given space to withdraw in that situation, but certainly to be able to reflect on connections, triggers, and responses. We may also face the possibility of experiencing an overwhelming sense of hopelessness, and secondary trauma, as we spend time with parents, absorbing their emotions; or an anger that needs to be named and understood – and put where it belongs! It can be important for our own integrity as well as our professional practice to have someone listen to us and help us make sense of what is going on.

If you are working with families in this situation, then I would strongly suggest you sort out your supervision as a matter of priority.

What can you do?

- Name it. Encourage colleagues to talk about this specifically as child to parent violence and abuse (or whichever name is more commonly in use where you practice).

- Reflect on the power you hold as an individual and as a professional in your relationship with families.

- Be aware of the power you hold in conversations with families. How good are you at really listening?

- Be aware of the power you have to make decisions about a family's future. How sure are you that you have all the information you need?

- If you felt another professional was undermining a parent in a meeting, by their words or attitude, assumptions or actions, what could you do about it?

- How can you positively promote the expertise that many families have in supporting and nurturing a child, despite the abuse and violence they experience?

- Perhaps you are in a position to make changes at a strategic level. Can you ensure that CPVA is included in documentation, in advice leaflets, in guidance?

- What about supervision? If it is not forthcoming, can you organise peer support to reflect on cases? Can you keep a reflective log to help you process events and emotions?

Find out more

For examples of information on local authority websites, see for instance **Leicestershire Safeguarding Board** which includes definitions, advice for professionals, and links to resources including video, as well as referral information: http://lrsb.org.uk/lmagrda-child-parent-abuse .

For examples of leaflets and information for parents and carers, see for instance the booklet by **Kent and Medway domestic abuse Strategy Group**, *Adolescent Violence to Parents*, an adapted resource booklet for parents and carers: http://www.domesticabuseservices.org.uk/APV%20booklet%202014.pdf This was based on the booklet by **Inner South Community Health in Melbourne**, http://www.sharc.org.au/wp-content/uploads/2017/06/Adolescent-Violence-to-Parents-Inner-South-Community-Health.pdf.

For more discussion about the current debates within social work, see work by **Featherstone, White and Morris**, for instance Featherstone B, White S and Morris K (2014) *Re-Imagining Social Work: Towards humane social work with families*. Bristol: Policy Press.

For more discussion about issues around power and culture, see the blog post on **Holes in the Wall**, *CPV: Working across other communities* (2016): https://wp.me/p1sWM6-Sv

An example of an empowering conversation as related by a parent: *A Little Help From My Friends* on the **Suddenly Mummy blog** (2016): http://suddenlymummy.blogspot.com/2016/12/a-little-help-from-my-friends.html.

References

Edenborough M, Jackson D, Mannix J & Wilkes L (2008) Living in the red zone: the experience of child-to-mother violence. *Child and Family Social Work* **13** 464–473.

Hillingdon Council (2010) *Parent Abuse: Report of the children and young people who abuse their parent and carers working group* [online]. Available at: https://modgov.hillingdon.gov.uk/documents/s4166/Appendix%20-%20Report%20of%20the%20Working%20Group.pdf (accessed February 2019).

Holes in the Wall (2017) *An Act Relating to Support for Parental Victims of Child Domestic Violence* [online]. Available at: https://wp.me/p1sWM6-11m (accessed February 2019).

Holes in the Wall (2018a) *Child to Parent Violence to be debated at the House of Commons* [online]. Available at: https://wp.me/p1sWM6-1bP (accessed February 2019).

Holes in the Wall (2018b) *Adolescent Family Violence: Good news from Victoria!* [online]. Available at: https://wp.me/p1sWM6-1hm (accessed February 2019).

Holt A and Retford S (2013) Practitioner accounts of responding to parent abuse – a case study in ad hoc delivery, perverse outcomes and a policy silence. *Child and Family Social Work* **18** (3) 365–374.

Home Office (2015) *Information Guide: Adolescent to parent violence and abuse (APVA)* [online]. Available at: https://assets.publishing.service.gov.uk/government/uploads/system/uploads/attachment_data/file/732573/APVA.pdf (accessed February 2019).

Howard J and Holt A (2016) Special considerations when working with adolescent family violence. In A Holt (Ed.) *Working with Adolescent to Violence and Abuse to Parents*. Oxford: Routledge.

Imperfectly Perfect Mother blog (2018) *What do you Actually Need?* [online]. Available at: https://imperfectlyperfectmother.wordpress.com/2018/02/09/what-do-you-actually-need/ (accessed February 2019).

Price J (1996) *Power and Compassion, Working with Difficult Adolescents and Abused Parents*. New York: The Guilford Press.

Royal Commission into Family Violence (2016) *Summary and Recommendations* [online]. State of Victoria. Available at: http://files.rcfv.com.au/Reports/Final/RCFV-All-Volumes.pdf (accessed February 2019). See p.123-128 for recommendations around APVA.

Chapter 11: Full family assessment

A family has been referred to you, or has come to your attention another way. Perhaps you are chasing them because of a poor school attendance record. It may be that they have asked for help with an 'unruly' or confrontational child, or they may be very clear about the levels of violence and abuse. You may have realised in the course of other work that a child or teenager in the family is causing havoc and stress. A separate agency may have made contact because of concerns about a child's offending behaviour, or because they are 'out of control'. The family circumstances will not always be the same. The work you are able to offer will vary according to your role and mandate. The family's needs, and what they are asking for, will be unique to their situation. But there will be certain commonalities in the way you work, and in the steps you take to offer a response.

At this stage you may be aware of difficulties, but not perhaps the extent – or even the existence – of the child or young person's violent, abusive behaviour. In order to know how to proceed you would, of course, begin an assessment of their situation, and needs. In many ways, an assessment in a situation where there is CPVA will feel exactly like any other you would complete. Ideally you will be exploring issues *with* the family, to enable them to come to a greater understanding of the problems and to start to identify with them what are the goals, and possibilities for change. You will be looking at strengths and protective factors, as well as where things are not going well. We have already seen how many different issues may be related to the abuse; and because of this, the assessment you do will look at the family 'in the round'.

What I would like to offer is the wisdom of others who have trodden this path already; an accumulation of pointers, guidance, and direction from those experienced in their work.

P is for pointer

Assessment, it has been said, can be summed up by the three Ps:

- What precipitated it?
- What perpetuates it?
- What predisposes it?

(Danya Glaser, personal communication)

But it is also much more than that, as we shall see.

When I started asking people about assessment tools for work with CPVA, I quickly learnt that different people mean different things when they talk about this; assessment *of* different things, assessment *for* different purposes. And the specific assessment processes and tools which go hand-in-hand with work involving CPVA may well be in addition to the standard measurements that any agency will already be employing for every family or individual coming to their attention.

I am going to assume that the agency you work with already has a set of initial referral/eligibility assessment criteria of some sort. If you are already engaged in work with children and families (in Britain) I will assume you are familiar with some version of the Common Assessment Framework (CAF), looking at the domains of (i) development of the child or young person, (ii) parents and carers, and (iii) the family and environment. The CAF was designed specifically to identify unmet needs early on, to more easily enable sharing of information and avoid multiple assessments, to enable a holistic picture of the child and their situation, and to facilitate referral on as necessary. It presents a useful foundational level assessment for all situations. The level of details on each side of the triangle has been specifically designed to obtain as thorough a picture as possible. I do not intend to lead you through the process of completing such an assessment. There is plenty of information elsewhere about that. Interestingly, Mainstone's text, *Mastering Whole Family Assessment in Social Work* (2014), includes the example of a family experiencing CPVA as one of the case studies.

Mainstone also reminds us of the way different assessment models and tools reflect varying styles and power relationships:

- **Questioning**
  Power held by the practitioner, who defines the problem, need or risk, and drives the assessment process.

- **Procedural**
  Standard tools are used to determine needs and risk, often using a deficit model.

- **Exchange**
  Individuals are understood to be experts of their situation. The practitioner brings problem-solving skills to the interaction.

The introduction of models such as 'signs of safety' has tried to shift the balance of power within the assessment, and to include the family's voice much more within the process of understanding and planning. It is worth reflecting on this as we consider the style and methods of assessment we might use.

What I will consider in this chapter are the various aspects of the assessment process that practitioners are employing, with discussion about their importance and value; and suggestions of things to include or consider. I offer my apologies now that this might involve a lot of lists. My first list:

- Who?
- When?
- How big, how long?
- Why?
- Risk assessments, to practitioners, and to family.
- Safeguarding.
- Dynamic assessment.
- Trauma-informed approaches.
- Is a diagnosis helpful or not?
- Scaling.
- Tools and framework.

Who?

This might seem a strange question to pose, but since I have called this chapter 'Full family assessment' I think it's worth asking who we include in the family. When an initial referral comes in, we may not hear about all the members, even of the immediate family. There may be important individuals who have already left home, perhaps for their own safety, perhaps following their own violence and aggression. Their absence may have left a gap to fill. There may be powerful individuals not living within the household, but who nevertheless command respect or fear. An absent parent may still wield considerable power and control. Are there other siblings living elsewhere? What members of the extended family are in regular contact, or are held in esteem? Are there community 'aunties' and 'uncles' who hold a position as if they were family members? A genogram is always a useful tool to help identify the key individuals, their relative influence, and the different alliances within a family. Completing one separately with different members of the family can yield interesting results. Similarly, an ecogram will include close friends and community support, as well as immediate family. By using straight or wavy lines, thick or thin, solid or broken to designate relationships, it is possible to map alliances and areas of conflict. Where there are positive roles, work can take place to strengthen these relationships to build resilience and self-esteem.

Identifying who is included in the family, who is respected, who holds power, may be more revealing than we first imagine. It will certainly be of value as we proceed.

When?

Some agencies offer a commitment to respond to a referral with an initial contact within 24 hours, before going on to make a more thorough assessment accordingly. Where there are already other agencies involved, and the referral is for a specific programme, with an expectation of ongoing work from the referrer, there might be a longer wait before engagement. Sadly, for some specialist services such as CAMHS, we have learnt recently that families may wait anything from a number of months, to several years for assessment and support (NSPCC, 2017; YoungMinds, 2019). Depending on what a family was asking for, some might have gone on to find help elsewhere, or to cobble together their own solutions. Some however, will undoubtedly have experienced a worsening of the situation as the behaviours become more entrenched, the child gets bigger, or the parents become more and more worn down. If you are considering referring on to a specialist agency where there is a long wait, you might like to think about what can be offered to a family in the interim.

How big, how long?

'After we receive a referral, we visit the family in their home to meet the parents and the child, to learn about their situation and to explain about our service. We try to meet each individual on their own, to hear their story.'

This is a common sort of response to a question from my Mapping Project, exploring specific CPVA programmes of work; often involving two workers (where there is a large enough team), and offering what might be deemed the 'standard assessment'. There may be multiple forms to be completed, which will drive the meeting. However, in the hands of a skilled practitioner, this meeting can provide valuable insights into the family situation and future work. Questions that are asked, and observations made, can help to determine the nature and direction of engagement, the type of help wanted or needed, and the appropriateness of a particular response.

- What is the family's story?
- What does the young person think is happening?
- How do individuals feel about agency involvement?
- What other agencies are already involved?
- Is everybody 'on board'?
- How serious is the violence and/or abuse?
- What particular circumstances are there for this family?
- What evidence of abuse is seen during the visit?

The visit may be just a couple of hours, but practitioners might now have a sense of the type of intervention needed, the urgency, other people to involve – and other information that is missing and still needs to be explored.

Forms: master or servant?

Within the YODA (Youth Offender Diversion Alternative) programme, described by Whitehill Bolton *et al* (2016), the assessment process involves an extensive range of issues, including aggression, mental health, resilience, substance abuse and knowledge of community resources. These are measured using a number of assessment instruments, with over 300 separate items to scale; and are administered both at the start and the end of the programme. More about assessment as evaluation later.

Forms can be a mixed blessing. Without them we may miss important information. With them we may miss important clues. There may be some we believe in and find really helpful, and others we complete because we are obliged to by our agency. How we use forms may be as important as the detail on them. Some people find that they are able to retain the details and questions of a form, and weave them into a conversation. Some take notes and rewrite later. But certainly much of the work will be completed in the meeting. Accuracy is important, and some forms are for completion by the family themselves – consent, and scaling for instance. But we should ask ourselves questions about how a young person with difficulties in concentrating might cope with a succession of questionnaires, and how we can adapt the process to better meet their needs; or how a family feels about divulging deep and personal information to someone they may never have met before, who does not make eye contact perhaps, or is so busy following a standard set of questions that they might not hear what is behind the answers, or recognise the supplementary details they might have sought.

Building trust

Without trust between family and practitioner, change – or even engagement – is likely to be seriously compromised.

There are times when we might have the luxury of allowing people to feel completely comfortable with us before we ask any of the big questions, perhaps if the sort of help we offer is less formal, and an individual has come with expectations of emotional support rather than immediate change.

> 'Personally, I think you have to build a relationship with them first. They have to learn to trust you. You need to build up a bond. Then it's a lot easier.
>
> When they've been coming long enough, most of our regular clients know it's a safe place to talk, and discuss what's going on. New people coming in need to gather, they need to find their own way, and they know when it's safe to speak.
>
> Eventually, after a few sessions, when I've gained their trust and they know that nothing's going to happen, I will say "Do you ever feel unsafe?" ... I'm not asking "Are you a victim of domestic violence?" – I'm asking if they feel unsafe, and sometimes they then disclose ...'
>
> (Galvani, 2010)

However, for many practitioners, the building of trust and the assessment of the situation need to go hand-in-hand. The young person may be mandated to attend, the family may be in crisis, there may be an upper limit on the number of sessions on offer. Then it is down to the specific skill and experience of the practitioner to enable a family, or an individual, to feel comfortable enough to follow through, to believe that they are in safe hands, and that change is possible.

A different agency; not such a different story

For Pereira (2016), using systemic family therapy at an outpatient clinic in northern Spain as part of a specialist CPVA service, the assessment process forms an ongoing part of the 'initial phase' of work, taking place over the course of four separate sessions. During these the therapist meets with the whole family: to enable them to feel comfortable and confident in the work and the relationship with the therapist, to explore the family's circumstances and the nature of the problems experienced, to see what else has been attempted, understanding each person's understanding of the violence and its role, forming a 'therapeutic system'. Finally the family agrees a 'pact of non-violence' to be maintained for the duration of the work.

So, while the assessment process may take place over a shorter or longer period of time, the range of information sought may be very similar. It will perhaps be in the depth of detail that we see the difference.

Why?

Why do you need all this information? If you are only offering a listening ear, or if your agency puts on a short, fixed programme for families, you may feel that in-depth questioning is intrusive, disrespectful or unnecessary. Fair enough! But if you think of your task as helping families to think through for themselves what might be happening, or what might be driving the violence, then helping them to explore and identify important issues becomes central. A respectful curiosity may be your most valuable tool.

Risk assessments

The more sources of information we have to inform risk assessments the better, if we are to ensure we have the full picture and are best able to keep everyone safe. Unapologetically, I will discuss risk to practitioners first.

Risk to practitioners

We do need to be aware of this, particularly if we have been asked to become involved in a situation which may, by its very nature, involve violence and harm. Practitioners need the support of their own supervisors in determining the likelihood of danger, the safest place to meet, whether to be accompanied by another, invoking policies around phoning in to the office or calling for support. This needs to be an honest conversation that understands why one practitioner might feel more at risk that another, whether physically or emotionally.

Ultimately, if a practitioner is in danger, then this highlights further the very real risks faced by the family on a daily basis. It should be of concern that children are sent home from school, for instance, because their behaviour is deemed to pose a serious risk to both other children and staff, but that there may be only one person then available to deal with a potentially heightened risk within the home.

Risks to families

The level of risk a family faces will form an important part of understanding their situation, and may be most usefully established as part of a structured questionnaire:

- What are the sorts of behaviours that a family has experienced?
- Who is targeted?
- Can people say what it is that usually sets something off, place, time of day, who else is present, antecedents?
- Are there clear signs that the situation is escalating?
- What has been tried already, has it worked at all or not?
- Are there pay-offs for the young person (or other family members) from their aggressive behaviour?
- Are threats carried out?
- Is there concern about damage to property or possessions?
- How can this be minimised?
- Are weapons involved?
- Have they been used?
- Does a parent already have a plan of how to respond when in danger?
- What can they be offered immediately as a way of reducing risk?

Risks to the child or young person

This should not be overlooked, just because we are focusing on the harm the young person is causing to others. It may be that the violence is a one-way street, but we should not necessarily assume so. A young person's harmful behaviour may be as a direct result of harm they are being caused elsewhere. Risks to the young person may be presented within the family, or within the community, or through the actions, or lack of actions, of the young person themselves. An understanding of contextual safeguarding is essential here in seeing the bigger picture, and in unpicking the risks involved.

Risk to a young person may be direct, through their harmful behaviour: running away, peer group involvement and risky behaviour, substance use, deliberate self-harm, likely harm when in a state of heightened distress. If the child has a particular health issue, there may be risks associated with that, whether in safe management, separation from parents and family while in hospital, potential pain and trauma. It may be less obvious, through missed education, the impact on future life chances, likely criminalisation, and homelessness.

As with all aspects of the assessment process, a risk assessment is more than a one-off event, much more than an item to be ticked off and filed away. It will be continually evaluated and updated as necessary. It forms a valuable understanding in determining the future direction of work. It needs to be thought of as a document that is fluid, dynamic, and central to formulating a plan of support and intervention. It will feed in to the development of a 'safety plan', which is discussed further in the next chapter.

Safeguarding

Much as families might prefer us not to go down this route, we cannot avoid this discussion. We have statutory responsibilities to consider, but the way we operate these will make all the difference.

Families complain that practitioners adopt a blinkered approach to safeguarding in cases of CPVA; that assessments are experienced as highly accusatory, and that the unexpected involvement of a stranger asking challenging questions in the home can serve to escalate the violence, making the family as a whole feel less safe.

- Is the family 'on side'?
- Are they also concerned about the safety of different family members?
- Are they already doing everything humanly possible to ensure safety?
- Who are the risks to and from?
- How can they be safely managed?
- If the investigation finds that there are no child protection concerns, is there anything else that can be offered to the family?

We might feel that there is room to explore the way child protection and safeguarding assessments are carried out for all families. When the family themselves are asking for help in achieving safety, then there is certainly space to consider whether the approach we adopt might instead have the effect of disempowering them further. There is further discussion of this in Chapter 13.

Trauma-informed approaches

A trauma-informed approach is not so much about the questions that make up the assessment interview itself, as about the whole approach to the process and intervention. It is a way of understanding the impact of trauma on a child and the family, and the way that might play out. It understands the effect of asking questions in a particular way; of meeting in certain places or at certain times. It changes the way we think about the behaviour of individuals in the family, whether the child or adults. But it does also ask a different sort of questions: not so much 'what is wrong with you?', instead, 'what has happened to you?' and 'who was there for you?'. The sensitivity and respect it offers can bring new insight to a situation, whatever the experience of the child and their family.

Dynamic assessment

There is a difference between constant re-assessment and 'dynamic assessment'. Constant re-assessment, going over the same ground, may tell us more about the uncertainty of the agencies or the practitioners involved. It may make us look busy, but it does not necessarily move the situation on at all.

Dynamic assessment takes place as part of the work itself. Not only is it unrealistic to assume that all the information needed will be available right at the start, but – with a hope and expectation that there will be change – the very circumstances for a family will be altering, demanding new assessments of risk, effectiveness, and plans. As more comes to light about a family's situation, a practitioner may choose to focus on a more thorough analysis of a particular aspect of their situation: the role of the extended family perhaps, a family member's health, a move or transition; and the focus on this becomes itself part of the intervention, as practitioner and family explore relevance, how it effects everyone, how people respond to each other, and how new understandings or interpretations might alter the situation.

Is a diagnosis helpful or not?

Having spent some time in earlier chapters considering the centrality of diagnosis for many families experiencing CPVA, this might seem a strange question. How you answer it might well depend on how this affects you directly. I have found over the years that there is a distinct difference of opinion, but that there are good reasons to treat the question with great care. What do we want it to achieve?

Any assessment will, and should, include an understanding of any diagnoses given to members of the family. They open up the understanding of what might be happening within relationships, both now and in the past. They may tell us something about blame, or 'responsibilisation'. They may indicate possible directions of intervention. Diagnoses may relate to attachment disorders, to psychoses, to developmental disabilities such as ASD, to disabilities affecting the brain and body such as FASD, to physical health. It might also be helpful to know when the diagnosis was acquired, or whether treatment so far has been beneficial. A child, or adult, may have one straightforward diagnosis, or multiple labels acquired over months or years. A child may resent a label, or they may be proud of it. A parent may feel stigmatised, they may feel their life has become a constant round of medical appointments, or they might be relieved that someone has taken them at their word. Given the difficulty in obtaining a diagnosis, and the waiting times that many people report, the absence of a diagnosis should not be taken as meaning an absence of a condition. It is worth remembering that it has only relatively recently been recognised that autism can be a significant issue for girls as well as for boys.

'At the end of the day, the list doesn't matter. All that matters is, he's the way he is and I know how deal with him. So you can forget the labels. All you need to know is how to deal with him. I didn't want him to have a label because that can affect your work life. But, without labels you don't get access to services. You don't get help. That is the most ridiculous way.'
(Interview with Rachel, 2017)

For parents like Rachel, being given a diagnosis opens up the possibility not just of medication or understanding, but also a route – perhaps the only route – to extra help for their child in school. Rachel's sentiments are echoed in a post on the We are Family blog (2017) where a parent talks about the sense of relief at finally being given an explanation for her child's behaviour, and of feeling vindicated for all the years of asking, at the same time as experiencing utter devastation at the realisation of what it might mean for her child, and the rest of both their lives. They also point to the cynicism of some, in questioning the thoroughness or accuracy of the diagnosis process. Herein is the nub of the dilemma. If a diagnosis is to be given, accuracy – and faith in its accuracy – has to be paramount.

A mental health diagnosis carries with it more than the possibility of support. It may suggest treatment and medication; it may also bring stigma and discrimination. We might not like that, but that does not necessarily make it something we choose to accept or reject. Some diagnoses may be based on observations rather than a definable medical test, such as a blood test or genetic screening, for instance, leading to the criticism that they may be tautological. Some people may feel that leaves more room for challenge.

Over the last months I have read articles claiming both that ADHD is over-diagnosed in *The Atlantic* (Ruiz, 2014) and that it is under-diagnosed in *The Independent* (Matthews-King, 2018). Certainly some countries appear more ready to offer a diagnosis than others. There is concern that medication is handed out in the absence of other therapeutic support, or alternatively that children are left without medication that could allow them to moderate their behaviour and fit more readily into the expectations of society. Others will argue that we should understand certain behaviour not as a 'disorder' requiring treatment, but as a message that a child is experiencing severe stress – requiring a different sort of response to help them feel safe.

Where different issues may present similarly, suggesting confusion, there is concern about a misdiagnosis, as much as missed diagnosis. Is it trauma or ADHD/PDA/ASD? Is it ASD or FASD? The distinction matters when different conditions may require different or even divergent approaches. It will matter a lot for parents, who may have been held responsible for having caused their child's behaviour while it was considered to be an attachment issue.

We should be wary of a diagnosis bandwagon as different conditions come 'in and out of fashion'. We should be open to the possibility of multiple diagnoses, and that things are not necessarily mutually exclusive even when they are confused with each other. Surely though, the most important issues must be the accuracy, and who it is that has offered the diagnosis; with an assurance that they are properly qualified to do so. For most of us, our responsibility is not to count ACE scores, to speculate or to offer a definitive diagnosis. What we can do though is to listen, to be curious and to care.

Scaling

I'm going to include here both 'before and after' evaluations, and the sort of scaling that might form an integral part of each session.

Before and after

There are many reasons for conducting 'before and after' assessments. It will be important for the family as well as the practitioner team to be able to identify changes and growth. It will certainly be important to justify continuing with a programme of work by being able to demonstrate its effectiveness at some level. Typically such assessments involve the completion of questionnaires and matrices detailing strengths and difficulties, the types of behaviour exhibited and its frequency, issues of self-esteem and mental health, social networks and connections with pro- as well as anti-social behaviour. The challenge is to find a way of including these in the process that feels helpful to all, rather than a tiresome task. Questionnaires can be adapted for younger children, or those with special needs through the use of symbols or pictures.

The YODA programme, already mentioned, uses a number of measurements to assess an all-encompassing range of issues:

- The young person's basic needs and risk factors (including all aspects of health, housing, safety, conflict, decision making, community involvement and stress management).
- The young person's solution finding abilities.
- Resilience and psychosocial resources available to the young person.
- Mental health, substance use and sociability.
- Dispositional hope.
- The experience of anger.

The Who's in Charge? programme uses a significantly smaller group of questions to which parents and/or young people are invited to show their level of agreement or disagreement over a five-point scale, for instance:

- How often in the past two months has this child done the following to you? (with examples, including hitting, throwing, pushing, yelling, verbally abusing and destroying possessions or property).
- How often in the past two months has this child done the following to your partner? (same examples).
- How often in the past two months has this child done the following to their siblings? (same examples).
- List other violence or abusive behaviours.
- Agreement/disagreement with a series of questions about stress, coping and resilience.

You will find a system that meets your needs, and the requirements of those funding you or commissioning the service!

Within the session

The 'solution-focused approach' to work uses scaling within a session as a fundamental aspect of the work, perhaps as a 'check-in' at the start, or in exploring changes that have taken place since the previous meeting. They – the questions – are a focus of motivation and accountability as individuals are encouraged to think about what has gone well, what needs to change to further increase the score – or why it might not be even lower. They are a valuable tool in placing responsibility on the young person for change.

Solution-focused work forms an integral part of many specific programmes, and approaches to work with CPVA. The emphasis on taking responsibility, and on supporting the family in finding their own answers, sits well with an understanding of families as experts in their own situation.

Tools and framework

Tools are there to assist us in our work. They can make an assessment more interesting and engaging. They can ensure we cover all the ground needed. They can be chosen or be adapted to meet different needs. They can be found relatively easily if you do not already have them.

Measurement

Mainstone (2014) provides a comprehensive list of clinical tools and measurements to inform assessment with children and adults (see Appendix 2).

Strengths and Difficulties Questionnaires are available to download here: http://www.sdqinfo.com.

There is discussion about scaling questions and their use on the Institute for Solution-focused Therapy website: https://solutionfocused.net/what-is-solution-focused-therapy/.

Behaviour inventories are a way of gathering information about the types of violence or harm, and its frequency. They might ask *how many times* in the last four weeks, the last week, today? They might also be used for measuring pro-social behaviours. There are examples available on the Uniting Kildonan website, a part of a forum with Lily Anderson (2017): https://www.unitingkildonan.org.au/programs-and-services/child-youth-and-family-support/family-violence/adolescent-violence/forum-lily-anderson/.

Genograms and ecograms

Templates, guidance, and instructions on completing and using 'genograms' (depictions of a family tree and relationships within the family) and 'ecograms', (showing wider relationships in a looser form) can be found easily online. You can use a ready-made version, or it can be more interesting and revealing to let the family design their own, whether with symbols, pictures, or buttons even.

A framework for assessment

We started this chapter thinking about the Common Assessment Framework, and I want to end by thinking about the framework that you might use to ensure that you have covered all areas, asked the questions you need to, thought about possible connections and links in every field. The three fields of child development, parents and carers, and family and environment present a ready-made template, with many issues to consider in each side of the triangle. Alternatively you could base your assessment on an understanding of the nested ecological theory, since that presents a useful model for thinking about the influences in a child's life. Or what about the typology suggested earlier, for a framework that considers all possible events that may be linked to violence and abuse, and the way they might play out. The framework you use may be chosen for you already by the agency for whom you work. If not, then use the one that seems most helpful, most encompassing, while bearing in mind that you may be called upon to share your assessment with others if you need to refer the family on for greater help.

But whatever else you use, you will be using first and foremost your own personality, skills and curiosity. Your most important tools.

Things to think about

- What information do you already have? Is it up-to-date?
- Who needs to be included in the process, within and outside the family?
- How can you enable to family to take ownership of the assessment process?
- How can you explain the need for particular assessments of risk?
- What tools and methods are best suited to the situation you face? Do they need adapting to meet a particular need?

Find out more

For discussion about diagnosis and labelling
A guest post on **Al Coates'** website; *Does Labeling Support the Notion of 'Divide and Conquer'?* (2018): http://www.alcoates.co.uk/2018/10/guest-post-does-labelling-support.html.

Taylor N (2018) *Adoption and Attachment: A parent's perspective*. The Association for Child and Adolescent Mental Health website: https://www.acamh.org/blog/adoption-and-attachment/.

Gayton J (2018) *Flip-Flop Season is Here!* A Disorder for Everyone! Website: http://www.adisorder4everyone.com/flip-flop-season-is-here/.

Smith M (2017) Hyperactive around the world? The history of ADHD in global perspective. *Social History of Medicine* **30** (4) 767–787.

Delahooke M (2017) *Deconstructing Oppositional Defiance Disorder*. Mona's Blog: https://www.monadelahooke.com/deconstructing-oppositional-defiant-disorder/.

Steph's Two Girls (2018) *Is Pathological Demand Avoidance Real?* https://www.stephstwogirls.co.uk/2018/10/is-pathological-demand-avoidance-real.html

A piece of research conducted in Norway asked children specifically about their experience of being given a diagnosis:
Rasmussen IL, Undheim AM, Aldridge-Waddon L & Young S (2018) Just being a kid, or an ADHD kid? A qualitative study of how young people experience receiving and living with a diagnosis of attention deficit hyperactivity disorder. *Journal of Psychiatry and Cognitive Behaviour* **1**: https://www.gavinpublishers.com/admin/assets/articles_pdf/1533187359article_pdf1255565452.pdf.

For discussion about the importance of distinguishing between attachment and autism/ADHD diagnosis, or between FASD and autism
see references at the end of the Chapter 2.

Assessment practice
Ross K (2018) *Risk Assessment of Violent Adolescents*. Talk from the Conduct Disorder Conference. The Association for Child and Adolescent Mental Health has made slides of conference presentations available online. There is a particularly interesting one about risk assessment of violent adolescents by Dr Kenny Ross (2018): https://www.acamh.org/freeview/conduct-disorder-conference/.

A report for the **Office of the Children's Commissioner** (2013) *'It takes a lot to build trust', Recognition and Telling: Developing earlier routes to help for children and young people*, pointed to the importance of building trust in enabling children to disclose abuse and seek help.

You can find out more about my **Mapping Project**, the process and the outcome, on my website: https://holesinthewall.co.uk/resources/directory/. For information about contextual safeguarding see the work of the **Contextual Safeguarding Network**: https://contextualsafeguarding.org.uk/about/what-is-contextual-safeguarding.

References

Galvani S (2010) *Supporting Families Affected by Substance Use and Domestic Violence*. University of Bedfordshire, Adfam and Stella Project.

Mainstone F (2014) *Mastering Whole Family Assessments in Social Work*. London: Jessica Kingsley Publishers.

Matthews-King A (2018) ADHD treatment may be needed by hundreds of thousands more children, experts suggest. *The Independent* **8 August**. Available at: https://www.independent.co.uk/news/health/adhd-ritalin-attention-deficit-hyperactive-disorder-medication-psychiatric-lancet-oxford-study-a8481701.html (accessed February 2019).

NSPCC (2017) *Over 100,000 Children Rejected for Mental Health Treatment* [online]. Available at: https://www.nspcc.org.uk/what-we-do/news-opinion/child-mental-health-referral-rejections-top-100000/ (accessed February 2019).

Pereira R (2016) Responding to filio-parental violence. In: A Holt (Ed.) *Working with Adolescent Violence and Abuse Towards Parents*. Oxford: Routledge.

Ruiz R (2014) How childhood trauma could be mistaken for ADHD. *The Atlantic* **7 July**. Available at: https://www.theatlantic.com/health/archive/2014/07/how-childhood-trauma-could-be-mistaken-for-adhd/373328/ (accessed February 2019).

We are Family blog (2017) *The Diagnosis* [online]. Available at: https://wearefamilyadoption.wordpress.com/2017/10/13/the-diagnosis/?utm_content=buffer49aad&utm_medium=social&utm_source=facebook.com&utm_campaign=buffer (accessed February 2019).

Whitehill Bolton K, Lehmann P & Jordan C (2016) The youth offender alternative (YODA). In: A Holt (Ed.) *Working with Adolescent Violence and Abuse Towards Parents*. Oxford: Routledge.

YoungMinds (2019) *Children Waiting Years for Mental Health Treatment* [online]. Available at: https://youngminds.org.uk/blog/children-waiting-years-for-mental-health-treatment/ (accessed February 2019).

Chapter 12: Whole family intervention

'As all able practitioners are aware, the quality of relational engagement between social workers and those who area constructed as their clients has a significant influence on subsequent outcomes.'
(Hyslop, 2016)

'Families, like individuals, resist efforts to change them by people they feel don't understand and accept them.'
(Price, 1996)

So you've done your assessment, through which process you have begun to build a relationship with the family; a lot will depend on this relationship. Parents really want to trust that you have their interests at heart, and that you know where this is going. I would like to offer an interjection at this stage; something that parents have stated has happened to them frequently, causing significant distress and distrust; something that has been highlighted in serious case reviews in Britain.

Don't confuse assessment with intervention, or action with impact.

The shape of the intervention offered will now depend on many things.

Practitioners encounter CPVA in all types of work. You may be employed by a statutory agency, delivering work with children and families; but equally you may work in a voluntary agency, be a housing officer, a learning mentor in a school, a nurse in the accident and emergency department of a busy hospital, a children's residential care worker, a police officer, a foster carer or someone working in the field of domestic violence. You may have many years of experience, or have just started. You may be a specialist, or you may meet people with a very diverse range of needs. You may be working with families with multiple complex needs, or you may offer a universal service. You may have unlimited resources, or you may have simply yourself. You will be subject to your own agency's policies and expectations, and may be required to refer something on, rather than engaging directly with a family yourself.

You may find that some of the guidance and suggestions outlined in this chapter do not seem to fit with your situation, but I hope that there will be *something* here that chimes for you – that helps you feel more confident in your work. Your intervention should have a focus on keeping people safe, and within that you are aiming to reduce the violence and to restore healthy relationships within the family. Not everyone will be asked, or expected to work with families where the levels of trauma, risk, exploitation and violence are at an extreme level. If you are, then you should be assured that you are not expected to do this alone, but as part of a multi-agency team with many other skilled workers, working together to keep a family safe.

I am going to arrange this chapter by some FAQs, questions that I am asked over and over again by people looking for guidance in this work. I tried other ways but it was getting too complicated and wordy! But first, two questions to ask you.

1. What have the family asked for?

Was it advice they sought? Did they come to you asking for a child's removal, whether permanent or as respite? Do they need support to access other services? Are they confused and uncertain, or fixed in their request? We should not assume that all families want or need the same thing. We should certainly not be offering the same answer to every request. It may be that the parents are doing everything right already, but simply need reassurance, or a quick pointer to something else. Do you know what the child or young person thinks about what is going on? What would they like to happen?

2. Is this family safe?

There is no silver bullet, no straightforward answer to the question of what to do when your child is on the rampage. But the most important thing we can all do is to work to ensure a family's safety. Sadly it may only be at the point when people feel unsafe that they come to our attention. Tragically it may only be at this point that they reach a required threshold in some agencies for work. Nevertheless, the removal of a child to ensure safety is by no means the only, inevitable scenario. The purpose of assessment and intervention is to identify risks and strengths, and to work with a family to find ways to ensure future safety. The family is an important resource to achieve this, but they can only function safely with the tools, skills and support that we can help them find.

Safety planning

In any other situation where there was violence and abuse within the home, devising a safety plan would be a standard part of the help offered. Working with families where the violence and abuse is from a child should be no different. If you work in a domestic abuse agency, then you will already have safety plan templates that can be adapted to this scenario. But in any case, there is a wealth of information, and even documents freely available online, which can be used for this purpose.

A safety plan is about understanding and reducing the risks faced by the family. It will be unique to that family, and may need to be differentiated further for each member. The Step-Up programme also includes a safety plan for the young person using violence, recognising their responsibilities and helping to hold them to account for their behaviour. A plan will be contextual, examining where and when the risk of violence is greatest, what happens, when and to whom. Safety plans will likely consider where to go inside the house when the individual is not feeling safe or in order to help others remain safe; similarly outside the home – who to call in different circumstances and who to make aware of the situation. They may involve additional steps taken to provide a safe space. But crucially each one should be a specific response to that family's, and young person's, needs.

- One family may use a 'codeword' to alert other members to an escalating situation, and someone then moves to unlock doors and gently move individuals into a space that is visible from the street.

- If a child is likely to run, putting themselves in acute danger when dysregulated, then it may be more appropriate to lock the doors to help contain them and their anxiety.

- Where neighbours are very close and likely to hear things kicking off, they can be asked to 'knock for a cup of sugar', if it is thought that distraction will help defuse a frightening scenario.

- A local 'uncle' may be identified who can be called upon for a swift visit to offer moral and physical support.

- In extreme situations, parents may install locks on internal doors, cameras, and panic alarms.

> *'At the instigation of Women's Aid, S's bedroom was turned into the "safe room" with a personal alarm, telephone and alarm fob for the safety alarm which was installed for us (but because my abuser was my son, not an ex-partner, I had to pay to hire it). S's bedroom door has 3 large bolts on the back of it after L chased her upstairs threatening her with a carving knife, and I thank God that she managed to get into her bedroom before he caught her. The 15 stab and slash marks in her door still bear testimony to what happened that afternoon when I was unfortunately still at work.'*
> (Michaela, personal communication)

A safety plan will not remove the risks, but it is an important part of maintaining some level of control in a dangerous situation. A safety plan may also include consideration of when it will be necessary to call the police, but more of that later.

When a child is presenting the violence, it would not normally be appropriate to encourage the one harmed to leave the home, although potentially partners and siblings might do so in an emergency. Parents may well have important caring responsibilities for other children. Sometimes consideration is given to accommodating siblings elsewhere, because of statutory responsibilities to keep children safe. This is a contentious response, meeting only part of a family's needs and potentially causing further trauma. It may be appropriate, for the safety of all concerned, to look at finding alternative accommodation for the young person.

Back to where we were then. What does an intervention look like? What might it include? Where do you start, and what do you do when it all kicks off! Can I offer some reassurance that, though this may be a completely new area of work for you, it is essentially about work with families with very complex problems, and you may already be doing this in another arena. You will use skills and knowledge that you already have regarding attachment, trauma, and brain development, understanding anxiety, family interaction, resilience, and collaborative working. You will base your intervention specifically on your assessment and, since every family's situation will be unique and uniquely challenging, your responses will be tailored to each family every time.

Just as other interventions might be staged by tier, according to whether it is a universal service, targeted, community, or residential /hospital, we should not assume that all support for families experiencing CPVA will look or feel the same. Neither will they all look the same in different countries or regions; but they will have certain features in common.

My FAQS:

1. What are the important elements of the work?
2. What theories underpin the work?
3. What approaches do people employ?
4. Who do you work with?
5. How long should an intervention last?
6. One-to-one or group work?
7. What evidence of effectiveness is there?
8. Are there circumstances that make intervention inappropriate or ineffective?

9. What do you do when it all kicks off?
10. What about restraint?
11. Should you call the police?
12. What happens when a child can no longer live at home?
13. Where can I find resources to use?
14. What are the costs involved?
15. How do people fund the work?

#1. What are the important elements of the work?

In 2015 I embarked on a short piece of work to try to map the specialist services, across Britain, for families experiencing CPVA. You can find more information about this project on my website Holes in the Wall, but one of the ways in which it was interesting was in showing up that, though there were many different programmes and interventions being used, they held many features in common. Other people have observed this too. Amanda Holt's book *Working with Adolescent to Violence and Abuse to Parents* (2016) brings accounts from a range of different programmes, approaches and nations, sometimes disagreeing over some aspects of the issue, but bound together by a focus on the importance of listening and of building relationships, the value of a needs-led, strengths based service – and of long term support.

Breaking things down further, there are certain elements that will be found within work with families experiencing CPVA, wherever it takes place, across the world.

Naming the problem

Parents acknowledging what is happening, to themselves and to others, including making it clear to the young person that this is not acceptable. Young people need to be confronted with the reality of what they are practicing, and to be able to acknowledge this. This might be through a formal process, with letters or announcements (for instance in NVR) or simply acknowledging it within the family and asking for help and support from others. Sometimes parents have not previously thought about what they are experiencing as abusive. The gradual build-up over years has normalised their experience. They should not be forced into a corner, but helped to reflect on their situation. It may be only when they meet other parents, or start talking about their day-to-day experiences, that they come to understand it in this way.

Identifying support for the family

A strong network that can be relied on to provide emergency help when things get tough, but also to affirm and encourage individuals daily, and even act as a mentor to the young person. Parents should be encouraged to think about people other than professionals. A teacher may be a wonderful support, but is not available 24 hours, or through the long holidays when problems may be worst. Extended family may be appropriate, so long as their interpretation of the situation does not add to the condemnation a parent already feels. If you have a large group of friends yourself, it might be hard to imagine not being able to identify someone you could call when things are tough. But families experiencing CPVA may well have become more and more isolated over the years, as the abuse has developed. They may need help to identify even one supporter.

'We have got a network. Maybe because of how I was brought up, I haven't got a problem with talking to people about stuff… So I've always been very open. Loads of "aunties". It's so great to have a network. Some people don't have that and so we need to provide people with a network.'
(Interview with Stephanie, 2015)

'The power of:
– simply being told "you are doing okay"
– positive reinforcement on approach
1 session. 1 week = seismic shift'
(Tweet from Mumdrah, @mumdrah, 2017)

Prioritising issues

Agreeing what are the important issues that have to stop. A zero tolerance approach is going to lead to a constant battleground with no winners; but identifying the red lines can help to focus attention and bring perspective.
Deal with the big things first, one step at a time! Within NVR this is part of the 'basket exercise' but it is a useful strategy whichever approach is being used. Leaving towels on the bathroom floor, or not helping with the washing up may be annoying, but they may need to take a back seat while attention is focused on not hitting people, or being back home by midnight.

De-escalation

Recognising when a situation is building to conflict, and learning new ways of engaging to bring things back down: helping parents to take back control by refusing to be drawn into an attempt to build the tension; and equally helping a young person to find ways to re-regulate their emotions. It can be hard to walk away from someone intent on using every technique to get under your skin. We seem to have an inbuilt need to either have the last word, or to make it clear that some things are intolerable.

'When little people are overwhelmed by big emotions, it's our job to share our calm, not join their chaos.'
(Knost, 2013)

> I heard an interesting illustration of escalation at a conference for special educational provision staff:
>
> A young person needs a reason to get out of a situation that they are finding uncomfortable, or perhaps they feel in need of being held, to help with regulation; and they know that hitting you will provide that escape or response. Yet they do not feel ready to hit you yet. There are certain codes by which they abide, and they need to feel they had no choice in the matter. So they state, through their confrontation: I need to hit you but I am not ready yet, can you help me reach that point please. You can respond to the insults with outrage, helping to move the child up to the next and next levels of rage, until they predictably explode and their desired outcome is achieved, or you can find a way to give the young person a safer and more appropriate exit.
> (Thanks to Bernard Allen, 2012)

Changing thought patterns, changing language used, changing behaviours and responses – what this looks like will vary from family to family. When we use the language of war and of battles in a situation like this, we can end up in a situation of believing there must be a winner, and a loser. In fact, we are hoping for a situation where a new peace is restored and all are winners. There will be specific techniques suggested within programmes such as NVR, or by a therapist, and often families will already have identified methods that are helpful or not. Just as distraction might work for a two year old working themselves up into a frenzy, the offer of a hot chocolate and a biscuit might effectively interrupt the direction of travel for an older child losing control. Another child might respond to breathing or counting practices.

Sometimes escalation happens in a way we feel totally confused about. We thought we were talking about one thing, making a reasonable point; but suddenly we are arguing fiercely about something completely different. One minute you were explaining why they had to be back home by 11.30pm, and now suddenly everyone is arguing about why you as a parent are unable to get a new boyfriend and go out yourself. By subtly changing the subject, a young person takes control of the discussion out of the adult's hands, undermining their right to make any decisions at all. Parents need help to remain clear, assertive and 'on message', without being drawn down side alleys with a brick wall at the end!

When it's written down, it all seems so straightforward, but of course in the heat of the moment we all get sucked in and then feel we have failed. Learning de-escalation needs practice, support and encouragement. If it is so important to a parent to have the last word, do what a friend confided that they do: wait till the child is asleep and then whisper to them in their bed – but best make sure they are really asleep first!

Children and young people may need to be helped or taught to recognise when their emotions are heightening, or when they feel particularly stressed, and offered alternative safe ways to 'let off steam'. This in itself can take many forms, whether finding alternative outlets for aggression, such as hitting a punch bag; or introducing the rhythmic effects of bouncing a ball or jumping on a trampoline; or of moving to a different space where their sensory needs can be safely met. For some children, with a diagnosis of autism for instance, or with a particularly traumatic history, there might only be a short moment between a stressful event and an explosive reaction. It will be important to bring in the experts to advise on support and techniques in situations such as this.

Understanding consequences

This is more controversial, and there is a strong voice lately against the use of reward and punishment charts, and strategies such as 'time out'. It may be that some families will adopt a scale of consequences for actions that are unacceptable to them, involving pocket money, or loss of 'services' within the home (lifts in the car, laundry etc). Families can be helped to work out what these might be and how to operate them. Price (1996) has a whole chapter on 'the secret weapon strategy', which is worth looking at and some families may find helpful. But all families, including young people, can be helped to consider the natural consequences of certain actions as a part of taking responsibility for their actions. If someone throws the television across the room, they will no longer be able to watch their favourite show. If they injure Mum's hand, she may not be able to drive them where they want to go, or to cook dinner. Committing certain acts 'in the real world' could lead to arrest and incarceration.

Rebuilding relationships

Relationships, which, despite seeming to be damaged beyond repair, have foundations that go back a long way and can still be restored. Finding things to do together might be an eventual goal, even if it feels way out of reach at the start. Parents may find it hard at the start to come up with positive aspects of a child's character or behaviour, but there will almost always be something they can remember from the past, or that continues even now. A number of programmes include aspects of restorative practice using video to facilitate conversations between parents and young people, with remarkable impact. Both parties can find it easier to say things when they are not face-to-face, and remark on the healing power of such interaction.

> Geraldine puts little notes in her child's lunchbox sending love and wishing him a good day.
>
> Dave refuses to speak to his mother, but she continues to text him messages to remind him of her presence.
>
> Janelle plans a pizza and film night every Friday, making sure all the children have a turn at choosing the film (and making sure there are sufficient places for everyone to sit right from the start).

Noticing the positives can disrupt negative patterns of thought and help to build a basis for further restoration. Within the practice of NVR, this might include reconciliation gestures. Sometimes this can feel anti-intuitive. Surely this is the adult acquiescing or even pleading for improvement? Alternatively you can understand it as a step for a parent in rejecting confrontation and retaking control of the narrative: 'This is how we behave in this house'.

Building parents' self-esteem

Like each of the other elements, this one feels like maybe it should be first in order to build the others around and on top of it. There may be a natural obvious order to work in each individual family, or you may end up working on all simultaneously. You will have seen from the chapter on impact, as well as the descriptions of what form CPVA can take, that a parent's self-esteem may be absolutely at rock bottom. Gallagher (2018a) introduced a questionnaire to help parents recognise their declining influence in a child's life as they age – this is not all your own fault! This directly contradicts and challenges the story being told in society at large. Ironically, it can sometimes be by hearing that there are other parents in the same situation that an individual can be helped to start the long climb out of despair and hopelessness. Then small changes can make it feel more possible, and the sharing of tips and advice can offer hope. Peer group support, whether online or in actuality, can be very beneficial here. Whether through acts of self-care, sharing with others, or learning new skills, there are many different ways of building self-esteem, but it is as a parent believes they are 'worth it' that they will start to feel equipped to reclaim authority in the home.

What else?

I would like to emphasise that while it is important to address issues of violence and abuse, it is not sufficient to work on this and to neglect other issues. The effects of early trauma can be life long and attention needs to be given to these as well as the actual violence and abuse. A young person at risk of gang exploitation or using drugs will need help with this separately and as well. Poor mental health will not necessarily magically improve as a relationship is restored. Where a child has a particular diagnosis the family will require help to understand this and work to support their child to overcome these additional hurdles. Equally, work on any of those without addressing the violence is less likely to bring about the improvements the family so desperately hopes for. Where patterns of behaviour have become established and normalised these need understanding and addressing as well. This is not a case of either/or. It is very much a both/and situation.

#2. What theories underpin the work?

Unsurprisingly, as our understanding of roots and routes to CPVA – of vulnerabilities and interventions – has developed, so too has the prominence of particular theories or work. Where once a focus on behavioural learning may have been pivotal, this will now be but one of your tools. When we understood CPVA in a much narrower way, it was easy to impose our interpretations and remedies through a blanket approach. Now we see many contributory factors and many needs, and our intervention will be informed by a range of theories and understanding of child development – cognitive, physical and psychological – of family relationships, and of the influence of the wider community and society, on a family's structure and integrity. An understanding of feminist theory will be helpful. You will draw on attachment theory, and understanding of trauma particularly, as you consider relationships within the family. You will also find a systemic understanding underpins good practice, as you work on supporting relationships within the context of a wider community of support.

#3. What approaches do people employ?

Just as there is no one-size-fits-all solution, there is no one individual approach to this work. Speaking with those running established programmes and interventions, you will find practitioners adopting and adapting a whole range of approaches, including: solution-focused work, CBT, narrative therapy, anger management (yes – this is an integral part of work with young people in a way that it is not usually recommended with adults perpetrating violence), systemic work, strengths-based approaches, trauma-informed work, restorative approaches. You may work in groups, or one-to-one, or both. You may feel concerned that you do not have the skill set needed to work with families, but you will almost certainly be familiar, through your training, with one or more of these components.

> Sandi received a minimum of training about domestic abuse when she was qualifying as a social worker, and none regarding CPVA; but she was able to make use of the skills she had developed through other work when she started to come across CPVA on a regular basis.
>
> *'I got a lot of similar cases. At one point I was the social worker who'd get those cases where teenagers were being relinquished into local authority care … part of it was the violence, usually the older ones – it seemed like parents were a lot more comfortable saying, "My kid's doing this to me, doing that - I'm scared of him." … I'd just finished my Restorative training and it's a model I like and see a lot of merit, and I did some restorative work with Mum and K and her siblings. So it was opening up conversations, helping each other hear what was going on for the other one. And that remorse. I remember that day when I brought Mum and K together and she saw her mum cry, there was a real remorse …'*
> (Interview with Sandi, 2018)

With so many links to trauma, a good understanding of this, and of the principles of trauma-informed work, will be invaluable. If you still feel anxious that you don't know where to start, reading the accounts of work from other practitioners can give encouragement – and ideas. There are suggestions for reading at the end of this chapter, and in the appendices.

The Royal Commission on Family Violence (2016) made recommendations on work with adolescent family violence, which included the possibility of work using 'family group conferencing'. There are concerns around such models because of the potential use of power within the process by the young person, but Howard (2017) comments that this need not be a problem if proper consideration is given to the issue, and that it could be a powerful restorative tool as part of a wider intervention programme.

#4. Who do you work with?

Time to adopt a pragmatic approach here. In an ideal world you would work with the whole family, depending on how they live and who is important to them, maybe even bringing in extended family members for support at appropriate moments. It's worth checking out early on who is identified as being part of the family. This is an issue that affects relationships, and so working in a relational way, as far as possible, is almost certainly going to reap the most benefits.

Being realistic, there may be all sorts of reasons why you end up working with some family members rather than others. It might be difficult for both parents to attend sessions outside of the home if there are other children to mind. Sometimes one parent in a couple might have difficulty in accepting the changes needed – and committing to the time. Siblings often get forgotten, but they might also be a target of abuse and violence; or exposure to trauma may mean that they might step up to take over the abuse without attention to their needs. The whole family needs to find a new way to enjoy healthier relationships.

You will remember from the chapter about engaging young people that it is generally not recommended to work with just the young person. While they clearly need to accept responsibility for their actions and choose not to use violence and abuse, such a change will be best supported by parents and other family members finding new ways to be together, whether in making requests, issuing statements, explaining consequences, or enjoying each other's company.

Some programmes work just with parents. You might choose to work in this way because of the particular agency you are in, or because of staffing, resource and timing issues, or simply because you like the programme of work. Who's in Charge? works in this way and is a well-established programme, running for many years in Australia and Britain. NVR programmes also work with parents to help them find a new way of developing and maintaining authority in the home. By supporting parents, building their self-esteem and encouraging new ways of understanding family relationships, it has been shown that it is possible to bring about transformation in the whole family.

If you work with the whole family, this might look completely different from one situation or agency to another, whether you are offering some sort of traditional family therapy, or a looser type of family intervention. If you are offering a specific programme of work, some of the work might take place in parallel sessions, joining together at key points. If you work on a one-to-one basis, work may take place with different family members as well as bringing everyone together at other times. If there are a number of workers engaged with a family (often adopted as good practice for the purposes of support, observation, feedback, modelling, and safety), they might work together, or one might focus on working with the adults, and another with the children, making the most of particular skills, as well as allowing deeper sharing of information. (But in this case, there would need to be clear protocols about confidentiality to avoid collusion; and well-structured joint planning and reflection.)

Don't forget your colleagues. The appropriate sharing of information, meeting together to review and plan, taking advice, and working together on an agreed pathway, are all potentially crucial to effective work in resolving deeply embedded patterns and frightening levels of violence. How can you include families in these meetings? Can their voice be heard directly? Do not confuse the sharing of information with the formulation of a plan; and be sure that everyone is aware of whose responsibility it is to act on the plan. If colleagues have different opinions and interpretations of child to parent violence and abuse, think about your role in education and awareness raising, and in supporting your family's integrity and human rights.

However you work, and whoever you work with, the key issues remain the same: reducing the levels of abuse and violence, keeping everyone safe, enabling the parents to find a new way to maintain their authority in the home, and restoring healthy family relationships.

#5. How long should an intervention last?

How long is a piece of string!

When I was comparing different programmes for my Mapping Project, I was interested to see that there was a range of time that families were engaged in work, anything from eight to 20+ weeks. Pereira (2016) describes working with families intensively for as long as 15 months. How can this be? Is it possible to achieve something meaningful in as little as eight weeks? Let's look at the context.

First of all, each family will be different, and at a different stage in their journey. If we are able to work with families early on, before patterns of abuse have become established, and before the abuse and violence becomes truly dangerous, then the chances of turning things around in a shorter length of time will be greater. It may even be that there is a straightforward cause and once this is 'fixed' the difficulties are resolved easily enough. Or it may be that the family asked for something quite straightforward that you were able to deliver in a short time.

A specific programme of work may be just one element in a longer engagement with a family. They might have been supported for a long time to bring them to a point of being ready to work intensively for an eight, 12 or 15-week period, and there might then be a long period of work following up, reinforcing and supporting the changes made.

If you work in a specialist agency, then your intervention might be completely open-ended, perhaps even with 24 hour emergency cover, and might include advocating for a family in meetings at school, with housing or welfare benefits, supporting them in obtaining legal advice or attending court, writing reports to other agencies, visiting a child in a residential home. There might be no limit to the time you can spend, until the work is complete.

If a child has very particular needs that mean the chances of totally eliminating violence appear slim, then you might end up dipping in and out of work with a family over a long period of time, as the situation evolves and their needs change too.

Something that is always difficult, and completely unsatisfactory for families, is when a piece of work is started, but resources are withdrawn before completion. In some agencies, where funding is renewed on a yearly basis, this might be a real concern. Wherever possible, we owe it to families, and to ourselves, to ensure we, or someone else, can see a piece of work through to the finish.

#6. One-to-one, or group work?

Another issue where opinion is split, and it may well be that you will have to decide this according to your own circumstances. Do you have a large number of families needing help, or just one or two? Are you based in a large anonymous town, or on a small island where everyone knows everyone else's business? How far will people have to travel if everyone meets together? Anxieties abound regarding the negative role modelling possibilities working in groups, while many people speak passionately about the opportunities this offers. Increasingly, I am hearing of people delivering programmes that were originally written for group delivery in a one-to-one setting, for a range of reasons. The resources are there, but they should be seen as a tool, not a straightjacket.

Group work does offer additional possibilities, and there are teams of people finding amazing and creative ways to supplement and reinforce the work, from sharing food together, to producing films, music and artwork, in order to bed-in the learning. These are not precluded by a one-to-one offer, but some of the energy and inspiration is lost.

There are some specific questions that are often asked in relation to group work:

- Is it sensible to work with siblings together?
- Is it appropriate to mix ages together?
- What about gender – should boys and girls be in separate groups?

I have heard strong arguments on both sides for each of these points, and once again it may all depend on each individual situation and your own skills and resources. Where siblings are very competitive or have different needs it might be crucial that they work separately. Older children can act as positive mentors – or they can teach younger children new ways to misbehave. If the age gap is very wide there may be issues about the nature of some of the material covered, or about levels of maturity and understanding, but equally, thought needs to be given not just to chronological age, but to emotional maturity too.

Some groups have been designed specifically to work with just girls, and the curriculum reflects this. One girl, or one boy, will be very different to another, but it is worth thinking about balance in a group. One young woman in a group otherwise dominated by young men may not be the most appropriate mix, yet there is no absolute rule that single gender groups are better or worse. If you have done a proper assessment of each young person referred, then you will be in a position to make the call.

> In an interview specifically about this issue, Chris Bolas, then Youth Offending Service Manager within Leicestershire County Council, acknowledged that he remained ambivalent about the wisdom of mixed groups, although he had seen benefits when this had been done:
>
> *'We removed the gender references in the material and neutralised them. In the young people's group we sought wherever possible to have male and female workers running the group. Role plays need to have different genders as the*

> "perpetrators", as all members of the group needed to see themselves in the role. We did not mix this up very well on the group due to some staff issues, but I think it would be important do better next time. I think that it is important for young people to see good working relationships between genders, as many who attend that group may not have witnessed this very much previously. Also they may not have witnessed women being able to be leaders or sharing power. Mixed gender group workers provide their own gender perspective on the group's behaviour, essential if you are exploring issues of risk of harm being caused to others in this type of group. As an aside, I think it is just as important for the Parents' group as the Young People's group.'
> (Chris Bolas, Holes in the Wall, 2016)

There is plenty of anecdotal evidence that parents benefit from being in a group. Once the initial difficulty of feeling exposed and intensely shameful has been overcome, the pluses of finding that you are not alone, of having an instant new network, and of the challenge of others to keep going are immensely powerful. The first documented work in Britain, the PEACE programme (Parents Enjoying A Changing Environment), established in the Wirral, spawned a separate group TULIP (Together United Living In Peace), as the parents continued to meet and support each other longer term. There are many examples of how parents have set up a WhatsApp group to continue to encourage each other after the sessions have finished, or have continued to meet in a less formal way.

On some occasions, the support on offer is *specifically* that of peers. Set up by parents with personal experience of CPVA, or facilitated by an organisation, these networks may or may not follow a set programme, and are usually open-ended. They can provide a brief respite, encouragement and guidance, and even a source of emergency help if needed. They may be connected with a particular issue, such as adoption or substance use, or they may be open to all.

> Adfam is a national UK charity with the aim of *'improving life for families affected by drugs and alcohol'*. They work with families as well as professionals to offer support, and are additionally involved in research and policy change. Adfam offers a directory of over 200 support groups for families dealing with drug or alcohol use, often by young people. Research into these groups (Adfam, 2016), showed how effective they were at supporting parents experiencing violence and abuse. Parents experienced the group as a 'safe space', and one where they would not be judged; *'I just depend on it, it's such a necessary part of my life…it's made me so much stronger. I mean I can't deal with everything, it's impossible, but I feel that much stronger'*.

Some parents did express concern though about confidentiality, or the degree of support they felt was needed, and preferred to receive help on a one-to-one basis. This model of provision makes it easier to tailor the support to each individual situation. Adfam have now developed their support to include a peer-to-peer volunteer service, funded through Comic Relief:

'We believe that the best people to support people affected by CPA are "experts by experience" – those who have experience of the issue themselves. We are therefore training family members with experience of this issue to become peer support volunteers.'
(Adfam, 2016)

#7. What evidence of effectiveness is there?

Desperate people will try anything. The charlatans of this world see them coming, and welcome them with open arms. Parents will spend hours of time or thousands of pounds on the basis of a misplaced trust in a solution for something that seems completely intractable. Many of us would do the same. Similarly there are many, many different therapies on offer these days, from reputable organisations but also from 'someone we've found online'. In times of cost cutting, it may be tempting to offer fewer solutions, whether or not they meet the exact need. It is very right and proper that we should be concerned about evidence of effectiveness for the approaches we use.

The bad news is that much of this work has been running for too short a period to have been rigorously assessed against the most testing of standards. A programme of work approved in one place may not automatically transfer to somewhere else with different cultural expectations, language or life style. If it has been 'tweaked' does that invalidate the assessment? The good news is that almost all the models available have been evaluated in other ways, have accumulated large amounts of material demonstrating a positive impact, and that some have been adopted nationally as models of effective practice. RYPP, Break4Change and Who's in Charge? are all promoted by the Youth Justice Board in England and Wales. I have provided links to material about different programmes in the Appendices at the end of this book.

We see increasing attention on a trauma-informed approach in work with young people, as we become more aware of the impact of early life experiences, and of loss generally. Not all families perhaps will feel that this is relevant, but all can benefit from the 'gentleness' of the approach.

> A number of programmes have interviewed parents and practitioners as part of their evaluation (and promotional) process.
>
> '…This programme is much more reflective and therapeutic. It gives them space and time to take a step back and think for themselves what's going on and how they can change and fix things. Rather than an outside person saying you must do this this and this, and it not necessarily working…
>
> The fact that it is quite different from a lot of programmes and it is more about helping the parent think for themselves rather than saying you're no good at this. It's much more positive and helping them think for themselves.'
> (Who's in Charge? 2018)
>
> 'All of a sudden I was talking to other people that were dealing with the same sort of thing – or worse – and I just thought, oh my god I can get through this. And all of a sudden I had hope. Break4Change gave me hope when I had none.'
> (Parent, Responding to Child to Parent Violence project launch, University of Brighton, 2018)

I am interested that when I have spoken with parents as to what has worked for them, it has not been the programme itself on which they have commented so much as their relationship with the practitioner. Where this has not been good, progress has been difficult. Where it has been positive, it is almost as if anything could have been offered.

'In terms of his relationship with me, that was rebuilt through [CAMHS] *and a lovely lady.'*

What sort of help was she giving you?

It was just … She really had a great relationship with A. I've had other experiences there that weren't so great. It's finding the person.

What was special about her?

We had the family session ….. then she just managed to find within A, she was very focused … they were trying to find out what else was going on.'
(Interview with Stephanie, 2015)

The Children's Social Care Innovation programme in the UK looked at developing, testing and sharing effective ways of supporting children needing help from Children's Social Care. Their evaluation of Step Change (2017), a partnership project working to improve outcomes for children on the edge of care or custody and their families, using functional family therapy or multi-systemic therapy, where 80% of the children referred had displayed aggressive or violent behaviour in the home, showed that what worked was *'the relationship with the therapist, the consistency, accessibility and intensity of the therapy, and the degree to which the therapy was empowering of the families'* (a sense that the therapists were on their side and this was a journey they were on together – done with them rather than to them).

'Where Step Change appeared to work particularly well, therefore, was the ability of therapists to get to know the families well: understand their difficulties, and build trust by consistency of contact, as well as empowering them to develop their own ways of repairing family relationships. This more intensive, personal, independent approach was seen as a useful lever for encouraging the collaboration of families that might have felt let down by services in the past.'
(Department for Education, 2017)

(It should be acknowledged that the period under investigation was relatively short term, and so it is impossible at this stage to comment on long-term improvements.)

When we were discussing, 'what works?' social worker, blogger and campaigner for better support following adoption, Al Coates, remarked, *'Nothing works'*. What he actually meant was that there is no one reliable answer that will work for every family, every time. Even with evidence-based programmes, something might work in one situation but not a different one, on one day but not the next, with one family but not another. It is a view echoed by Jenny Ginger, Partnership Project lead on peer support, with Adoption UK:

'Parents will be disappointed to know that there is no silver bullet to addressing this. When your child is having a meltdown, or is on the rampage, the most important thing in that moment is for people to stay safe.'
(Ginger, 2017)

Something to ponder as we make decisions about the type of work we offer, and the impact we hope to make!

#8. Are there circumstances that make intervention inappropriate or ineffective?

Most agencies or programmes will operate referral criteria, as a way of determining if a family will benefit from the help on offer. These criteria might recognise that a particular offer is better suited to early intervention for instance, or for families in clearly defined circumstances, or that the practitioners have a specific skill set. Other exclusion criteria might typically include the age of the child, the presence of an adult abuser in the home (so if there is ongoing intimate partner violence), if the parents are using physical chastisement with children (the supposition that their choice of punishment might be escalating the violence, and it will be hard to encourage them to look at other means of discipline), if a child is adopted (recognising that bigger issues might be at play beyond the scope of a particular programme), or if there are additional diagnoses for which the team do not feel qualified to offer assistance. Routt and Anderson (2015) suggest that where a parent's own behaviour is contributing to the young person's violence, or where there is parental domestic violence or substance use, it may be important to address these issues first, as they are likely to get in the way of an individual's full participation in the programme.

It is important to be honest about these criteria right from the start, even though it might seem that the very neediest families are those who are being excluded, but by offering something inappropriate we might be adding to the danger. It is disingenuous to suggest that there is only one level of response that will suit all comers, even though we might have hoped this was the case early on. We do need to recognise that some families will be experiencing far greater levels of violence and abuse than others, that some families will put up with certain levels for longer than others before seeing help, or that some children, and their parents, will face a cocktail of circumstances that require the assistance of specialisms beyond the scope of most workers.

This is not the moment to walk away, NFA, assessment completed but no suitable help available. This is the time to dig deep; to work with families to identify specialists in other fields to work on some of the other issues; to ensure safety; to make sure families have access to emergency phone numbers, whether the police, the Samaritans, the out of hours mental health team, or even Uncle Joe up the road.

What about a situation where a parent does not agree with our assessment, maintaining a belief perhaps that the issue is solely with the child and they have no need to change anything themselves? Or they find it too difficult and painful to examine the other issues in the home that may be contributing to a child needing to 'speak so loudly', and so seem uncooperative or disengaged? Another question: how sure are you of your assessment? Does the child indeed have needs which are not being sufficiently met, causing them intense pain, anxiety or anger? Is the parent actually already doing everything humanly possible to manage the situation? Sometimes we just need to be patient, to spend time working on a relationship with all family members, and listening further to their world, and their life. Parents may have many reasons not to trust our judgement. They may have very many reasons not to feel safe. We may need to spend time building confidence, before they can do so. Without this, our intervention may fall at the first hurdle.

#9. What do you do when it all kicks off?

Yet again – it all depends!

Is everyone at home, at the shops, at a party, on public transport? How big is the child? Are there onlookers (who could perhaps be brought in to help)? Does a parent feel supported or judged, calm or panicked, energised or exhausted, safe or at risk? Much as we might want to be able to offer a perfect solution, and certainly much as parents would like us to, this is the moment to be honest. Peter Jakob's wry comment, *'When it all kicks off, it all kicks off,'* is based on many years of work supporting families in this situation.

I have heard suggestions of parents being encouraged to disarm a child. I have read accounts of parents talking a child down and successfully removing a weapon, but the truth is that very few of us have been taught how to do this safely. If a child is coming at you with a knife, the important thing is to prioritise safety, minimise risk, and, if necessary, run away. If the situation looks different to this, then parents will need to be helped to identify solutions that work for them in that moment to ensure safety. It may include engaging others to care for younger children temporarily, or moving everyone to a different room. Parents may have learnt a way themselves to help their child come back to a place of calm. It may mean learning to ignore looks, comments and unhelpful interventions, but the impact of them will add to the exhaustion and trauma already experienced.

One of the fundamental principles of NVR is 'strike while the iron is cold'. The moment of most intense conflict and heightened emotion is not the time to rationalise or remonstrate with a child. When parents feel stronger and able to resist in a non-violent way, the need to control the child is lessened. The parent is able to use their presence later to help move things forward. If everyone is safe and there is no prospect of calm returning imminently, parents of older children may simply remove themselves from a situation and wait for a more appropriate time to address the issues concerned.

> What to do in that situation as you wait for a calmer time?
>
> *'Things I do when it's kicking off and there is nothing I can do:*
> - *make some new experimental weird fermented vegetables*
> - *deep clean the cupboards*
> - *cook dinner*
> - *catch up on emails*
> - *take refuge in twitter*
> - *take the dog for a walk*
> - *shut myself in my bedroom.'*
>
> (Tweet from Mumdrah, @mumdrah, 2017)

#10. What about restraint?

It is probably fair to say that there are few things more contentious than the restraint of children, and yet, at the same time as we have pressure to reduce the use of restraint within the youth justice system and within health and education, we have parents campaigning to be taught how to use it within their own homes. The response to this seems to vary around the country and from agency to agency. Some families report that they have been met with extraordinary understanding and compassion. Others have been told that restraint is inappropriate – but without suggestions of what to do instead. It is a complicated issue, made worse by a lack of clarity about what we are actually talking about.

When we hear the term 'restraint' we may well think of children being held face down, of spit hoods, locked doors, injury and even death. There are certainly reports in the media that emphasise this understanding. The word has overtones of control, and coercion, and we picture perhaps several large adults using force to contain a much smaller child. The term is sometimes also used in discussions of discredited practices such as 'Rebirthing' or 'Holding therapy'. It is understandable that, as practitioners, we might feel very ambivalent or hostile to the use and promotion of restraint within the home if this is what we understand. But whether we like it or not, where children are considered to be out of control and posing a danger to themselves or others, it is certainly happening on a regular basis in many settings.

> Annual statistics published by the Youth Justice Board and Ministry of Justice (2018) show that in 2016/17 there were a total of 4,527 incidents of physical restraint – compared with 4,315 in 2015/16 – a rise of 4.9 percent. The 2016/17 figure equates to a restraint rate of 32.1 per 100 young people held in custody – the highest figure on record. The statistics show that 100 young people required medical treatment after being restrained. Eight were so badly injured that they needed to be taken to hospital for treatment, while 92 were treated on site for 'minor' injuries. This despite a drop in the number of children entering youth custody.
>
> An investigation by BBC Five Live (2017) found there had been more than 13,000 incidents of restraint in special schools in last three years, involving 731 recorded injuries.
>
> Campaigners have brought to wider attention the number of young people with learning difficulties, whose original escalating challenging behaviour, in the absence of any support, made it difficult for them to remain at home; but who are now held in seclusion in residential settings for months or even years, because of ineffective and inappropriate alternative methods of behaviour management.

Where people work with young people, whether in the secure estate, in education, health, or within foster care, guidance is issued regarding the use of restraint, including the fact that it should only be used as a measure of last resort. We may believe very strongly that restraint is used inappropriately on many occasions in these settings; and where different models of care and management, such as positive behaviour support, are put in place, the need to restrain young people can decline dramatically, suggesting that this is not simply about children being dangerously out of control. Children have attested to the fear and pain experienced, as well as the physical injuries incurred through being held at school or in other settings, when no other measures were available to staff.

Within family life, we would undoubtedly want to support parents to maintain a safe and healthy home life, to enable children to understand their feelings, to help them regulate their emotions and behaviour; and this should always be the first intention. But we also know, from listening to parents, that there are many situations when a child suddenly 'explodes' with pain, or anxiety, or rage, and there is no time for a carefully staged intervention. Or a brooding mood reaches a point where it boils over; or a much larger teen approaches with a knife. What then? What is a parent supposed to do in that moment, to keep everyone safe?

Let's deal with the knife question first. I think there are very few people who would recommend any response other than removing yourself – and others – from the immediate situation. Some parents may feel confident to talk their own child down. A child threatening to use a knife to harm *themselves*, or a sibling, may need a different response, which will vary according to age, place, other people, or degree of risk. Within Britain firearms are not easily available to most children, and so the risks are different to those experienced by families in other countries. I am not qualified to comment on the use of guns.

What if a child is throwing furniture at you, or hurling a television across the room? Do you just duck and dodge? Do you wait for it all to calm down and risk the total destruction of the home? What if a child is smashing all the windows in the house with a baseball bat – with bare feet? Or what if they are punching, kicking and biting you, adding insult to the injuries you suffered earlier in the week? What if they are distressed and disturbed in their bedroom, slamming cupboard doors, and working themselves into a frenzy? At what point, and how, would we want or expect an individual to intervene to keep themselves and others safe, and to protect property? Most parents will not be standing by, waiting for policy and guidance to be written covering these situations. They will have cobbled together their own responses based on knowledge of their particular child, their background and training, their instincts and need to survive. It may, in fact be working quite well.

'I used to hold Josh because he would flip his lid and attack me, just doing what any parent would. Eventually he'd calm down. That's how it started. When I went to school and said I need to be taught how to hold him safely, nobody would. I've only done what comes naturally as a parent.'
(Interview with Rachel)

For other parents though, the anxiety and fear of causing more harm through restraining their child, or of the legal consequences of doing so, may mean they hold back and seek professional guidance. And of course there are times when the tried and tested methods may cease to work as a child gets bigger. What then?

What are we actually talking about in these situations? What do we mean here by restraint? In 2017, adoption charity The Open Nest and SecuriCare organised a national survey of adoptive parents about their experience of the need for restraint and training. *'The findings from this survey revealed that physical restraint was very much a lived reality for a significant majority of the parents who participated. There was a sense that "Restraint wasn't a choice", it was a necessity'*. It was also a significant ethical issue for many parents – they didn't want to have to do it.

In the final report (Hollins, 2017) the definition of restraint being used is made clear: *'Just enough intervention to ameliorate immediate harm, done in a way that communicates love and empathy and one that is never a replacement for striving to provide the sort of support that helps a child regulate themselves and go on to reach their full potential'*. The restraint advocated here is generally about a safe way for one or two people to hold a young person, in a way previously agreed with the child themselves, adapted to the individual's needs, and until they feel safe to be released.

'We need to be really clear on this. We are not advocating therapeutic holding but safe physical intervention in a safeguarding crisis. We are talking about training to react calmly, sensitively and confidently in the presence of extreme violence so that parents can effectively manage safeguarding within their homes.'
(Boorman, 2016a)

Securicare, and other similar organisations, offer training to parents in this manner of safe holding. A full history is taken and a plan devised with all concerned, tailored to the individual needs and reviewed over time. The hold remains a matter of last resort, after other methods of de-escalation have been tried. This sort of holding feels less problematic if it can be made to work!

Young people themselves, as well as their parents, have attested to the importance of being helped to regain calm and composure through being held in an appropriate way.

> 'In our case it was a hold that is standing and using core body strength not aggression. It is safe and kind and involves verbal reassurance to the child throughout. My daughter was involved in conversations about why we were learning, what would happen during a hold and the end goal of safety for all. She was so relieved. Finally somebody had taken control of her safety. Our lives were changed immeasurably from that point.'
> (Boorman, 2016b)
>
> 'I have bursts of betting them up ad calling them hobble names ad when they do the safe hold I like it because I no thear thear ad I'm safe but I can get quite a gresive but I no its all going to be ok and now we don't have to do the safe hold much.'
>
> [I have bursts of beating them up and calling them horrible names, and when they do the safe hold I like it because I know they're there and I'm safe, but I can get quite aggressive. But I know it's all going to be OK, and now we don't have to do the safe hold much.]'
> All Aboard the Trauma Train, 2015)

> 'You can actually feel him. When you've got him like that. And you've cocooned him you can feel him starting to melt. You can feel the relaxation in him. It must be like "I can calm down now".'
> (Interview with Rachel)
>
> And from an adult with a diagnosis of foetal alcohol spectrum disorder (FASD)
> 'Sometimes he has to just hold me down and use extended breathing techniques and calmly stroke my hair and tell me I am loving and loved, all is well and I am safe in a soothing voice over and over again while I kick and scream and cry until I am exhausted and its all gone and I've let go of my fear, urgency and panic.'
> (Pietrantonio, 2017)

Parents who are not given advice on safe ways to help their children are perhaps more likely to adopt inappropriate methods. One example might be a family who employed security guards to intervene every time their child started to escalate their behaviour. In fact, their very presence made the situation more risky and when they were removed and more thoughtful and understanding interventions were initiated, it was possible to work with everyone to bring about change. Alternatively, without any support, patterns of behaviour simply become entrenched so that an out of control seven year old grows into a hurting and dangerous fourteen year old. Hurt children hurt others, is one maxim, and it is one that we see played out regularly. When we understand a child's so called 'out of control' behaviour as a response to hurt, then we owe it to all concerned to help bring about an increased level of safety in which a family can be supported to heal.

I have heard the argument that children and young people who have been subject to violent restraint in the past – as young children – should not be held in this way because of the risk of re-traumatising them. This seems to have merit, but we must acknowledge that none of us lives in complete isolation, and the danger posed by not intervening may well traumatise others. It is also argued that it is of positive value for young people to know and experience that their anger can be contained.

The bottom line will always be that restraint is a last resort, as a part of a specific management plan, and once all other approaches to managing behaviour have been exhausted. Hopefully, the need for restraint will diminish or cease over time. However, not intervening gives messages to a child or young person that we might want to avoid: 'We feel powerless, we don't care about the hurt you are doing to yourself and others, we are afraid of you, we don't care about the hurt you feel'.

'First ever successful strong hold (or whatever it's called) today. It worked. Still breaking stuff now but less like "a thing possessed".'
(Tweet from Mumdrah, @mumdrah, 2017)

#11. Should you call the police?

Calling the police may seem to be the most obvious thing to do, or it may be the very thing a parent would never dream of doing, depending on how long the abuse has been going on, how serious it is, how you understand it, previous experience of the police, what they hope to achieve, or what friends and family think and recommend. All families are different. All police officers are different too!

While some parents would wish to use the police as a form of discipline and punishment, or to make clear that there are consequences to certain actions for a child over whom they no longer have any residual authority: a look at the cells, a taste of the hand cuffs, a sharp warning; many parents are understandably reluctant to do anything that might involve criminalising their children, fearing the immediate as well as the long-term consequences. Will the child be taken away? Will they get a criminal record? Will it affect their future life chances? Will they be even more aggressive when they return home?

I have read some pretty hideous stories myself – and spoken with the parents concerned – about a situation being made worse by clumsy, ill-informed police action (and indeed that of other professionals), which has had the effect of further angering or empowering a young person. *'Don't do it again, or we'll come out and tell you not to do it again'* was how one police officer summed up the limit of their powers when I was first looking into how parents could access help.

'They [the police] were very trying. That was the first violent altercation that I had. When I confiscated her phone she fought me. "Give me back my phone." She lunged at me and tackled me down to the ground to the point where my son called the police … It was only the police when they arrived took her off me … I couldn't believe it … Oh, my gosh! Is this really happening? The police were nice enough, but they were like, "Oh, give it a couple of weeks and you'll be best friends again." OK! So there was no input. It was just like …'
(Interview with Demetria, 2018)

I draw comfort from the fact that most of these stories are now several years old, that there is now greater awareness of CPVA among police forces (as among all professionals). Recently an adopter tweeted *'Once again police were kind & helpful … Police said our types of calls are common.'* (Hushabye Mountain, @Tobetherefor,

2018). Awareness is not the same as substantive intervention of course, but training in child to parent violence and abuse is now more commonplace within police forces in Britain and policies are being drawn up.

Detective Superintendent Simon Retford became aware of child to parent violence in his work and went on to study for a Masters and Professional Doctorate, looking at responses to child to parent violence in the Greater Manchester area. His work has been published (cited elsewhere in this book), and has helped to contribute to the growing understanding and improved response.

In addition there are examples of imaginative proactive work taking place by the police around the country.

> A family moved to a new area and sought out the community police officers with the explicit purpose of alerting them to their complex home situation, should they need to call for help in an emergency. The local officers went out of their way to befriend all the members of the family, calling in regularly, playing games with the children; all the while keeping an eye on levels of tension and offering comments and guidance to both parents and young people, and making it clear that certain behaviours were unacceptable. The friendships forged, and the heightened awareness of the whole situation, meant that when things did kick off the police were able to respond more sensitively and their intervention was met with greater respect by the young person concerned.

There have been particular concerns about young people in residential care being criminalised at unacceptable rates. Residential workers may regularly face aggressive and abusive behaviour from children in their care. The Howard League (2017) report that children aged sixteen and seventeen years old living in children's homes are 15 times more likely to be criminalised than others of the same age, with police sometimes being called for relatively minor incidents that it was felt staff should have been able to deal with. Others suggest that this is not necessarily a deliberate, explicit policy, but actually about staffing levels, about training, about understanding young people's needs and about flexibility in responding to situations; with good practice also highlighted on many occasions. In his review of residential care in England, Sir Martin Narey (2016) writes,

'While I believe that most homes are slow formally to involve the police in responding to poor behaviour sometimes, for example, when a child has been seriously violent toward another child or member of staff, managers will conclude that they have little choice other than to seek police help. The key then must be to

ensure that, unless the child's behaviour has been so serious that no course other than prosecution or other formal action is appropriate, that the police deal with the behaviour informally.'

Reassuringly, we see increasing moves towards diversion from the youth justice system where this is possible, whether in formal structures such as the Step-Up programme developed in Seattle for exactly this purpose, or through the individual work of officers, in offering warnings and more restorative approaches to young people and their families.

Police data shows us that parents *do* call the police about the actions of their young people, whether in damage to property, or assaults on an individual; and we see the beginnings of better systems of logging CPVA as a unique issue. Broader understanding suggests that by the time parents call the police, matters will have reached an extreme level whether in terms of the risks to the parents or the young person. The police have particular powers which mean they may well be the most appropriate people to be involved at a moment in time, for instance if a young person has gone missing or is at risk from other people in the community. But, as with all such instances of CPVA, their involvement should be as part of a collaborative, multi-agency response, with shared understanding and shared goals.

Should you call the cops? When people ask me that question I make it clear that that will always have to be their own decision. But that there are right and proper times for seeking such help. If a parent fears for their life, or the life of a member of their family, and there is no one else they can call in that moment, then there should be no hesitation.

#12. What happens when a child can no longer live at home?

There are a raft of reasons why it may no longer be safe for a young person to remain at home. The levels of violence may have reached an unpredictability level, or a point at which, despite support from practitioners and friends, and all the safety measures of locks, cameras and even dogs, safety cannot be guaranteed. It is possible that adopted siblings should never have been placed together because of their severe and competing needs, and one will need to be found a new home before anyone can be safe. Some children's trauma experience is so great that it seems they cannot cope with the structure and demands of a normal family. Such a decision is hard to reach, and parents may be overcome with guilt at the loss for all concerned.

> 'Mary isn't home. My little girl is flourishing in her residential therapeutic school. I am so glad she is making progress. I am also so heartsick that she couldn't get better here in our home. It shouldn't matter as long as she is healing, but somehow it still matters to me. I am grateful but I am also resentful. It isn't as if they are doing anything different than we ever did. It isn't as if they are even using a different treatment model. It's literally the same language, same sensory tools, and the same coping strategies. It's just that when she's removed from the pressure of a family structure, Mary is able to respond to treatment.'
> (Herding Chickens, 2018)

It could be that the level of trauma, mental illness or special needs are so great that no family could be expected to support a child alone and in their own home. It might be that a parent's own needs are too great to allow them to support a child and cope with the levels of aggression. A child may choose themselves to leave, or they may have become vulnerable to exploitation in the community and need to leave for their own safety. A parent may simply have had enough and sees no future without a substantial change in circumstances.

Often, families will find their own solutions. A child might be sent to live with grandparents, aunts and uncles, or an absent parent. This may work for a while, or that too may break down eventually. A young person from an immigrant family may be sent 'back home'. An older child may be moved into a flat, end up sofa-surfing, or may take themselves to a girlfriend's or boyfriend's family home. If there are issues around schooling, some families find the respite of residential school can help them remain together, but other young people may end up in the secure estate or hospital, within residential or foster care, hopefully with a therapeutic component to their ongoing care.

With a focus on a child's place within a family as the preferred option, we need to be sure that sufficient support is going to families to keep them together if that is a safe option; and equally, where a child has left home, we should not be rushing to return them without being sure that there are steps in place to help decrease the levels of violence and abuse. We have already heard from Sandi about the work she undertook to support families with young people 'on the edge of care' where there were high levels of violence.

> *'The youngest case I had, a girl, was nine years old, very, very angry. Mum had five kids. It was a real struggle for her but she was desperate to keep her child but she was getting to that point where she thought, I don't know if I can, I don't know if I can keep her safe … One day with her I was doing a home visit, and I witnessed it and it was horrible. It was, you saw this mum … was taking it all upon herself and really felt she was to blame and she didn't know what to do. But she had these two babies … and then her teenage daughter and a little boy as well, and she was just screaming at Mum, throwing stuff at her, throwing herself on the floor, just crying, it was so desperate. And you saw Mum, "I don't know what to do," She kept looking at me. "I don't know what to do" … She was just so devastated by that disconnect she had with her child, and that desperation to both love her and want her and keep her, but knowing her need to look after the other ones too … She looked at me with desperation and was like, "What am I going to do?" Care, for her, was the only alternative. Luckily we didn't get to that stage. We did more work, as much as we could.'*
> (Interview with Sandi, 2018)

Respite care was once an option that many people now say is harder to access because of budget cuts. Yet if this can give families breathing space, and maintain a family together, the much greater costs further down the line are potentially avoided. Kinship carers have stated clearly their hope that respite care might be an option for families who have stepped up to the plate in an emergency, and have often placed their own hopes and dreams very much on hold, as their lives take an unexpected turn. It should not be solely about cost, of course. Much better to understand the value of maintaining family coherence, where this is possible.

Parenting at a distance

And when a child is removed, what is our expectation of continuing family involvement? There will be some parents who have been counting the days until this moment, who feel so ill-treated that they see no other option, and wish for no further contact. But it may come as a surprise to hear that for many families, while trust and safety have broken down, the bond of love continues as strongly as ever; with a continuing hope and expectation of involvement in a young person's life, and, if possible, their eventual return home. Families may need help and support still, to reflect on their own loss, and the needs of other members, as well as preparing for a future reconciliation if possible.

'Please do not believe that all children in the care system have no loving families that care about them when many do. We can battle in vain for years for our children to get the help they need, in a system that stigmatises and shames us.

Having to make the decision that we cannot safely look after our children is heart wrenching and we need support more than ever in this scenario if we are to survive as families and help our children navigate through life after children's services have long gone.'
(Schroer, 2018)

#13. Where can I find resources to use?

You will be relieved to hear that there is no need to reinvent the wheel. And with the wonders of the internet, many resources are relatively easy to find and free to download. You can find manuals for particular programmes, guidance in specific approaches, and libraries of books with printable resources.

Do you know what you are looking for?

If you have a specific programme in mind, it might be possible to find the materials somewhere yourself, or you may need to sign up for a facilitator training package which includes manuals, licences, and perhaps supervision. Some programmes insist on fidelity, in order to use the name. There are others that can be adapted by you to fit local situations, and cultures. I have listed a number of programmes, with details of how to obtain materials etc, in the Appendices. Holt (2016) introduces a number of approaches and programmes in her book, and so if you are not sure where to start, this might be an interesting place. It's worth speaking to someone else already using a programme if you can, to hear from them what works and what might need some adaptation. Use the online map (https://holesinthewall.co.uk/resources/directory/) to identify someone appropriate.

If you are looking for specific forms or documents, these too can generally be found easily. Suggestions for assessment documents are to be found at the end of the assessment chapter (Chapter 11). Templates for safety plans, for instance, can also be found via a number of websites, with some suggestions listed at the end of this chapter. The Duluth wheels, as adapted for use with young people using CPVA, are introduced and discussed by Routt and Anderson (2015) and are also available online. These are particularly useful for 'check-in' at the start of a session, or to compare the experiences of parent and child as they reflect on the past week. Scaling forms and questionnaires about thoughts, feelings and behaviour could be used in a similar way. There are vast numbers of books offering worksheets for a range of ages on feelings, anger, safety etc.

Work with particular groups of young people

If you are involved with a family where there are specific additional issues then it is wise to explore materials that will be more relevant in this area of work, as you will almost certainly find that there are additional things you can use, or to take into account. Whether this is work around addiction, adoption, loss and trauma, or special needs – or any number of other things, there will be plenty to think about. Some of these factors may radically alter the approach you take, and so it is important to be up to speed. Organisations such as Beacon House, in Britain, have a wealth of resources to help practitioners understand trauma and design their work accordingly. Google the issue, contact specialist organisations, search publisher's lists, speak to families to learn directly from them what works. Think too about linking families up with specialist websites, phone lines, online communities, and peer support meetings.

When you have finished looking up everything else, your most valuable tool will remain yourself: your openness, your empathy, honesty, reliability – humour even – and your curiosity. You need to get this right first, and the rest can then follow!

#14. What are the costs involved?

You may need to provide costings before a new piece of work can be agreed. Though these will inevitably be somewhat speculative, there are examples drawn up which compare the lifetime costs of not intervening for children exhibiting the behaviours we often find in this group, with the actual budget for running the work over a set period of time. The RCPV project demonstrated the financial costs and savings of specialised CPVA programmes in their final report (Wilcox & Pooley, 2015). Over a six month period, they calculated a total saving of €195,362 through provision of the Break4Change programme. You will find a full breakdown in the report. More recently, Thorley and Coates (2018) have attempted to calculate the overall costs to families, as well as the state, of living with CPVA. They suggest that any figures need to also include an acknowledgement that many parents will find themselves unable to work, falling back on the benefits system at an additional cost to society.

#15. How do people fund the work?

One person I know facilitates Who's in Charge? groups as part of her job description. She and a colleague have time factored into their workload for this – but that's all. She has to beg and borrow any other resources she needs, including space to meet and refreshments. But, as she says, *'Once they know I can do it, why would they fund me more?'*.

Other people spend an inordinate amount of time applying for grants, often for their own salaries, as well as all the other costs of running an office, meeting with families, attending meetings, providing reports – and then more reports to funders to justify the money taken.

Most people are probably somewhere in the middle: part funded by their employer, with management applying for specific grants to support expansion or test out innovative ways of working. If the work is recognised as important then there will be a time allowance or a protected caseload.

In terms of funding, things to think about particularly include the training of facilitators. It might appear sensible to offer blanket training, skilling up a large part of the workforce to recognise and respond to CPVA whenever they meet it. In some agencies this would enable quick recognition, a promising first response, and then more in-depth support as necessary. However, where training has been offered in a particular programme, but without the space allowed to run the programme itself, practitioners have reported that they lost confidence over time, and this then becomes a particularly costly exercise with little reward. Furthermore, within some agencies, practitioners might find that their time is not protected, and they are 'whisked away' for statutory tasks in an emergency, making it difficult to commit to regular availability. With such considerations, there may be a reliance on sessional workers to deliver the programme as the preferred option.

So long as work specifically targeting CPVA is seen as new, and not part of a core offer, it remains vulnerable to budget cuts. Sadly we see new work springing up, only to fold as the funding stream dries up; or pilot projects proving successful, but without sustainable means and commitment. We can only hope that greater awareness of the wider issues will lead to an understanding of the ubiquitous nature of CPVA, and the benefits of a more sustained response.

We have neglected one big question: is this a child protection issue?

I will be looking more at this in the next chapter. Suffice it to say here, that there may well be clear child protection elements involved, with, at the very least a commitment to resources and regular review.

I will conclude with some things to think about as you contemplate the way forward, but first some comments from parents about things that they believe have made a real difference to them and their families.

'Professionals prepared to listen, accept it happens and being empathetic would be a good start.'
(CPVA survey, 2016)

'I feel much more supported now that I have a GP who wants to listen and understand without judgment.'
(Imperfectlyperfectmother blog, 2018a)

'I really dislike this need to find strategies for me. For full disclosure it makes me upset. It has connotations that suggest that it is my parenting which requires fixing. The way I parent small person therapeutically works. For them. For me. For therapy … There are not magic strategies here, if there were someone would have thought of them already … This morning I talked to a lovely friend who asked the right question: what do you need to keep going?'
(Imperfectlyperfectmother blog, 2018b)

Things to think about

- What help did the family ask for? Can you deliver this, or something similar?
- What does this family need to keep going?
- Is this family safe?
- How will you build a relationship to facilitate the work?
- Do you understand all the issues involved?
- Can you refer to specialist organisations for support for any of these issues?
- If you are planning to offer a specific programme, have you received the appropriate training?
- Does the child or young person have specific needs which make it difficult for them to access a 'regular' programme of help?
- Have you done your homework? Has this family already attended a similar course to the one you are suggesting?
- If you've tried something and it isn't making a difference, what else can you try?
- What other expertise can you make use of locally?

Find out more

Further discussion about gender issues in group work can be found in the chapter by **Howard J and Holt A** (2016) Special considerations when working with adolescent family violence. In A Holt (Ed.) W*orking with Adolescent to Violence and Abuse to Parents*. Oxford: Routledge.

Information about the **Mapping Project** can be found on the Directory page (under Resources) at: Holesinthewall.co.uk.

Kate Iwi talks about restorative elements of work, including the use of video in this video *Innovative Restorative Justice in Practice* (2014): https://www.youtube.com/watch?v=oeqtPBpF3l0.

More about the **PEACE programme** here:

- *Model Students Perpetrating Abuse* (2013) Holes in the Wall: https://wp.me/p1sWM6-mi.
- and here: *Parents Face their Violent Children* (2003): http://news.bbc.co.uk/1/hi/england/2824537.stm

Members of the Adoption community in Britain contributed their ideas of 'what works' to the magazine **Adoption Today**: *Aggressive Behaviours, You Tell us What Works*, August 2017, followed up by a special edition in October 2017: *Trauma-fuelled Violence*.

The 2017 report by the **HM Inspectorate of Probation** into the work of youth offending teams comments specifically on the value of a trauma-informed approach: https://www.justiceinspectorates.gov.uk/hmiprobation/wp-content/uploads/sites/5/2017/10/The-Work-of-Youth-Offending-Teams-to-Protect-the-Public_reportfinal.pdf

Jack Brookes blogs at Lost in Care (https://lostincare.co.uk). He grew up in care and has since worked as a residential care worker, training foster carers and residential workers, and as a child therapist. His posts are interesting and informative from his unique perspective of the experience of violence, and the response of staff and police.
A particular blog about having to restrain a young man in a residential care setting: *Violence, Boundaries, Control and Physical Intervention* (2014): http://lostincare.co.uk/2014/05/25/violence-boundaries-control-and-physical-intervention/.

More about restraint
All Aboard the Trauma Train, two posts from 2016, Support for Violent Children, what next? Parts 1 and 2 https://allaboardthetraumatrain.com/2016/12/04/support-for-violent-children-what-next/ and

https://allaboardthetraumatrain.com/2016/12/04/support-for-violent-children-what-next-part-two/.

CoramBAAF and NAFP Practice (2017) *Note 63, Restraint and Physical Intervention in Foster Care*. Published by CoramBAAF.

BBC News (2018) *Placement of Children with SEN in Seclusion*: https://www.bbc.co.uk/news/uk-wales-45489464?fbclid=IwAR1XwxdkhgeY82CqJvsZIKfVT0GbtzQu5lXgwaioRs-mRh1o3jOW2YBsudw.

NICE Guidance (2015) *Challenging Behaviour and Learning Disabilities: Prevention and interventions for people with learning disabilities whose behaviour challenges* (NG11): https://www.nice.org.uk/guidance/ng11.

See a blog by **Al Coates** for what it can feel like as a parent when 'it all kicks off' in public: *Understanding, Misadventures of an Adoptive Dad*: http://www.alcoates.co.uk/2018/07/understanding.html.

Many specialist organisations with a web presence offer advice, leaflets and links to other supportive agencies. Some also have confidential helplines:

- **Adoption UK:** https://www.adoptionuk.org
- **PAC UK:** https://www.pac-uk.org
- **Adfam:** https://adfam.org.uk
- **YoungMinds:** https://youngminds.org.uk
- **Family Lives:** https://www.familylives.org.uk
- **Autism Awareness:** https://autismawareness.com/about/

The Home Office issued a guidance document in 2015, *Information Guide: Adolescent to parent violence and abuse (APVA)*, with advice on responding to cases for those working in healthcare, education, social care, housing, the police and youth justice: https://assets.publishing.service.gov.uk/government/uploads/system/uploads/attachment_data/file/418400/Final-APVA.pdf.

Individual authorities have also begun to issue guidance documents relevant to their own area, for instance:

- **Leicestershire and Rutland**: http://lrsb.org.uk/lmagrda-child-parent-abuse. Leicestershire also have a child on parent abuse (COPA) 'first aid kit', available on their website: http://lrsb.org.uk/search?query=COPA.
- Some authorities have information booklets for parents, for instance **Kent**: *Adolescent Violence to Parents, A resource booklet for parents and carers*: http://www.domesticabuseservices.org.uk/Adolescent%20violence%20to%20parents%20Feb%202016-1.pdf.

Evidence-based practice
Community Care (2018) *What is the Place and Meaning of 'Evidence-based Practice' in Real World Social Work?*
https://www.communitycare.co.uk/2018/10/26/place-meaning-evidence-based-practice-real-world-social-work/.

If you haven't already done so, take a look at **The Family Rights Group** *Mutual Expectations Charter*, for a way forward in developing more helpful relationships: https://www.frg.org.uk/images/YFYV/Mutual-Expectations---Parents-Charter.pdf.

NSPCC (2016) *Evaluation of the Domestic Abuse, Recovering Together (DART) Service*: https://library.nspcc.org.uk/HeritageScripts/Hapi.dll/search2?searchTerm0=C6566

Step-Up Curriculum available at: https://www.kingcounty.gov/courts/superior-court/juvenile/step-up/curriculum.aspx.

A Safety Plan template is available as part of the **Step Up** programme: https://www.kingcounty.gov/courts/superior-court/juvenile/step-up/what-to-do/safetyplan.aspx.

Chapter 7 in **Routt and Anderson**, is all about ensuring safety; Adolescent Violence in the Home (2015) Oxford: Routledge.

There are links to documents, PowerPoint slides, tips and checklists for work with young people on the **Uniting Kildonan** website, as part of a forum with Lily Anderson (2017): https://www.unitingkildonan.org.au/programs-and-services/child-youth-and-family-support/family-violence/adolescent-violence/forum-lily-anderson/.

Nowakowski-Sims E and Rowe A (2015) Using Trauma Informed Treatment Models with Child-to-Parent Violence. *Journal of Child and Adolescent Trauma* **8** 237–244.

Eva Nowakowski-Sims and Amanda Rowe discuss the value of a trauma-informed approach to work with families experiencing child to parent violence, and the importance of looking at the 'correlates of such violence', rather than starting from a conceptualisation that the CPVA dynamic mirrors IPV

More about costing
Early Intervention Foundation (2016) *The Cost of Late Intervention: EIF analysis 2016*: http://www.eif.org.uk/publication/the-cost-of-late-intervention-eif-analysis-2016/.

Khan L, Parsonage M & Stubbs J (2015) *Investing in Children's Mental Health: A review of evidence on the costs and benefits of increased service provision*. Centre for Mental Health: https://www.scie-socialcareonline.org.uk/investing-in-childrens-mental-health-a-review-of-evidence-on-the-costs-and-benefits-of-increased-service-provision/r/a11G0000009JpW1IAK.

Marczak M (2018) A video from an ACAMH conference; *The Costs of Conduct Disorder and Evidence for Parenting Interventions*: https://www.acamh.org/freeview/conduct-disorder-conference/

More about parenting at a distance
The POTATO group website: https://thepotatogroup.org.uk and **Special Guardians and Adopters Together** website: https://specialguardiansandadopterstogether.com.

References

Adfam (2016) *Child to Parent Violence: Project consultation and background* [online]. Available at: https://www.adfam.org.uk/files/docs/CPV_background_and_consultation.pdf (accessed February 2019).

All Aboard the Trauma Train (2015) *The Teenager Who Felt Nothing but Scared* [online]. Available at: https://allaboardthetraumatrain.com/2015/03/08/the-teenager-who-felt-nothing-but-scared/ (accessed February 2019).

Allen B (2012) *The Legal Framework for Restraint*. STEAMING.
(Includes on a helpful 'script' to be used to explain to children why restraint is used page 44.)

BBC Five Live (2017) *Investigates: Restraint in special schools*, Presented by Adnan Goldberg. Available as a podcast: https://www.bbc.co.uk/programmes/b08ljdhy (accessed February 2019).

Boorman A (2016a) *Support for Violent Children: What next (part two)* [online]. All Aboard the Trauma Train. Available at: https://allaboardthetraumatrain.com/2016/12/04/support-for-violent-children-what-next-part-two/ (accessed February 2019).

Boorman A (2016b) *Support for Violent Children: What next (part one)* [online]. All Aboard the Trauma Train. Available at: https://allaboardthetraumatrain.com/2016/12/04/support-for-violent-children-what-next/ (accessed February 2019).

Department for Education (2017) *Step Change: An evaluation* [online]. Available at: https://assets.publishing.service.gov.uk/government/uploads/system/uploads/attachment_data/file/585194/Step_Change_an_evaluation.pdf (accessed February 2019).

Gallagher E (2018a) *Who's in Charge? Why children abuse parents and what you can do about it*. London: Austin Macauley Publishers.

Gallagher E (2018b) *Who's in Charge?* [online]. Available at: https://vimeo.com/194021479 (accessed February 2019).

Ginger J (2017) *Peer-to-peer Support for Violent and Aggressive Behaviours* [online]. Adoption Today: Trauma fuelled violence. Available at: https://www.buddies4fc.org.uk/app/download/13957739/Adoption+Today.pdf (accessed February 2019).

Herding Chickens (2018) *When the Chickens Don't Come Home to Roost* [online]. Available at: https://heardingchickens.wordpress.com/2018/10/16/when-the-chickens-dont-come-home-to-roost/ (accessed February 2019).

Holes in the Wall (2016) *Parent Abuse: Gender issues in group work* [online]. Available at: https://wp.me/p1sWM6-NR (accessed February 2019).

Hollins L (2017) *The Reality of Physical Restraint: An online survey for adoptive parents "a cry for help"* [online]. Available at Holes in the Wall: https://helenbonnick.files.wordpress.com/2017/04/the_reality_of_restraint_for_adoptive_parents_2017_final.pdf (accessed February 2019).

Howard J (2017) *Restorative Justice and Family Violence* [online]. Available at: https://www.linkedin.com/pulse/restorative-justice-family-violence-jo-howard/ (accessed February 2019).

Hyslop IK (2016) Where to social work in a brave new neoliberal Aotearoa. *Aotearoa New Zealand Social Work* **28** (1) 5–12.

Imperfectlyperfectmother (2018a) *Support* [online]. Available at: https://imperfectlyperfectmother.wordpress.com/2018/10/23/support/ (accessed February 2019).

Imperfectlyperfectmother (2018b) *What Do you Actually Need?* [online]. Available at: https://imperfectlyperfectmother.wordpress.com/2018/02/09/what-do-you-actually-need/ (accessed February 2019).

Knost LR (2013) *Whispers Through Time: Communication through the ages and stages of childhood*. Little Hearts Books.

Narey M (2016) *Residential Care in England: Report of Sir Martin Narey's independent review of children's residential care* [online]. Available at: https://www.gov.uk/government/uploads/system/uploads/attachment_data/file/534560/Residential-Care-in-England-Sir-Martin-Narey-July-2016.pdf (accessed February 2019).

Pereira R (2016) Responding to filio-parental violence. In: A Holt (Ed.) *Working with Adolescent Violence and Abuse towards Parents*. Oxford: Routledge.

Pietrantonio S (2017) *Let's Understand the #FASD Meltdown – 8 Reasons and How to Help Us* [online]. FASD with Hope. Available at: https://jodeekulp.wordpress.com/2017/11/14/8-reasons-for-fasd-meltdowns/ (accessed February 2019).

Price J (1996) *Power and Compassion, Working with Difficult Adolescents and Abused Parents*. New York: The Guilford Press.

Routt and Anderson (2015) *Adolescent Violence in the Home*. Oxford: Routledge (see p.91 for Duluth abuse and respect wheels).

Royal Commission into Family Violence (2016) *Summary and Recommendations* [online]. Available at: http://files.rcfv.com.au/Reports/Final/RCFV-All-Volumes.pdf (accessed February 2019).

Schroer S (2018) *Superkids with Superadoptive parents and Superspecial guardians* [online]. Special Guardians and Adopters Together. Available at: https://specialguardiansandadopterstogether.com/superkids-with-superadoptive-parents-superspecial-guardians/ (accessed February 2019).

The Howard League (2017) *Ending the Criminalisation of Children in Residential Care, Briefing Two: Best practice in policing* [online]. Available at: https://howardleague.org/wp-content/uploads/2017/12/Ending-the-criminalisation-of-children-in-residential-care-Briefing-two.pdf (accessed February 2019).

Thorley W and Coates A (2018) *Let's Talk About: Child-parent violence and aggression (CPVA)* [online]. Extended summary. Available at: https://www.academia.edu/37078253/Lets_Talk_About_Child_to_Parent_Violence_2018_Summary (accessed February 2019).

University of Brighton (2018) *Responding to Child to Parent Violence Project Launch* [online]. Available at: https://www.youtube.com/watch?time_continue=4287&v=j_38E0dcMiE (accessed February 2019).

Wilcox P and Pooley M (2015) *Responding to Child to Parent Violence: Executive summary* [online]. Available at: http://www.rcpv.eu/78-rcpv-executive-summary-may-2015-english/file (accessed February 2019).

Youth Justice Board and Ministry of Justice (2018) *Youth Justice Statistics 2016/17 England and Wales* [online]. Available at: https://assets.publishing.service.gov.uk/government/uploads/system/uploads/attachment_data/file/676072/youth_justice_statistics_2016-17.pdf (accessed February 2019).

Part 4:
Two conflicting paradigms

Chapter 13: Two conflicting paradigms

We are used, in the western world at least, to thinking and talking in terms of binary opposites: good or bad, winners or losers, victim or perpetrator. We see it in the fiercely adversarial nature of our politics, in the tribal approach to sport, even in our approach to diet: 'naughty or nice' – and of course Santa's list! The implication is that the two are poles apart and incompatible with each other. It has become a practice that is replicated every day within the social care system. First, within Britain, we divide between children and adults, with different staffing budgets, different training expectations, different emphases and priorities. You are one, or you are the other. We work with one, or the other.

When we start to look at approaches to practice, we again see fiercely contested territories. A struggle between a zero-tolerance attitude and a trauma-informed approach, as regards discipline and behaviour management in schools, is mirrored in the youth justice and the prison service: welfare or punishment, care or control. Two approaches, two distinct philosophies, two sets of adherents who believe passionately in their own data and evidence. Over the years we have swung from one to the other, as different political opinions gain ground, as budgetary constraints impact on delivery, as new learning and emerging scientific understanding brings pressure for reform.

Widening our gaze, do we concentrate resources on work with individuals, or with the community? Do we seek personal change, or to eradicate structural inequalities and barriers to engagement and development; work with trauma, or with poverty; social work, or community work; a deficit model, or a strengths-based model? We are encouraged to believe that we cannot easily have the two in parallel, yet in reality poverty and psychological issues may be more closely linked than we acknowledge.

A particularly insidious split can be the one between practitioner and service user/client. We must be watchful if we are to avoid the 'othering' of families, which becomes so easy when risk averse, defensive practice gains a foothold: the morally pure professional vs. the corrupt and dissolute individual; the family as devious or demanding; them – and us. And then the choice, presented to us all too regularly: do you load funding towards early intervention or child protection, a choice that makes no sense other than in an environment where budgets are cut, funding is short term, and need on the rise. And not even then either.

And so it is with CPVA

Child to parent violence and abuse does not escape this propensity, whether it is in finding someone to blame for the conflict (is it the child's fault or the parent's?) or in the way we construct and respond to the issue. While I understand the sentiment behind attempts to distinguish between challenging behaviour that has its roots in trauma, and that fuelled by intent, it concerns me that this too is a false dichotomy. Children often move between the two, and there need be no distinction in the way we respond: with compassion, curiosity – and a good deal of support. An overarching understanding that looks for the unique circumstances of each family, while recognising the similarities of pain and anguish experienced, has room for all within its orbit.

Hunter *et al* (2010) looked at the three separate domains of youth justice, domestic/family violence, and child welfare in an attempt to position CPVA within a legal and policy framework. Each had its own image of the child and family, the way parents are represented, and the manner in which victims and perpetrators are constructed; but in their own way each pits child against parent in both their understanding and response. The focus is inevitably on one to the exclusion of the other, with an explicit assumption of need, worth, and responsibility. More recently, Holt and Lewis (2018) found four separate ways in which practitioners working with families experiencing CPVA thought about the issue:

- Like IPV, so requiring a police response.
- Caused by poor parenting, so requiring a parenting programme.
- Caused by a wider context and family dysfunction (the perfect storm), driving a response such as multi-systemic therapy (MST).
- The outworking of trauma and more complex needs.

It is clear that there is far from one distinct way of looking at the issue of CPVA, and each approach may have its merits or problems. Indeed, all single paradigms seem to prove problematic!

And another dilemma, as we listen to parents who have asked for help and been turned away, as services become more and more targeted and fragmented: do we understand this as a problem that needs an early help solution, or as a child protection issue? Whose responsibility is it to get involved? As thresholds rise in the face of increased demand and limited resources, has the boundary with 'early help' also moved up, or is there contested territory between the two where there is uncertainty, magnified by this being an unfamiliar problem? As services pass the buck, not recognising child to parent violence and abuse as part of their responsibility; and parents want protection for the WHOLE family, it becomes a serious question, with potentially life-changing consequences all round.

> 'They had never shown any interest in us at all. But when it came to the stage at school where he was that bad … I had asked for help a long time ago. I said, "I don't know what to do. I love my son to pieces but I don't know what to do to make things better". They basically told me there was nothing they could do. Then, when it got so bad at school the Headmistress asked me "Would you like me to phone social services? I'm not reporting you. I'm asking for help".
>
> I said, "Yes please. You're not coping. I'm not coping. None of us know what we're doing". Then I phoned social services because I heard nothing from them. I spoke to a guy who said, "We haven't got the resources to put into place for incidents before – if he actually stabs you then we can put things in place … We'd love to prevent it but we do not have the money". And that's what I was left with. They did not intervene at all. So I was still left on my own … I didn't want him taken into care, I wanted help.'
>
> (Interview with Rachel, 2017)

So, is child to parent violence and abuse an early help issue?

Early help can mean different things to different people and in different situations. Sometimes the term is used to refer to help in the early years of a child's life, the first 1000 days in particular. There is an expectation that if families can be supported to lay good foundations, then all will be better, if not actually well.

More often it refers to help given to families and individuals that is more complex than the universal offer of support, but not so extreme as to need statutory intervention. Early help acknowledges that some children have needs that are above and beyond what can be provided by universal services. They will need professional guidance and support; and some children might have multiple or complex needs, requiring a specialist service from a range of agencies. Early help focuses on providing support before problems become acute, and as a way of preventing them reaching such a level, improving outcomes for children and families (and saving money at the same time). The term 'early help' might seem perfectly apposite in some situations, where a problem is identified and support can be given quickly. It can seem less appropriate if the difficulties a family faces are multiple, complex and deeply entrenched, yet they fail to reach a statutory threshold.

There is a risk of playing 'Top Trumps' in any area of need, and CPVA is no exception. Some families will experience far greater levels of violence, over a more protracted period, and with worse outcomes, than others. But this is not to deny each individual family's experience of anguish, or their rightful expectation of help. There will be differing levels of need, with differing types of response called for. For some families, help might be so easily accessed that a potential problem is nipped in the bud, and everyone goes home safely. For others, the route for support will be via a range of non-statutory agencies, albeit to frightening levels of need, but all the time with a clear understanding of safeguarding responsibilities and of when it might be necessary to refer on for statutory intervention.

When we understand CPVA as linked to multiple other issues, then support early on in any of these areas can help families to change patterns of behaviour before they become deeply embedded or seriously dangerous. For instance, children who have lived with domestic violence have been found to benefit from support, with their parent, to understand and move beyond the experience. Where families are experiencing violence because of trauma, or where a child has a particular diagnosis, help early on can offer medication and different styles of parenting and relating that support emotional regulation. Enabling families to communicate better, to understand each other's needs, and to try new ways of being together has been found to lower levels of tension and aggression within the home.

In the current climate of budget cuts, and the impact of these documented through report after report, it is concerning that access to early help is diminishing, and some families will be left to contend with rising levels of need and violence without external support. Norman Lamb, former care minister, said on the *I Feel Really Bad When I Hurt My Mum* film (2018) '*The NHS fundamentally, together also with other public services – Education, Social Care, are just massively failing these families; and in a way we're abandoning families to try to cope on their own with extraordinarily complex circumstances*'. In this environment it is all the more important that all agencies, all practitioners, have a working knowledge of the issues and appropriate responses. Where there is understanding of the complexities of parenting a child who is using violence and abuse – and where help can be accessed – with good support it can be possible to keep a family safe and to restore healthy relationships. It is sad to hear on an almost daily basis of families who have been unable to find this, whether because of a lack of understanding or of resourcing.

> *'Our studies took place against a backdrop of rising social work demand and diminishing supply. Significant reductions in preventative family support and early intervention services (such as Sure Start Children's centres) have substantially altered the availability of vital supports for families, leaving many without the help they need. As the rate of referrals to social care increase, social workers find themselves increasingly making potentially life changing decisions with limited time and resource.'*
> (Mason and Walsh, 2018)
>
> *'This is part of the problem, where to ask for diagnosis and support. PAS say it's not PAS, disabled services say we don't meet the threshold, CAMHS are unable to assess complexity. So here we are with the police and safeguarding SWs knocking on our door.'*
> (Tweet from HushabyeMountain, @Tobetherefor, 2018)

Nothing else to add?

When we see parents struggling to manage a child's behaviour, or worn down by the demands of coping daily with living in 'a war zone', it is tempting to assume that everyone will be better off with the intervention and support of public services. Even as I type that it seems so self-evident. But what knowledge and resources do we have to offer, to add to the situation, that parents are not already contributing? Best to be clear in our own minds what we can add to the situation, before we try to intervene.

> *'It is extreme violence. Children's Services have said numerous times that there is nothing that they can do to improve or change our situation and we remain open with them in the hope that they will fund respite; but unfortunately I have to source that.*
> *The local authority told us, "It's not always possible to find the services parents want or need, but they will continue to look at options for families".'*
> (BBC Two, 2018)

A realisation that we do not have anything else to offer does not absolve us of the need to respond, but it should inform the manner in which we do so, the attitude with which we approach families, and it should fire our professional curiosity and creativeness.

A situation may be escalated as a child protection concern because of genuine issues, or simply because no one knows what else to do. On many occasions investigation may well establish that an inappropriate referral has been made. A clear-sighted analysis of the situation reveals that a child is not at risk, and that the family are doing all they can to provide safety and promote welfare. A lack of resources and provision is the more pressing issue. Understanding of the specific areas of need, input around de-escalation, the development of a support network, and strengthening the position of the parents: all these things have already been considered and should enable a family to remain together safely. But there will be some occasions when a child's specific needs are so extreme, or a parent's position is so compromised, that more radical intervention is called for, and investigations will then rightly take place to establish whether the threshold for statutory intervention has been met.

Child protection – but not as we know it

- A child may be placed at risk of significant harm by the behaviour of their sibling.
- A child may be actually harmed by a sibling.
- A child may be harmed by a parent, in self-defence.
- A child alleges harm by a parent as part of the pattern of control.
- A child may be deemed 'beyond parental control'.
- A child may be harmed, mentally or physically, by their own actions, whether in the short or long term.
- A child's education may be disrupted.
- A child potentially faces homelessness.
- A child's actions may have criminal elements.
- A child may already be at risk of significant harm for other reasons, and is using their behaviour as a way of conveying distress.
- A child's abusive behaviour places them at risk of becoming vulnerable in other areas.
- Without intervention, there is a risk that a child's behaviour will be repeated in future relationships.
- A parent's life may be threatened by the actions of the child.

When investigations are instigated, what do we assume to be the place of the parents in this? We need to be aware that a professional conceptualisation of this as a 'child protection issue' may not match with a parent's understanding or assumption of the help they sought and might receive. It is worth remembering that the internet is full of parents warning others not to go down this route because of the response they received themselves. At one extreme families might experience confusion, disbelief and despair. At the other, a righteous anger may jeopardise hope of future reconciliation or of joint working, as professionals are perceived to have acted arbitrarily, and without justification.

> Within England and Wales, it has been established in law that a child may be beyond parental control without blame being attributed to the parents in this respect. The relevant case is WBC v A [2016] EWFC B70:
> 'The approach adopted by Butler-Sloss LJ is precisely the one which HHJ Bellamy adopted in the Re K case. He did not find any culpability on the part of the adoptive parents but held that the child's behaviours justified a finding that she was beyond parental control and that threshold was satisfied on that basis. The combination these authorities and the Guidance seems to me to be clear that there is no requirement on the part of an applicant Local Authority to show that there is a causal link between the parenting the child has received and the child being beyond parental control for the purposes of section 31(2)(b)(ii).'
> (Bailii, 2016)

Approaching an agency whose main raison d'etre has become to protect children from harm inflicted by adults can be a risky undertaking, with a baseline working assumption that a parent must be in part responsible for the harm the young person is dealing out. Seeking help with behaviour, asking for respite or other services in order to keep going, and then meeting with a philosophy of 'child rescue', parents can find the response was not one they were expecting.

> '… under a section 47. So for us this is like a massive cloud … And still somewhat confused as to how the hell we ended up here when all we asked for were strategies to manage the behaviour and help with the dynamics with two of the children … He is only 6, but a large boy for his age … I have never felt so isolated in my life. All my children are on CP. Because of the risks from our youngest, and the youngest putting himself in danger. We are deemed to be failing to safeguard them all. Kind of ironic when the other two children are flourishing and achieving well.'
> (Jocelyn, 2015, personal correspondence)

It is entirely appropriate that we place safety at the heart of this conundrum. The problem is that the legislation available to provide structure and rigour was designed for a different situation all together. It may be that there is simply no help available to support a child or a family with their situation. It may be that a lack of awareness and understanding has blocked conversation and skewed the intervention. Whatever the underlying issue, the shame of experiencing the violence is now compounded by the shame of being found wanting by the state; and there may be very real consequences for an individual in terms of where they can live, or of their employment situation.

Finding a position that recognises the needs of the child, without an automatic assumption of parental culpability, would lead to a process that feels more protective and less punitive: parents as part of the solution, rather than part of the problem; and by implication would help create a shared response that parents feel able to sign up to and matches more closely their expectations of help. The testimony from Sandi, and many others like her, remind us importantly that there is good supportive work going on around the country. Where practitioners understand the issues and work with the parents with real compassion, there is no place for antagonism, distrust or despair. Instead, relationship-based work listens to the family, respects their narrative, and walks alongside the parents as a solution is found and safety achieved.

Who goes where?

If Section 47 enquiries (in Britain) establish that there is a need for action to be taken, the question remains: what should this look like? What support is on offer? If someone needs to move from the home to ensure safety, who should this be; and when they are placed somewhere else is this a long-term or short-term solution? Do they need to be in hospital, residential school, or foster care, for instance? Is the help they will get elsewhere available to them if they are not removed? Indeed, if they are removed, will they receive the help they need in their new setting? Do people there have the specialist knowledge and understanding to bring about change? Does there need to be a court process, or can arrangements be made on a voluntary basis? What are the expectations about continuing parental involvement? These are all important questions that cannot and should not be side-stepped.

A continuum of safeguarding

So yes, CPVA needs family support and early help, and for some families it also needs a child protection response. Thinking about it as a safeguarding issue may be more helpful than trying to position it at one end or another. We do people a disservice when we ask them to wait until things have become worse before we can help. From early on, siblings may be at risk of harm, through actual acts of violence or control, or the emotional impact as attention is focused so much on the violent child. The harm caused to the adults, to their mental, physical and economic well-being, has a huge impact on their capacity to parent safely and may well contribute to their ability to offer care and protection. The harm to the young person themselves, through their own words and actions, cannot be overlooked. The significance of harm to each party will only increase over time without support and intervention. When seen through this lens, CPVA becomes very much a child protection issue. But in order to be able to offer a response suited to the circumstances of the family, one that is compassionate, honest, and constructive, a conceptualisation of the problem that includes a full understanding of the issue of child to parent violence and abuse becomes absolutely imperative. Not liking the way that things are done at the moment is not necessarily an argument for stopping doing them. It may be an argument for doing them better.

The problem is the problem

I suggest that focusing on choices, and on apparent opposites, distracts from the real issues. It is a false dichotomy. The problem with CPVA is that it cannot be split so easily. It is a both-and problem. It refuses to conform to one understanding or another, to one solution or another, to binary models of delivery. A child may be both victim and aggressor. Parents hold in tension the unacceptability – a hatred even, of the behaviour – and an uncompromising love of the child. The problem is not in the child, or in the parent – the problem is the problem.

CPVA does not fit neatly into one agency's remit. It looks very different in different families. We need to think in terms of both family support AND child protection. This is absolutely a safeguarding issue; and yet it looks very different to that we are used to. It needs elements of care AND control; welfare AND protection. As Coogan (2017) states, this is a wicked problem, one without straightforward causes, understanding, or solutions. Safely positioning it at one edge of a divide, we are blind to the complexities of family situations and a young person's story. We need all of us: the whole family, parents and professionals to work together, if we are to stand any chance of bringing about change.

Where to now?

We are perhaps at an interesting moment for work with families and children in Britain today. Some aspects of what we face may well be familiar to those in other countries and cultures. We are told that austerity is coming to an end, and yet there is little evidence of greater funding at the same time as need apparently increases. But there are strong calls for change: from campaigners shouting loudly for human rights to be respected; from practitioners in children's social care exhausted by the demands made on them, and the sense that social work has lost sight of its roots; and from academics challenging the delivery models and priorities that have taken over as social work has felt ever more under siege. The gains of clear and thorough data entry and justification of every action became losses themselves, as there was less and less time for actual contact. Speedier removal of children to places of safety and permanence has created new problems – perhaps unforeseen.

Now we see interest in strengths-based work, rather than a focus on a deficit model of intervention. Innovative practice is supported, albeit in the short term. Established attitudes to the separation of children from their families are being challenged. Respected voices in the field are calling for a refocusing on family support, real engagement, time spent – and money saved in the long run. Ironically, as resources are in short supply, the most important tool becomes the self; the worker and what they bring in terms of empathy, knowledge and understanding, and a hunger for change. Perhaps we see the pendulum swinging back the other way. Perhaps we are at the perfect moment to build services that understand and respect the needs of all experiencing this issue.

Rejecting the binary

As a complex problem, this needs a complex response. Family support will be needed, often long-term, that challenges, nurtures, teaches, plays and cries together, support that places the family at the centre, and listens to the voice of all concerned. A response that brings together experts from relevant fields and agencies, rather than being the remit of just one profession, and which includes the family in that body of expertise; all the while ensuring the safety of all members of the family, both now and in the future. Small wonder perhaps that it is often independent providers who are more easily able to adjust to such a model, unconstrained by the slowly grinding wheels of bureaucracy. Yet we see that there are increasing numbers of social workers, and of departments, that understand this issue, and that have developed a response that is both appropriate and timely. Innovative work needs belief to sustain it, as well as training, the support of management and of enabling structures. But intervening early, with therapeutic family work, is rewarding for all parties, and, in the long run saves not just money, but family lives as well.

The challenge for us is to reject the binary, to design such a model of work, and to deliver it in an environment that is still not yet entirely sympathetic.

Things to think about

- How does the agency you work in determine the model or type of work you are able to offer?
- How does this determine your thinking about the issues for which families seek help?
- How does this impact the aims of your intervention?
- Who do you work with? Who are you protecting by your intervention?
- What can you do to be more inclusive in the way you work?
- What can you add to the interventions the family themselves have already tried?

Find out more

For exploration of the difference between adults' and children's services in terms of philosophy and safeguarding practice, see this from **Dez Holmes** (2018) *Transitional Safeguarding from Adolescence to Adulthood*: https://www.rip.org.uk/news-and-views/blog/transitional-safeguarding-from-adolescence-to-adulthood/.

Trauma-informed work briefings are available from **Research in Practice**: https://www.rip.org.uk/news-and-views/latest-news/new-publications-on-trauma-and-transitional-safeguarding/.

For discussion about a strengths-based approach, see the **SCIE** (2018) *Strengths-based social care for Children, Young People and Their Families*: https://www.scie.org.uk/news/mediarelease/sba-children.

The report, *Realising the Potential of Early Intervention* from the **Early Intervention Foundation** (2018) includes discussion about the value of early intervention (and what this means), what sort of work is effective, the costs to society, and barriers to effective work: https://www.eif.org.uk/files/pdf/realising-the-potential-of-early-intervention.pdf.

For comment from a parent about the importance of parents and professionals working together rather than as adversaries, see **Sally Donovan's** column in Community Care (2018) *Sally Donovan: Adoption services should work with, not against, parents to learn from 'near misses'*: https://www.communitycare.co.uk/2016/03/02/sally-donovan-adoption-services-work-parents-learn-near-misses-failures/.

For commentary and challenge on the direction of travel of 21st century social work, a call to involve families in decisions, and a more compassionate, relationship-based model of work, see the writing of **Brid Featherstone, Kate Morris** and others, for instance:

- **Morris K, Featherstone B, Hill K & Ward M** (2018) *Stepping Up, Stepping Down: How families make sense of working with welfare services*. Family Rights Group: http://www.frg.org.uk/images/YFYV/Stepping-Up-Stepping-Down-Report.pdf.
- **Featherstone B, White S and Morris K** (2014) *Re-imagining Child Protection: Towards humane social work with families*. Bristol: Policy Press.
- **Featherstone B, Gupta A, Morris K and White S** (2018) *Protecting Children: A social model*. Bristol: Policy Press

For information about, and findings of the recent Care Crisis Review, facilitated by the **Family Rights Group**, see documents available here. http://www.frg.org.uk/involving-families/reforming-law-and-practice/care-crisis-review.

For examples of how alienated some people feel by the child protection system in England and Wales, and the voices of parents who have felt let down, see the website and blog from **Special Guardians and Adopters Together**: https://specialguardiansandadopterstogether.com.

Local authorities are required to publish guidance on thresholds for early help, and documents such as these can be easily found online if you do not already have access to them. For instance: **Doncaster Early Help handbook**: http://doncasterscb.proceduresonline.com/pdfs/early_help_handbook.pdf, **Hampshire Thresholds Chart**: http://www3.hants.gov.uk/thresholds.htm.

The **Child Protection Resource** website is particular to England and Wales, but is full of philosophical debate as well as that pertaining to legislation and guidance. For discussion about the threshold for care proceedings see this post: http://childprotectionresource.online/what-does-threshold-criteria-mean/. Discussion can also be found in the post *Beyond Parental Control: No attribution of blame*, on **Holes in the Wall** (2016): https://holesinthewall.co.uk/2016/11/07/beyond-parental-control-no-attribution-of-blame/.

For discussion about the lawfulness of Section 20 arrangements see this article on **Community Care** (2018) *Supreme Court Outlines Nine Key Principles of Section 20 Practice*:

https://www.communitycare.co.uk/2018/07/20/supreme-court-outlines-nine-key-principles-section-20-practice/.

For discussion about the way cuts to early help services have had an effect, see the report from the **Association of Directors of Children's Services** (2018) *Executive Summary, Safeguarding Pressures Phase 6*: http://adcs.org.uk/assets/documentation/ADCS_SAFEGUARDING_PRESSURES_PHASE_6_EXECUTIVE_SUMMARY_FINAL.pdf.

References

(Bailii, 2016) WBC v A [2016] EWFC B70: http://www.bailii.org/ew/cases/EWFC/OJ/2016/B70.html.

BBC Two (2018) *'I Feel Really Bad When I Hurt My Mum'*, a film by Noel Phillips for Victoria Derbyshire. Available at: https://www.bbc.co.uk/programmes/p06rlt19.

Coogan D (2017) *Child to Parent Violence and Abuse, Family Interventions with Non Violent Resistance*. London: Jessica Kingsley Publishers.

Holt A and Lewis S (2018) *Constructions of and Responses to CPV in England and Wales*. Presentation to the N8 policing conference on responses to child-to-parent domestic violence, organised by Durham University, 2018.

Hunter C, Nixon J & Parr S (2010) Mother abuse: a matter of youth justice, child welfare or domestic violence. *Journal of Law and Society* **37** (2).

Mason W and Walsh J (2018) *'Reproducing the Stereotypes': Family complexity, resource scarcity and social work decision-making* [online]. The Social Policy Blog. Available at: https://socialpolicyblog.com/2018/11/07/reproducing-the-stereotypes-family-complexity-resource-scarcity-and-social-work-decision-making/ (accessed February 2019).

Part 5:
One thing everyone can do

Chapter 14: One thing everyone can do

'Overall the main recommendation from respondents is that they require non-judgmental support, being believed and listened to and respected as a parent who is seeking help …'
(Thorley and Coates, 2017)

'Take the time to listen to the parent. Just take the time to listen. Because parents have so much to say sometimes. And I still feel now, they say "tell me about JJ, you've got 5 minutes". But no, listen to the way I deal with my son and listen to what I'm saying works. Because then they can do that, because if they don't they've got a blank page of a child. And they don't know. They've got their rule book and their skills but, you know what, it doesn't always come together, and some people say they're listening but I know they're not and I find that so frustrating.'
(Interview with Rachel, 2017)

Having got this far, I hope you might be feeling better equipped to support families experiencing violence and abuse from their children. I recognise though that you might feel that there is little within your own power or remit, or that of your agency, that can be done. Not everyone works in a fully equipped department with supportive colleagues, bountiful resources, a large training budget, and structures that make long term engagement with families with this issue possible. You might be the one family support worker employed directly by a school; a minister of religion, single-handedly supporting a hundred families all with unique needs; or you might in fact be a parent in the process of setting up a peer support service because you have been unable to find anything else that helps. Let me reassure you that there is one thing everyone, and anyone, can do.

It is about the way we listen.

Good listening is a skill that is more complicated than people sometimes appreciate, and yet is one of the most straightforward things we can do. It is also fundamental to any work with another individual, and a foundation stone of professional practice.

Good listening is respectful, non-judgemental, empathetic, honest, patient and kind. But we are required to stop, and to take time. Too often we are racing against the clock, or thinking about the next question on the form; or an object in the room catches our eye and we disappear in a reverie about something altogether unconnected. Or, we go with a list of resources in mind that we can offer regardless of whether they actually meet the need, and our ears are only open to the things that match that list. Good listening is exquisitely easy, and fearsomely complicated.

Good listening raises presence.
It is empowering and builds the person's self-esteem.
It gives respect and acknowledges the trouble the other person feels.
It validates the experience.
It acknowledges the expertise of the person speaking.
It educates us.

'Living with substance use is isolating. Family members often experience stigma and shame, and may not have a supportive social network. Being heard empathically and without judgement can immediately alleviate stress and help problems seem less overwhelming. Listening carefully to the individual's story and experience is also crucial for the practitioner to understand the family context and provide effective and relevant on-going support.'
(Adfam, 2016)

The literature is unsurprisingly full of people exclaiming that to have someone truly listen was the most important thing for them in moving forward.

Can simply listening ever be enough?

That depends of course on the situation. We can probably all think of times when all we needed to do was think out loud, and the answer presented itself to us without other help. Or it may be that in speaking about what we intend to do we somehow commit ourselves to it in a stronger way. Undoubtedly, for some people, to have someone listen will enable them to come to their own solution. For others it may be that speaking about the issues is an important first step that they have not yet taken. They may need to spend time processing their thoughts before they are able to move on beyond recognition to action. Then it becomes a privilege to be that person who holds their words and thoughts, to be able to contain their fears and anxieties.

The social enterprise IRISi was established to promote and improve the health care response to gender based violence, rolling out the IRIS (Identification and Referral to Improve Safety) programme. Originally conceived as meeting the needs of victims of partner perpetrated violence and abuse, advocates are also seeing more and more instances of women seeking help with experiences of abuse from their children. Feedback from women indicates how important it was for them that someone took the time to ask about their mental health, to listen and to take an interest in their situation.

'This support is the best thing that ever happened to me. You guys [advocates] are the only ones who believed me. Although they didn't say so I felt everyone else looked at me as if I make things up and have mental health problems. You listened to me.' (Johnson, 2018)

Furthermore, as well as the advocates themselves, women benefited from their GPs being trained to listen, ask questions, respond appropriately, and then refer on as necessary.

When listening is not in itself enough we have the opportunity to signpost or to refer to someone else, more experienced or qualified, whether that is an in-house service (such as IRISi in a health centre), or a local service, a specialist organisation, or a confidential helpline. Unsurprisingly, parents find that speaking to someone familiar with the issues, removing the need to explain everything from the start, is so much easier and more helpful.

Everybody Hurts: just a listening ear

Everybody Hurts is a not for profit parent support group, established in 2013, where parents can speak to somebody else who understands what it is like to be faced with abuse from their child. 'Empathy – not sympathy'.

Sarah, had struggled to cope with abuse from her son for almost twelve years before she realised that there were other people also experiencing violence and aggression from their children in the home. Finding nothing locally in the way of support, she set up the group to offer hope to other parents and their families.

*'We are a group who are aware of the devastating effect this form of abuse can have on the whole family. It takes a lot of courage to accept and admit that you are experiencing abuse, and then even more to feel able to talk about it! We're not here to offer solutions as such, **just a listening ear** which can often be the start of the parent opening up to others, and helping them to access whatever counselling or other support that can help them to get stronger. Hopefully strong enough to survive living with their abuser.'*

> *Sarah adds:*
>
> 'The group is called **Everybody Hurts** because everyone affected by child to parent violence is hurting: the mum, the dad, the sister, the brother, the grandparents, the carers. And let's not forget the young person who is being abusive or violent. They are likely to be feeling just as lost and frightened as anybody else in the family.'
>
> Everybody Hurts aims to provide sibling-to-sibling and general online support and monthly 'tea and empathy' groups for parents to be able to meet others who have sadly found themselves in similar situations. With a no blame, non-judgemental culture, meetings are held in a safe and secure environment. One-to-one meetings are available for anyone who is uncomfortable in a group setting.
>
> (Everybody Hurts case study, personal correspondence)

I have collected boxes of notes, a laptop full of quotes and links, and hundreds of thoughts in my head, but there are always a few that stand out. The 'Suddenly Mummy' blog (2016) lists the attributes shown by a friend who offered a listening ear in a time of difficulty:

- *'She did not freak out.*
- *She listened to what I had to say, without judgement.*
- *She acknowledged what had happened and did not try to brush it off with a dismissive 'all kids do that' sort of comment.*
- *She did not try to defend the indefensible.*
- *She acknowledged my feelings about it all.*
- *She asked me a few open questions with a view to heading towards a plan.*
- *She let me work out the plan for myself, out loud, while making the odd encouraging noise.*
- *She expressed full support for the plan, and promised to check in with me to see how it was going.*
- *She urged me to speak to her any time about it, and reassured me that it was right for me to be supported while I do what I have to do.'*

Sometimes it can be enough simply to listen. Parents have plenty to say about people who have not listened, who have made assumptions, who have not understood or who have blamed them from the start for the abuse they experience.

> Coates (2017) asked parents what would be the most valuable help – what would improve support for families living with CPVA?
> - *'Professionals prepared to listen, accept it happens, and being empathetic to it would be a good start.'*
> - *'To be believed.'*
> - *'Belief that it could be true.'*
> - *'Believe the parents and not blame them.'*

That is not to say that listening will be sufficient in every case, by any means, but that it is an important start; and if you have nothing else to give, then that is the best you can give.

Once we have listened, we can ask again, 'What is it you need?'.

Listen AND believe?

In the course of working with families experiencing violence and abuse from their children you may be told things that are so alien to your own experience of life – family life in particular – that it is hard to give them credence. But why not? From the point of view of the speaker, coming forward to disclose painful and embarrassing stories, whether or not they feel they have been believed may be the difference between them finding the strength to carry on, and a decision to throw in the towel and walk away. How you respond may affect whether they feel able to ask for help another time, whether they continue to view services as supportive, or as 'the enemy'.

What do we mean when we say parents need to be believed? Within the field of domestic violence or sexual assault, there has been a lot of discussion lately about the assertion that all allegations of assault should be believed as a fundamental right; with suggestions that instead we should be offering a commitment to listening respectfully and investigating fully. With families experiencing CPVA, I would suggest that we are still a long way off from here, when the initial reaction may be to hear something different to that said, or to assume exaggeration or blameworthiness. Then again – perhaps not so very far removed! I would suggest again, if we do not first listen, then we are not in any position to make any further judgement or offer any further help.

But what if they're wrong?

Yes, there may well be times when we listen to people and are very concerned by what they say. When violence has become normalised within a family, things can be missed, or dangers minimised. We may become aware of risks that a family faces that demand further intervention. Or it may be that a parent's attitude to the situation seems to be a contributory force itself to risk. Then listening is not enough. Then we will understand what steps to take. But if we do not first listen, we can never be sure of the reality as experienced by this individual, this family, at this time.

As professionals we may not always have been seen as allies. Sometimes there are difficult roles to fulfil, but there are never excuses for disrespect. Families have spoken about the lack of help they have received, the hopelessness they have felt, and the anger at the attitude of those they relied on to bring about change. But they have also spoken about those that helped, that were available, that took the time, and listened. If we want to move to a place where practitioners are understood to be a source of support rather than the enemy, then we need to start with ourselves. We may feel there are no resources, the budget is stretched already, or there are too many things on our plates; but we all have something we can give – a listening ear, a relationship, ourselves.

I hope that you will feel you are now more equipped to support families experiencing violence and abuse from their children. Listening may be the first step on a long road of support; or it may be the only kind of help that you feel you can offer, but it is perhaps one of the most important things that you can do.

I would like to finish this chapter with some words from Sandi.

'That's the feedback I've had from my parents. It's a skill that's really misunderstood. Listening is hard. I remember being really tired after my sessions. Listening properly, for two hours in quite deep emotional things is knackering! When I think about the parents that I've worked with, and got their child back home, that was for them they didn't feel judged. They were surprised I wasn't coming in and telling them what to do, or telling them off, or blaming them as a bad parent. That's where my Restorative training played a massive part. Because it wasn't me trying to fix it. It wasn't me trying to give them the solutions. It was me listening to understand how it got to this situation and now what we needed to do from their perspective … You really saw the merit in them coming to those conclusions themselves. It took a hell of a lot longer! I used to spend hours and hours with these families … Some of those families I was with 12-14 hours in the space of a month, and if you have 8 other families it's hard to do that and justify

it … But if I got that kid back home and they were happier, that was something … When I had to close the case to myself, she was quite emotional, I remember I was feeling quite emotional … I felt quite privileged to be let in on so much. You could tell, she was a mum who was really fighting for her kids, but she was just so low … And she said, I'm going to miss just being able to talk to you … I got her a really good family support worker. She was one of the best … It's tough. You feel like you can't really do as much as you'd like.'
(Interview with Sandi, 2018)

Things to think about

- What are the circumstances that make it easier for you to listen to someone properly?
- What can you do to facilitate this happening?
- What would need to happen for you to feel OK about 'just listening'?

Find out more

See this TED talk from Sophie Andrews (2017) *The Best Way to Help is Often Just to Listen*, about the power of having someone simply listen to you (rather than offering advice) in effecting healing: https://www.ted.com/talks/sophie_andrews_the_best_way_to_help_is_often_just_to_listen.

References

Adfam (2016) *Making it Happen* [online]. Available at: https://www.adfam.org.uk/files/docs/Making_it_happen_final_PDF.pdf (accessed February 2019).

Coates A (2017) *Results of the CPV Survey*, 2016.

Johnson M (2018) *Navigating the Language – listening to the words women use to describe their mental health and hearing what they need* [online]. Safe Lives. Available at: Blog. http://safelives.org.uk/practice_blog/navigating-language-listening-words-women-use-describe-their-mental-health-and-hearing (accessed February 2019).

Suddenly Mummy (2016) *A Little Help from my Friends* [online]. Available at: http://suddenlymummy.blogspot.com/2016/12/a-little-help-from-my-friends.html (accessed February 2019).

Thorley and Coates (2017) *Child–Parent Violence (CPV): Grappling with an enigma* [online]. Available at: https://www.academia.edu/32167527/Child_-Parent_Violence_CPV_Grappling_with_an_Enigma (accessed February 2019).

Conclusion

Chapter 15: A final word, and where to next?

One issue which I have not really touched on here, and indeed which has received less attention overall, is the matter of parricide.

Children who kill their parents

Is this the extreme end of the same issue, or are we looking at a separate group of children? Parents regularly speak of fearing that they will be killed, but the actual number of cases where this happens is thankfully small, and is more usually connected with children who are legally adults. In countries where guns are not so freely available, this is even less common.

When incidents do occur, they tend to attract significant attention in the media, and the sensationalisation does not always move our understanding forward.

'Possessed' teen accused of disemboweling mum with scissors 'because she was a witch'.
(Rkaina, *Mirror Online*, 2014)

Some research has been undertaken in this field. Heide (1994) was instrumental in opening up this work and identified a number of scenarios which it was suggested might lead to parricide. Notably she includes the presence of mental illness, a retaliatory attack in the face of extreme of persistent violence towards the child, a sibling or the other parent, and extreme anti-social traits. More recently, Holt and Shon (2016) examined the tendency to view non-fatal and fatal abuse separately, suggesting that the division of interest in adults and young people by disciplines, and the attribution of violence in one to dysfunctional families, and in the other to mental illness or criminal violence, has prevented a comprehensive understanding.

Holt (2017) explored this further, finding that of 693 parricides in England and Wales over a 36-year period (1977-2012), approximately 9% of the principle suspects were juveniles; with the majority of suspects being male, but an even spread of victims by gender. However, looking across the life course, juveniles were more likely to have killed their fathers; mothers were more often the victims in later years. This might support the notion that this is a separate issue, given that the majority of those experiencing harm from their pre-adult children have been found to be female. Holt suggests rather that the distinction made up to now, between non-fatal and fatal violence towards parents, needs to be re-examined in the light of new understandings about violence within the family throughout the life-course, with a focus not simply on the psychopathology of the individual, but the inclusion of societal, political and developmental pressures.

Moving forward in policy and practice

Bringing together the ground already covered, I offer a summary of suggestions for the future:

- More attention is still needed to naming this as a distinct issue, separate but linked to other forms of violence within the family, and distinct to other adolescent criminality, at a national as well as local level.
- Once there is an agreed name and method of coding, then it becomes possible to count in a more realistic way.
- Awareness is needed among all universal services, whether health, education or housing, in order to cultivate a less judgemental service and environment, in which parents are able to seek help and receive support.
- A multidisciplinary approach is needed, recognising that this cuts across traditional boundaries and is not confined to one area or service, making use of the full range of skills, knowledge and structures, in partnerships between agencies.
- Early intervention needed to respond in a way that recognises the impacts of trauma on relationships and well-being; that seeks to support families before a crisis is reached, and before patterns of behaviour become embedded.
- Violence within the family should be part of education about healthy relationships within schools.
- Support is recommended for peer networks, making use of a community's capacity as experts in their own right, enabling support that works.
- Avoiding criminalisation of young people, seeing this as last resort, and developing diversionary approaches to work.
- Responses to be therapeutic in nature, supporting the whole family.

- All separate issues to be addressed.
- Services to be individually designed, and appropriate to age, culture and gender.

Our understanding has come a long way, but we can see that interpretation of data and the conceptualisation of issues has changed over time. Based on where we are now, a number of researchers have gone on to identify gaps in knowledge and understanding of child to parent violence and abuse, and to suggest some future directions for further study.

Future research

Up to now, research has been very much focused on counting, and looking at the characteristics of families where this has been an issue, whether in terms of individual traits and situations, parenting practice and approaches, or the young person's wider behaviour. With a focus on data from the justice system, or clinical practice, we are still failing to capture the experience of families who have not sought help, or who have so far been rebuffed. Holt (2016) calls this the 'dark figure' and there is a sense that it may well be much bigger than the data we do have already, though how to achieve this is still somewhat unclear.

We do not as yet have a wider sense of how CPVA fits into society as a response to bigger issues, and the impact of other social, philosophical and cultural contexts, such as attitudes to violence generally, or the support structures available to families.

We have been adapting and adopting a number of theories to understand this issue, but there is still no one clear expression or explanation.

Are there distinctions between those who carry out more trivial and more extreme acts of violence and aggression, or is this a continuum over time?

At a micro level, there is relatively little work on the impact on fathers, in particular.

We are starting to see the beginnings of research that acknowledges that individuals other than parents are frequently both caring for and subject to violence from children (grandparents, other kinship carers for instance).

There is a new sense that child to parent violence and abuse should be understood not just as a phenomenon of a particular age group, but as a relational issue that transcends age bands and stretches through to old age. As such, the need to offer a response early on becomes all the more urgent. Future research is likely to adopt this sort of longitudinal framework, starting to make connections between CPVA, IPV and elder abuse, and other aspects of violence between family members.

For more suggestions for future research, Simmons *et al* (2018) suggest a wide range of issues which could be investigated, across each field of the nested ecological theory.

The Monash University *Context Report* (Elliot *et al*, 2017) also includes discussion about future considerations for research, including methods of data collection and analysis, as well as subject matter.

Look out for current research to be published soon on:

- grandparents and kinship carers
- longitudinal work
- the understanding and experience of practitioners.

Holding understanding and uncertainty in tension

While we have indeed come a long way relatively quickly over the last five to ten years, there is still a lot we do not fully understand; and many new possibilities in terms of development and research. Recently I was looking for an image for a slide presentation and came across a stunning photograph of a dandelion head. The clustering of seeds perfectly illustrated for me the way everything is so interconnected – quite apart from their similarity to brain neurons; but it was the way the image was captured which spoke most strongly to me. The centre was perfectly in focus, but the outer edges completely blurred. It struck me that when we understood much less about child to parent violence and abuse, we had a clarity in our explanations and responses that we now understand was somewhat unwarranted. As we have broadened our gaze, we have come to see that the issue is more complex and varied; and we speak less categorically, with regard both to its genesis and in the range of responses we offer. I hope we are more humble. I hope we are more accessible. I hope we can offer more hope to others.

Find out more

Yexley M (2016) *Domestic Homicide Review Relating to the Death of CJ*: https://www.towerhamlets.gov.uk/Documents/Community-safety-and-emergencies/Community-safety/Domestic_Homicide_Review_4.pdf

Maclean K (2016) Reflections on the non-accidental death of a foster carer. *Adoption and Fostering* **40** (4) 325–339.

References

Elliott K, McGowan J, Benier K, Maher J & Fitz-Gibbon K (2017) *Context Report, Investigating Adolescent Family Violence: Background, research and directions* [online] Monash University. Available at: https://arts.monash.edu/gender-and-family-violence/wp-content/uploads/sites/11/2017/12/Investigating-Adolescent-Family-Violence-Background-Research-and-Directions.pdf (accessed February 2019).

Heide K (1994) *Why Kids Kill Parents: Child abuse and adolescent homicide*. London: SAGE Publications.

Holt A (2017) Parricide in England and Wales (1977-2012): an exploration of offenders, victims, incidents and outcomes. *Criminology and Criminal Justice* **17** (5) 568–587.

Holt A and Shon PC (2016) Exploring fatal and non-fatal violence against parents: challenging the orthodoxy of abused adolescent perpetrators. *International Journal of Offender Therapy and Comparative Criminology* **62** (4) 915–934.

Rkaina S (2014) 'Possessed' teen accused of disemboweling mum with scissors 'because she was witch' [online]. *Mirror Online* **24 September**. Available at: https://www.mirror.co.uk/news/uk-news/possessed-teen-accused-disemboweling-mum-4317098 (accessed February 2019).

Simmons, McEwan, Purcell & Ogloff (2018) Sixty years of child-to-parents abuse research: what we know and where to go. *Aggression and Violent Behaviour* **38** 31–52.

Appendix 1: Acronyms used

ACAMH	Association for Child and Adolescent Mental Health
ACEs	Adverse Childhood Experiences
ADHD	Attention Deficit Hyperactivity Disorder
APA	Adolescent to Parent Abuse
ASD	Autism Spectrum Disorder
APV	Adolescent to Parent Violence
APVA	Adolescent to Parent Violence and Abuse
AVITH	Adolescent Violence in the Home
CAMHS	Child and Adolescent Mental Health Services
CCVAB	Childhood Challenging, Violent and Aggressive Behaviour
CD	Conduct Disorder
CPA	Child to Parent Abuse
CPV	Child to Parent Violence
CPVA	Child to Parent Violence and Abuse
DA	Domestic Abuse
DV	Domestic Violence
FASD	Foetal Alcohol Spectrum Disorder

Appendix 1: Acronyms used

IPV	Intimate Partner Violence
IRIS	Identification and Referral to Improve Safety
NFA	No Further Action
NVR	Non-violent Resistance
OCD	Obsessive Compulsive Disorder
ODD	Oppositional Defiant Disorder
PAARS	Parent Abuse and Reconciliation Service
PDA	Pathological Demand Avoidance
RCPV	Responding to Child to Parent Violence
RJ	Restorative Justice
SEND	Special Educational Needs and Disabilities
SES	Socio-economic Status
SYSS	Surrey Youth Support Service
VCB	Violent and Challenging Behaviour
YODA	Youth Offending Diversion Alternative

Appendix 2: Programmes of work

The main programmes designed for work with young people using violence and abuse, and their families, in use in Britain at this time.

Break4Change

One of a number of programmes designed with parallel elements for parents and young people, Break4Change was conceived and is run as a multi-agency project, with input from the local domestic abuse agency, children's services, youth offending and a local arts and media organisation. This is considered crucial for ownership, design and delivery.

'A skills-based and restorative practice group intervention for young people and their parents/cares that focuses on non-violence and respect between family members. The program includes a young people's group with a creative aspect, parent group and a film dialogue process that enables communication between young people and parents.'

The team has experimented with different lengths for the programme. It currently extends over 12 weeks, for families with young people aged 11-16, and with an expectation that referring agencies will maintain contact throughout and beyond. Break4Change is delivered around Britain in a growing number of authorities. Although different models of management have been adopted, the multi-agency input remains central.

The Brighton team offer training, licensing and support for those interested in adopting this approach.

Break4Change was recently the subject of an international research project based at the University of Brighton. The project compared the outcomes of this model with the non-violent resistance model, across a number of European countries.

You can read more about this programme on the Break4Change website: http://break4change.co.uk and on the RCPV website: http://www.rcpv.eu.

Appendix 2: Programmes of work

Non-violent resistance (NVR)

Not so much a programme of intervention, but a different way of 'being' as a family. Parents commit to non-violence and are trained, often but not always, one-to-one, in methods of recognising signs of abusive interactions and their own role in its escalation, and in adopting alternative resistant strategies. There is emphasis on promoting positive aspects of the relationship and a network of supportive friends and relatives is established.

Anecdotally, many people (in the adoption community for instance, but also within residential care) report that this approach has been transformational in their families, bringing the tensions down and allowing then for other types of more specific therapy to also take place where appropriate.

It was evaluated in 2008 by Weinblatt and Omer, and also formed part of the Responding to Child to Parent Violence research (part funded by the Daphne 111 programme), which reported in 2015. There are links to research material as well as other resources on the RCPV website: http://www.rcpv.eu/research; and to a large amount of reading material on the reading list page of my website: https://holesinthewall.co.uk.

NVR is now adopted widely in Ireland, following the work of Declan Coogan (2017), and training by him and Eileen Lauster (2015). Together and separately they have produced a number of guides and other materials.

Training is offered within Britain by a number of organisations to both practitioners, and to families.

Useful links include:

- Partnership Projects: http://www.partnershipprojectsuk.com
- New Authority Network International: http://www.newauthority.net
- New Authority Parenting Ireland: http://www.newauthorityparenting.ie
- NVR Practitioners Consortium: https://nvrpractitionersconsortium.com
- NVR UK: http://nonviolentresistance.org.uk

A downloadable leaflet from Partnership Projects lists references supporting the evidence base for NVR: https://www.partnershipprojectsuk.com/wp-content/uploads/2017/03/PartnershipProjectsA4DS-NVR_.pdf.

Haim Omer explains the principles of NVR in this YouTube video: https://www.youtube.com/watch?v=I_39pn1Rf7E

References

Coogan D (2017) *Child to Parent Violence and Abuse, Family Interventions with Non Violent Resistance.* London: Jessica Kingsley Publishers.

Coogan D and Lauster E (2015) *Non-violent Resistance Handbook for Practitioners – Responding to Child to Parent Violence in Practice* [online]. RCPV. Available at: http://www.rcpv.eu/46-nvr-handbook-for-practitioners/file (accessed February 2019).

Weinblatt U and Omer H (2008) Non-violent resistance: a treatment for parents of children with acute behaviour problems. *Journal of Marital and Family Therapy* **34** (1) 75–92.

Respect Young People's Programme (RYPP)

The Respect Young People's Programme emerged as a specific piece of work from the Respect Young People's Toolkit. In common with many other programmes, it consists of parallel groups of parents and young people, running for approximately 12 weeks, and adopts a range of approaches, with a strong focus on restorative work.

It was funded as a specific piece of work by Realising Ambition to test replication and effectiveness, and found to produce statistically significant improvements to young people's mental well-being and behaviour.

'Analysis of these outcomes indicates a statistically significant improvement in nearly all areas, including of emotional wellbeing, conduct, pro-social behaviour, and overall mental health – with only hyperactivity and peer relationships showing no change according to children's self-report, but positive change according to parent-report. Of particular note is the overall improvement in mental health and behaviour of young people, which two thirds of parents reported as being improved by the end of the programme. Additionally, parent reported scores within the "high need" threshold range of mental health and conduct problems reduced by 23% and 27% respectively, which is particularly positive given the focus of the programme on addressing children's violence against their parents.' (Realising Ambition, 2016)

Originally focused on agencies in the north, it is now being rolled out around Britain, by a range of different agencies. Respect does not offer work with families itself, but trains providers. The offer includes full delivery manual, and guidance in relation to implementation, referrals, case and risk management, video materials, and on-going implementation support for 18 months.

You will find further information on the Respect website: http://respect.uk.net/information-support/young-people-using-violence-and-abuse-in-close-relationships/.

The Realising Ambition evaluation is also available: http://respect.uk.net/wp-content/uploads/2018/08/Respect-Respect-Young-Peoples-Programme-1.pdf.

References

Realising Ambition (2016) *Respect Young People's Programme* [online]. Available at: http://respect.uk.net/wp-content/uploads/2018/08/Respect-Respect-Young-Peoples-Programme-1.pdf (accessed February 2019).

Step-Up

Step-Up is a restorative justice programme, developed in Seattle, Washington in 2000, and now being adopted more widely in other North American states, with at least 75 agencies having used the curriculum across the country as of 2012. Originally developed as a means of diversion from the criminal justice system for court mandated youth, this programme now takes voluntary referrals, and some areas run it purely as a voluntary provision. Parents and adolescents have time to work separately and together. The focus is on self-awareness, stopping of violent and abusive behaviour, and safety planning. The curriculum was originally devised as a 21-week programme, but a shorter, 12-week programme also exists.

More information about Step-Up, including the curriculum and various tools, can be found on the King County website: https://www.kingcounty.gov/courts/superior-court/juvenile/step-up.aspx. Also in a journal article from Routt and Anderson (2011), and in their book (2014).

The model has been evaluated by the University of Illinois, and addressed by Buel in a 2009 article.

This programme has now been adapted and adopted widely across Britain and Australia in particular, under various different names.
For more information about the programme in Australia, see the work of Jo Howard, and the Uniting Kildonan website: https://www.unitingkildonan.org.au/programs-and-services/child-youth-and-family-support/family-violence/adolescent-violence/

References

Buel S (2009) Why juvenile courts should address family violence: promising practices to improve intervention outcomes. *Juvenile and Family Court Journal* **53** (2) 1–16.

Routt G and Anderson L (2011) Adolescent violence towards parents. *Journal of Aggression, Maltreatment and Trauma* **20** 1–19.

Routt G and Anderson L (2014) *Adolescent Violence in the Home, Restorative approaches to building healthy, respectful family relationships.* Oxford: Routledge.

Who's in Charge?

Who's in Charge, which has been running in Australia for many years, was designed by Eddie Gallagher (a social worker, family therapist and psychologist, with a clinical sample of nearly 500 families in the field of child to parent violence) as a group programme for parents lasting nine weeks, developed from the recognition that parents benefited from working together, supporting each other to effect change.

Who's in Charge is delivered in collaboration between local youth and family services and community health services. The programme takes a solution-focused brief therapy approach and is organised in four parts:

- Clarifying the nature of abusive behaviour.
- The use of consequences.
- Anger, assertiveness and self-care.
- A follow up session for parents to consolidate learning.

The programme was evaluated and found to be meeting its objectives (O'Connor, 2017).

Further information can be found on Gallagher's website: http://www.eddiegallagher.com.au. As well as his own book (2018), Gallagher has published journal articles expanding on the principles, and has contributed a chapter to *Working with Adolescent Violence and Abuse Towards Parents*, edited by Amanda Holt (2016). The course materials have since been adopted and adapted to form other group programmes in Australia, for example, Who's the Boss and Out of Bounds, and again, more details about these programmes can be found on Gallagher's website.

In the UK the programme is also in widespread use, and has been recognised as Emerging Effective Practice by the Youth Justice Board. More information about the programme itself, about evaluation, and about training as a facilitator, can be found on the Who's in Charge? website: https://whosincharge.co.uk

References

Gallagher E (2018) *Who's in Charge? Why children abuse parents and what you can do about it*. London: Austin Macauley Publishers.

Holt A (2016) *Working with Adolescent Violence and Abuse towards Parents, Approaches and Contexts for Intervention*. Oxford: Routledge.

O'Connor R (2007) *Who's in Charge? A group for parents of violent or beyond control children: Is this group achieving its aims?* Department for Legal Studies, Flinders University.

Other programmes and approaches

The book, *Working with Adolescent Violence and Abuse Towards Parents* edited by Amanda Holt and published in 2015, comprises information about a number of programmes, some already detailed in this appendix, but others too, as well as a section considering underlying theories and approaches, and analysis of a number of overarching questions. Some of the chapters include specific resources and tools which can be helpful

Details of a number of other resources can be found on the Directory pages of my website: https://holesinthewall.co.uk/resources/directory/ or on 'The Map' at https://community21.org/partners/cpv/.

Parenting a Violent Child, by Islay Downey and Kim Furnish, published in 2015 by Darton Longman and Todd, takes the reader through a 'virtual group programme' and was written with those parents in mind who were unable to find other help. As such it also offers some guidance to practitioners looking for ideas. It will be more suited to situations where the violence and abuse has not reached an extreme level.